IMMIGRATION AND SCHOOLING
IN THE REPUBLIC OF IRELAND

Manchester University Press

Immigration and schooling in the Republic of Ireland

Making a difference?

Dympna Devine

Manchester University Press

Manchester and New York

distributed in the United States exclusively
by Palgrave Macmillan

Published by Manchester University Press
Oxford Road, Manchester M13 9NR, UK
and Room 400, 175 Fifth Avenue, New York, NY 10010, USA
www.manchesteruniversitypress.co.uk

Distributed in the United States exclusively by
Palgrave Macmillan, 175 Fifth Avenue, New York,
NY 10010, USA

Distributed in Canada exclusively by
UBC Press, University of British Columbia, 2029 West Mall,
Vancouver, BC, Canada V6T 1Z2

British Library Cataloguing-in-Publication Data
A catalogue record for this book is available from the British Library

Library of Congress Cataloging-in-Publication Data applied for

ISBN   978 0 7190 8101 9 hardback
ISBN   978 0 7190 8102 6 paperback

First published 2011

Typeset
by Carnegie Book Production
Printed in Great Britain
by CPI Antony Rowe Ltd, Chippenham, Wiltshire

This book is dedicated to Séamus Devine
Do Dhaid – Réalt Óir

Contents

Figures and tables

Figures

Tables

Acknowledgements

My initial interest in the field of ethnic and migrant studies in education began from my work with student teachers toward the end of the 1990s. There was limited research available on ethnicity and schooling in Ireland, yet profound changes were occurring in classrooms and schools. I would like to acknowledge the contribution of Máirin Kenny and Eileen MacNeela to that earlier work. I have revisited some of these schools to do further work over the years and am grateful to the teaching staff, principals and children for their time and patience in working with me. Since then I have also been involved in a number of other studies, most notably with the Immigrant Council of Ireland and I would like to especially thank Sarah Sheridan and Fidele Mutwarasibo for their co-operation in that project. Over the years I have had the benefit of warm friendship and support from colleagues and students in UCD, in the Educational Studies Association of Ireland (ESAI) and the editorial team of the journal, *Irish Educational Studies*, as well as in the wider educational and research community in Ireland. Please forgive me for not mentioning you all individually. Míle Buíochas. I have also had the privilege of working with colleagues from outside of Ireland who continually inspire me to look from the outside within, shaping the sociological imagination. Special mention for all the encouragement, wisdom and support goes to Anne Trine, Wendy, Jannette and Charles who have become valued friends. A special acknowledgement to Marguerite, Gina, Giff, Gerda and Máire and my wonderful 'star' friends – you provided me with a welcome relief from the challenges of writing through solid and sustained connections. I am especially indebted to my family. My inspirational mum, Margaret, and my precious sisters Ca, Úna and Máiread who wrap me with their love and friendship. And last but certainly not least: Patrick, Cian and Oisín who tolerate the intrusions of mom's working life with such good humour. And Ger. Thank you for travelling the road with me with such love and patience. I am for ever grateful.

1

Setting the context: immigration, ethnic diversity and schooling in Ireland

Introduction

Irish society has undergone substantial change since the 1960s typified by membership of the European Union, a rapidly changing social and economic structure, urbanisation and competition within a global economy. Coupled with such developments have been changing demographic patterns, with massive emigration in the 1980s replaced by increasing immigration, following the unprecedented economic growth of the 'Celtic Tiger' in the mid-1990s. The period since 2008 has witnessed a sea-change in economic circumstances, the openness of the Irish economy making it especially vulnerable to the global economic down-turn, coupled with the bursting of a property bubble that has given rise to massive personal and public debt. Net outward migration is once again a feature of Irish society (CSO 2010), yet available records and anecdotal evidence suggest that while the number of immigrants is in decline, the number of immigrants continuing to work and reside here remains relatively high, especially among those with school aged children (OECD 2009a). While there have been numerous studies conducted in Ireland on the economic impact of immigration (e.g. Barrett et al. 2006), less attention has been given to how key institutions within the Irish state have responded to and coped with immigration, nor of how immigrants themselves have adapted to Irish structures and systems.

Sociologically, education systems have a pivotal role to play in society, not only because of their potentially formative power on young minds but also because of their significance in regulating and (re) producing patterns of power and control between social groups in society. In other words schools are not neutral spaces, and 'schooling' is not a neutral process. Education is submerged in cultural politics, a key instrument in defining identity, belonging and nationhood. The title of this book, *Immigration and schooling in the Republic of Ireland: making a difference?*, signals the focus, locating the analysis in terms of how difference is itself construed and worked with in and through education. Core to the analysis is the tension between production and reproduction in education, between transformative and more conservative tendencies and how these tensions are mediated by dynamics of power at national, local and increasingly European levels.

This chapter sets the general context, documenting the nature of demographic change, and the characteristics of the immigrant population, especially those of educational interest. In order to fully appreciate responses and reactions to change, the chapter also outlines the structure of the Irish education system, focusing especially on patterns of governance and control. This is important, not only because of the impact on access to and enrolment in different types of schools, but also on processes of identity formation and meaning making – central elements in the education process.

Immigration and social change in the Republic of Ireland

While there has been much attention given to the level of economic and social change in Ireland in recent years (Fahey et al. 2008; Nolan et al. 2000), the population remains relatively small, standing at 4.1 million, the highest in over one hundred and fifty years (CSO 2006). What is unique about the change in the past ten years is not only the level and intensity of immigration (the population increased by 8% between 2000 and 2006) but also the extent of immigration by those who did not traditionally belong to the Irish Diaspora. According to the 2006 census, 15% of people normally resident in Ireland were born outside of the State and 10% are of foreign nationality, including almost 130, 000 people between the ages of 0–24 years (CSO 2008). What is also significant about these patterns is the diversity of countries from which immigrants have come, with non-Irish nationals coming from 188 countries, the majority from non-English speaking countries, the regions of which are indicated in Table 1.1 below, followed by ethnic classification of those with Irish nationality in Table 1.2.

Table 1.1 *Population in the Republic of Ireland by nationality*

Irish	3,706,683
United Kingdom	112,548
Rest of EU[a]	163,227
Rest of Europe	24,425
Africa	35,326
Asia	46,952
America	21,124
Other	16,131
Not stated	45,597

Note: [a] This includes those in the EU accession countries of 2004.
Source: CSO 2008.

Table 1.2 *Ethnic background of those with Irish nationality*

Total Irish	3,706,683
Irish	3,549,243
Irish Traveller	21,769
Other white background	19,115
African	11,440
Other black background	1,546
Chinese	3,078
Other Asian background	6,190
Mixed background	12,934
Not stated	36,368

Source: CSO 2008.

While there have always been some minority ethnic groupings in Irish society, including indigenous Travellers, and small Jewish, Italian and Chinese communities, the vast majority of the population has traditionally been classified as white, sedentary and Roman Catholic. While showing some decline, the latter group remains in a considerable majority as indicated in Table 1.3.

Table 1.3 *Population by religious identity*

	N	%
Total population	4,172,013	(100.0)
Catholic	3,644,013	(87.3)
Church of Ireland	118,948	(2.8)
Other Christian	28,028	(0.7)
Presbyterian	21,496	(0.7)
Muslim	31,779	(0.5)
Orthodox	19,994	(0.5)
Methodist	10,768	(0.3)
Other	54,033	(1.3)
No religion	175,252	(4.2)

Source: CSO 2008.

While comparatively small, it is worth noting the percentage increase in minority faith traditions from the previous census in 2002 – an increase of 9% in the Protestant (Church of Ireland) communities, 70% among the Muslim grouping, and 67% and 90% respectively for those within the Buddhist and Hindu communities (CSO 2008). These increases, as we will see, are significant for access and enrolment to schools, especially in the primary sector. Of note also is the geographical dispersion of immigrant communities. While the CSO (2008) indicates that immigrant populations are distributed throughout the country, there is also evidence that certain groups of immigrants are 'clustering' in particular areas. The census indicates for example the high proportion of immigrant families from Brazil in Gort, Co. Galway (comprising 40% of the population), while certain urban centres, most especially in Dublin, have undergone rapid expansion to accommodate significant numbers of immigrants who often tend to be clustered in areas of low rental/housing (Fahey and Fanning 2010, NCCRI 2008). Such patterns are also reflected in the confirmed higher enrolment of immigrant students in schools in economically marginalised areas (Smyth et al. 2009).

These patterns become especially interesting when the educational profile of immigrants is also considered. What is notable is the high level of educational qualifications immigrants hold, relative to the native population, as indicated in Table 1.4.

Table 1.4   *Educational qualifications by ethnic status*

Ethnicity	*Education Level*					
	Total	*Primary*	*Lower secondary*	*Upper secondary*	*Non-degree*	*Degree or higher*
Irish	2,863,428	484,934	526,253	691,743	271,651	426,514
Irish traveller	13,098	6,905	1,621	369	42	33
Other white	253,835	9,419	29,088	77,299	18,572	59,749
African	23,835	833	1,516	3,454	1,741	4,098
Other black	2,342	136	248	501	187	399
Chinese	14,474	828	1,023	1,797	747	1,840
Other Asian	28,041	767	1,055	2,593	1,621	9,781
Mixed background	34,032	2,396	3,851	7,342	2,219	6,778
Not stated	48,648	4,856	3,612	4,035	970	2,059

Source: CSO 2008.

Such patterns suggest comparative levels of education between immigrants and the Irish population (when considered between the ages of 15–44 yrs), although the table also indicates significant variations between different nationalities. When mapped to the population with children, subsequent analysis confirms that immigrant parents have on average higher levels of education than native parents, including doctorate, post-graduate and professional qualifications (CSO 2008). The findings in general suggest comparative immigrant profiles with countries such as Australia and Canada, who have also attracted immigrants with high skill and educational levels (OECD 2006).

Some criticism has been levelled however at the construction of immigrants primarily in economic terms (Allen and Loyal 2006), without due attention to the broader familial and social dynamics that are embedded in the immigrant experience (Allen 2007). Yet the census data also gives some indication of the numbers of children born into immigrant families, as indicated in Table 1.5 below.

Table 1.5 *Ethnic background by age*

Age	Ethnicity						
	Irish	*Irish Traveller*	*Other white*	*African*	*Other black*	*Chinese*	*Other Asian*
0–4	252,499	3,298	12,100	9,378	836	939	3,630
5–9	253,369	2,126	2,452	220	496	1,731	3,152
10–14	245,903	2,954	11,196	2,452	220	496	1,731
15–19	262,505	2,529	11,709	1,931	201	758	1,250

Source: CSO 2008.

The patterns confirm highest proportions of children across most age groups among 'Other White', and African groups, especially in the pre-school years, and for 'Other White' in the later stages of primary and secondary school years. These patterns have clear implications for future enrolments in schools, as well as access to higher education. The fact that many immigrant children are clustered in communities and schools in poorer areas, yet their parents may have levels of educational capital substantially higher than the native population, raises interesting questions about the impact of immigration on community dynamics, as well as on dynamics within schools. From an educational perspective, such patterns have important implications for setting the context for levels of motivation, orientation to and integration in the education system by immigrant parents and their children, which will be discussed in more depth in later chapters.

Immigration and demographic change across the school sector

One of the difficulties with respect to the formulation of policy on immigration and schooling is the absence of precise information on the number of immigrants on a school by school basis. While Table 1.5 highlights the significant number of children who are defined as 'Irish' in Census data, it also gives some indication of the number of children of minority ethnic/immigrant background of school going age who are currently in the education system, as well as the numbers who may be entering the formal system in the coming years. There Table 1.6 below indicates the distribution of children by nationality for the primary school sector, with just 12% identified as having nationality other than Irish. Of course those who have Irish nationality may also include children born in Ireland to immigrant parents.

Table 1.6   *Total pupils enrolled in mainstream primary schools by nationality*

	N	%
Nationality Ireland	439,231	88.0
Other European Union	26,627	5.3
European other than EU	4,413	0.9
North America	1, 410	0.3
Latin America/Carribean	970	0.2
Asia	8,874	1.8
Australia Oceania	604	0.1
Africa	13,925	2.8
Unknown	3,039	0.6
Total	499,093	100.0

Source: Dept of Education and Skills 2010. Personal correspondence August 2010.

A further measure of the distribution of children of immigrant background is the allocation of language support teachers in schools. In 2009/2010 there were 1500 language support teachers serving the English language needs of between 25,000 – 30,000 migrant children. Again this is only a rough estimate given that not all immigrant children are in receipt of language support or may have already completed the two year allocation they are allowed under the scheme.

According to the DES, in 2009/2010, the total number of Secondary students was 342,486 and approximately 7% of these were immigrant pupils from nearly 160 countries. As Table 1.7 below indicates, the highest proportion of those who come from within the EU are from the UK, followed by Poland, Lithuania and Spain, while outside of the EU (Table 1.8), students whose families come from Nigeria, the USA and the Philippines make up the greatest number of immigrants.

Table 1.7   *Top ten countries of origin of immigrant students in secondary schools from the EU (2009/10)*

Country of origin	No. of students
United Kingdom	6,359
Poland	3,861
Lithuania	1,608
Spain	1,196
Germany	884
Romania	802
Latvia	786
Slovakia	378
France	246
Hungary	202

Source: Department of Education and Skills 2010.

Table 1.8   *Top ten countries of origin of immigrant students in secondary schools from outside the EU (2009/10)*

Nigeria	1,819
USA	1,188
Philippines	1,152
South Africa	560
India	524
Russia	345
Pakistan	479
Congo	314
Australia	249
China	235

Source: Department of Education and Skills 2010.

Governance and control in Irish education: the significance of denominational status

Immigration does not take place in a social or cultural void but becomes mapped to pre-existing structures and systems. This is one of the undeniable challenges that confronts societies in periods of rapid and intensive social and economic change – the extent to which social systems and institutions are equipped to deal with such change and the very patterns and structures that pre-date the social and economic shifts themselves. To an outside observer, what strikes as unusual about the Irish education system is the level of Church involvement – the fact that we have a state funded 'aided' system where ownership and control rests predominantly with Trustees/Patrons, the latter almost exclusively defined in denominational terms.

At primary level, there are two main types of school – national schools which cater for children aged from 4–12 years, and special schools; while at Secondary (also referred to as Post-primary schools) level there are three types of school: Secondary; Community and Comprehensive; and Vocational schools. These are indicated in Table 1.9.

Table 1.9   *Number and type of schools at primary and secondary levels*

National schools	3,165
Special schools	124
Total primary	**3,289**
Secondary school	394
Community and comprehensive	91
Vocational	247
Total post-primary	**732**

Source: Dept of Education and Skills 2010.

The ultimate control over primary schools rests with the Patron, who delegates managerial authority to each school board and has majority representation on each board through Patron appointees and the Chairperson. Of the primary schools under Catholic patronage, these are divided into those that are owned by religious orders – convent and monastery schools, but a majority are parish based and owned by the local Diocese. As Table 1.10 below indicates, an overwhelming majority of primary schools are under Catholic patronage.

Table 1.10 *Primary Schools by religious denomination*

School type	Number of schools	Number of pupils
Catholic	2,888	463,742
Church of Ireland	181	14,666
Presbyterian	14	661
Methodist	1	89
Jewish	1	86
Inter-denominational	8	1,093
Muslim	2	406
Multi-denominational[a]	69	11,425
Quaker	1	93
Totals	3,165	492, 261

Note: [a] The multi-denominational schools listed include: 56 under the patronage of Educate Together; 2 community national schools under the patronage of the VEC; 8 Gaelscoileanna under the patronage of An Foras Patrúnachta; 1 John Scottus School and 2 Steiner Schools.
Source: Dept of Education and Skills 2010.

More recently a new model of inter-denominational schooling has been developed, under the aegis of the Vocational Education Committees called community national schools. At the time of writing, two of these schools have been established on a pilot basis and under the temporary patronage of the Minister for Education and Skills. When the amending legislation is in place, County Dublin VEC will assume patronage. Approval has also been granted for additional Multi-denominational (Educate Together) schools.

At post-primary level the system is more diverse (see Table 1.11), following relatively traditional lines of vocationally oriented vs academic oriented curricula. Secondary schools belong to the tradition of academic grammar schools – although the curriculum today is broader. Secondary schools are privately owned and managed mainly by Catholic Religious Orders; Vocational schools while technically under 'secular' management and inter-denominational, in practice they are mainly Catholic – with Catholic clergy sitting on the Vocational Education Committees. Community and comprehensive schools developed in the 1960s as new models of secondary education, some of which are denominational (Church of Ireland) and most of which are under the control of the Vocational Education Committees.

Table 1.11   *Post-primary schools by religious denomination (2008/09)*

School type	Number of schools	Number of pupils
Catholic	363	174,656
Church of Ireland	25	12,549
Quaker	1	350
Jewish	1	142
Inter-denominational	340	154,789
Totals	730	342,486

Source: Dept of Education and Skills 2010.

Irish society is characterised then by a high degree of state funded faith based schooling, especially at primary level. The issue must be considered in light of the contradictory legislation governing Irish Education, especially the Education Act of 1998, which enshrines the right of all children to equality of access to and participation in education, while simultaneously enshrining the right of school Patrons to protect their religious ethos. In practice what this means is that primary schools have the right to refuse admission to children outside of the denomination of the school, if such admission undermines the ethos of the school, or if the school is already over-subscribed with children who belong to the denomination of the school. Given that over 90% of our primary schools are currently under Catholic patronage, this can create difficulties for children who are not Catholic in gaining access to a school in their locality. While subsequent chapters will highlight how many of these schools have embraced and welcomed children from a range of religious and cultural diversities, this should not undermine the challenges that exist in reconciling the need to respect and maintain a Catholic ethos, while respecting the traditions and faith of those children who are outside the Catholic norm. The situation is further complicated by the emphasis within Catholic education on an integrated system of faith formation that permeates the entire school day. For children who are not of the Catholic faith, it is virtually impossible for them to 'exclude' themselves from religious based activities, most especially in school years where preparation for both first communion and confirmation is intense, but also during the everyday recital of prayers, and the celebration of Catholic feast days and traditions throughout the school year. While this is an issue that poses challenges for children of minority beliefs, both indigenous Irish and immigrant, the increasing diversity of beliefs noted earlier in this chapter as a result of immigration, consolidates the problem.

Methodology and layout of the book

It is these tensions between context, history, norms and practice that are more fully developed and conceptualised in subsequent chapters. They document in a detailed manner the lived experiences and narratives of those who spend a considerable amount of time in schools – principals and teachers who are charged with the professional responsibilities for education and the children and young people who spend a considerable proportion of their childhood and youth engaging in learning as it is shaped and provided for by the Irish state. For immigrant parents too, the education system is the one institution of the state with which they must interact, some to a greater extent than others, but which conveys through the feedback and efforts of their children, a sense of what living in Ireland culturally and socially is about. The analysis presented is primarily qualitative in focus, drawn from interviews, classroom observations and field visits to a range of schools over the past ten years. A central tenet in qualitative method-ologies is to capture the meanings and intentions of those involved in the research, to tell their 'stories' in a manner which conveys the depth, complexity and subjectivity of their experiences (Hammersly 1999; Luttrell 2009). However such research also needs to move beyond description, to a contextualisation of those responses, meanings and experiences in the broader social milieu in which they occur. This is done in a number of ways throughout the book.

Chapter 2 presents a conceptual analysis of power, identity and governance in Irish education. Drawing on the work of Foucault it shows how dominant discourses in relation to ethnic and cultural identity provided the backdrop for state policy in relation to immigration as well as educational practice in terms of religious values, modes of governance and patterns of power and control. In more recent years these have been reshaped to align with a modern neo-liberal fashioning of Irishness in line with consumer capitalism (Inglis 2008), that situates migration firmly as serving the needs of the (then) rapidly expanding economy. While the discourse draws upon the language of inclusion and recognition of diversity, contradictions in the implementation of policy in practice are evident at the inter-face of poor urban/social planning and lack of investment in diversity training across the public sector. The impact on education is especially profound, structurally embedded patterns of segregation in terms of social class compounded by governance systems which endorse the separation of children on the basis of religious/faith background. It argues that the establishment of further 'layers' of schooling, while pluralist in intent by broadening 'parental choice' in certain urban centres, potentially demarcates 'immigrant' schools from those which are the 'norm' for the white, Catholic, population.

Issues related to parental choice and access to different types of schools are also significantly influenced by social class and Chapter 3 extends the analysis to the influence of resources (economic, social and cultural) on the adaptation and positioning of immigrants to the education system. The 'neutral' stance of the Irish state to governance issues in Irish education, positioning itself as mediator between powerful stakeholders, contrasts with its very explicit policy on the recruitment of immigrants with high educational capital, reflected in the census statistics outlined earlier in this chapter. Such policy can be located in the broader competition for 'global' talent among western developed states, underpinned by EU/OECD policies which emphasise the human capital value of immigration to economic success and advantage. This sets the context for responses to immigrants in the host society, both in terms of the status of those who add 'value' and those who do not, as well as in the level and nature of support that is provided to facilitate immigrant integration on the ground. The economic, cultural and social resources which immigrants themselves bring also has considerable implications for how they adapt and accommodate to education in the host society. Chapter 3 considers outline findings in relation to patterns of immigrant achievement in Irish schools. It details the factors which contribute to educational success with reference to the work of Pierre Bourdieu and considers the interplay of societal as well as individual level factors in shaping immigrant responses to, and outcomes in education. It highlights the centrality of power to processes of action and reaction in the field of education, as broader international and national policy contexts in relation to immigration crystallise in the dispositions, identities and responses of principals, teachers, parents and children in classrooms and schools.

The remaining chapters present the voices of each of these actors in education, providing a picture of the often competing dynamics and tensions around inclusion/exclusion that are currently being worked out in newly multi-ethnic Irish schools. Chapter 4 considers the impact of immigration on the work of school principals, who in their leadership roles are central to shaping and defining school culture and practice. It highlights how their leadership practices are influenced not only by each principal's prior dispositions (habitus) and management experience, but also by the local context of their schools and the nature and intensity of immigrant change. It explores the contradictory tendencies in their practice, as classed and racialised constructs of immigrant groups sit alongside a commitment to care for migrant children and their families. It points to clear distinctions however between leadership for social justice and leadership which is grounded in more paternalistic forms of concern and of the ethical and identity challenges faced by principals who seek to embrace real change.

Constraints in their practice are highlighted not only in terms of the continual struggle for additional state supports and resources – worsening with the economic recession – but also in managing local dynamics related to the reputation and public profile of their schools, especially in middle class communities.

While principals have a key role in shaping whole-school policy for diversity and inclusion, it is what takes place in the classroom, between teachers and children that makes a real and meaningful difference to the life chances and educational well-being of migrant children. Teacher 'effect' in this sense derives from the manner in which teachers engage with their teaching, connect with their students and place learning at the centre of their practice. However this is not a matter of simple 'transference' that takes place un-problematically in the school and classroom. Teacher practice is itself embedded in complex processes of identification, affiliation and normalisation that derive, as with principals, from their own location as gendered, raced and classed beings. Further it takes place against a backdrop of state policy, both in terms of curriculum and assessment requirements, as well as resourcing and professional development to support practice in the classroom. Chapter 5 explores these issues with reference to how teachers think and talk about migrant children, as well as how their own constructs of 'integration' shape their practice with all children (both immigrant and indigenous Irish) in the classroom. It highlights the personal and professional challenges which confront teachers as their assumptions about what is 'normal' are disrupted through their engagement with those who are ethnically different. It notes the a-critical approach to the education of migrant children which characterises many teachers' responses and the need for deep immersion in the life-worlds and perspectives of such children for real pedagogical change to emerge. This latter tends to be more evident among language support teachers.

Chapter 6 considers the perspectives of immigrant parents on their engagement with the education system. It explores the significance of class, gender and ethnicity to such engagement and highlights the resources immigrant parents draw upon in an effort to navigate and learn the 'rules' of the education system in Ireland. Some do so more successfully than others, influenced by their access to capitals and the accompanying sense of entitlement and expectation that they will benefit from the time and investment in education they make. Others struggled with lone parenthood and long work hours, often in the absence of social and cultural supports. Racialised dynamics are also highlighted however, in anxieties around 'visible' difference by parents from Africa especially and their reluctance to become actively involved in school activities. Prior experiences of more authoritarian systems of education in their home countries also influenced parent responses. The chapter also explores the different responses by schools to these issues and the key role they can play in the generation of both social and cultural capital among and between immigrant and indigenous parents.

All of these chapters highlight how significant stakeholders have adapted, adjusted and positioned themselves with respect to the social and cultural change that occurred in schools in Ireland during a period of intensive immigration. Be it at the level of macro level responses through European/OECD /national state policy initiatives or micro level responses in terms of principals, teachers and parents perspectives, what is in common among these stakeholders is their adult status, and by implication their (varied) capacity to direct, form and shape the everyday lives of children and youth in schools. Chapter 7 focuses on the perspectives of migrant children and youth and highlights how they actively construct and contribute to processes of integration, accommodation (and indeed assimilation) through their work in schools. In this sense children are central players in the adaptation and integration of immigrant communities into the host society. For many it is 'like living another life', as they move between contrasting social and cultural worlds of home and school. Two central themes are developed, related to the experience of learning and how this is influenced not only by issues related to class, gender and age, but also the desire to manage their ethnic identities with teachers and peers. This latter is developed further with respect to social and racial dynamics in schools.

Chapter 8 draws together the main themes of the book and revisits the explanatory model outlined in Chapter 3. It re-emphasises the significance of education as a field of power in society, shaping, regulating, preserving, transforming – identities, meanings, belongings through the manner of its engagement with children and young people in schools. Education is never neutral and the action or indeed inaction of those who work in and for schools has considerable consequences for the educational well-being of children. It sets the context for experiences of inclusion or exclusion that bears out for present and subsequent generations. This is most especially true with respect to migrant children.

2

Shaping the nation: power, identity and governance in Irish education

'It's mid week of the first full week of new term and Kenyan born Philippe Njoroge has arrived at the gates of Balbriggan's Educate Together school to collect his five year old daughter, Natasha. Njoroge has been in Ireland for five years, most of that time living in north Co. Dublin, and he had problems finding a school place for Natasha before she was accepted by Educate Together. The family had tried Catholic schools first. 'We are not Catholic, and your religion is one of the questions that appears most prominently on the application form. They should not be so tight on what your religion is because the country is opening up and we should embrace everybody', he said. (*Irish Times*, 8 September 2007)

This quote is taken from a report into the crisis that emerged in Balbriggan – a suburb in North Dublin, in September 2007. It encapsulates issues related to power, identity and school governance that are the focus of this chapter. I present a socio-historical analysis of the patterns of representation and control detailed in Chapter 1, outlining the significance of education in reproducing patterns of cultural belonging and national identity, most especially in emerging nation states (Green 1997). Framing the analysis is Foucault's conceptualisation of the exercise of power in modern societies, and the key role of institutions – such as schools – in both the production and circulation of discourses of belonging and 'other'. The focus is on structures as disciplinary mechanisms/technologies which classify/signify (how are you defined and understood?), divide (into different school types) and normalise (are you the exception or the 'rule'?).

Racism and power in society

Traditionally, accounts of race have emphasised biological differences between people, giving rise to perceptions of a hierarchy of races that neatly accorded with colonial oppression and white European supremacy (Gillborn 2008). More recently, with the benefits of genetic testing, the idea of inherent genetic differences between races has been challenged.

This has given rise to the use of the term 'ethnic' as more appropriate to mark distinctions between groups set apart by a shared cultural identity. Ethnic identity is itself construed as fluid and changeable, something that is constructed in interaction with others over time. Race continues to remain a powerful signifier however of identity, belonging, discrimination, identification and affiliation. Racism itself has undergone changes in how it is conceptualised and expressed. While 'old' racism articulated prejudice and discrimination on the grounds of assumed (genetic) inferiority of one group over another, 'new' racism is framed in terms of an emphasis on cultural difference between ethnic groups and the impending threats such difference can make to national solidarity and cohesion (Modood 2007). This cultural racism, while more subtle in its articulation ('I'm not racist but …') is nonetheless equally effective in marginalising and discriminating against those who differ from the dominant ethnic group. Fundamentally it is embedded in ideas of belonging and identity that privilege one form of ethnic expression and identity over another. Certain ethnic groups are thus minoritised, deprived from full participation and recognition in the society. They are stereotyped and racialised according to fixed and prejudicial attitudes which are assigned to the entire ethnic group. Such patterns are especially invidious when reflected at an institutional level, giving rise to a form of institutional racism which MacPherson, in his critique of the police force in the United Kingdom defined as:

> the collective failure of an organisation to provide an appropriate and profes-
> sional service to people because of their colour, culture or ethnic origin. It
> can be seen or detected in processes, attitudes and behaviour which amount to
> discrimination through unwitting prejudice, ignorance, thoughtlessness and
> racist stereotyping which disadvantage minority ethnic people. (MacPherson
> 1999: 321)

Colour racism is rarely overtly drawn upon in public discourse. Nonetheless discrimination against those who are black persists, typically by averting to difference in culture and lifestyle, rather than overtly to skin colour. Such racism should not detract from racism that is also directed at other non-white ethnic minorities, including for example Muslims, especially post-9/11 (Modood 2004). Neither should it detract from considering how factors related to class, gender, religion and sexuality influence the experience of racisms, intersecting with other forms of inequality and non-recognition (May 2009). More recently, attention has turned to an analysis of 'whiteness' and the privileging and embeddedness of 'whiteness' in society (Gillborn 2008; Leonardo 2002/2009). 'Whiteness' in this respect not only refers to skin colour but is symbolic of the access to resources and recognition that is taken for granted in a way that does not need to be named. Whiteness can be considered as a form of property, which when mobilised confers privilege and entitlement on those perceived and defined as 'white'. In this respect references to the 'whitening' of the Irish through their strategic mobilisation and economic development (Garner 2007) convey the symbolic as well as material value of 'whiteness' and how this is framed in terms of a distancing from black and minority 'others'.

Recent analyses of racism in Ireland highlight the prevalence of discrimination against those who are black and Asian: in housing, shops and services, public transport and job searches (Russell et al. 2008). Levels of discrimination against the Traveller community, previously identified as subjected to a form of 'caste like apartheid' in Ireland (MacGreil 1996) confirm the privileging of white sedentary Irishness in national constructs of belonging and recognition (Lentin and McVeigh 2006, 2002). Consistent prejudice against an indigenous minority ethnic group such as Travellers belies the view that racism in Ireland is new, an 'imported' phenomenon as a result of immigration. Yet the extensive agreement of the Irish electorate in 2004 to change the citizenship rights of children of immigrant parents is indicative of a culture of anxiety around immigration, that as Fanning (2009) notes had especially negative consequences at the time for black Africans who had come to Ireland predominantly through the asylum process. Making a clear distinction between those with a right of affiliation to the Irish nation through the blood line (jus sanguine) rather than as formerly through birthplace (jus soli) Lentin and McVeigh (2006) argue that the referendum 'constitutionalised' racism under the guise of 'common sense' citizenship. It reinforced the ethnically exclusionary provisions in the constitution at the time of its inception.

Differing viewpoints are proposed in relation to the role of the state in the production and promotion of racism and its genesis in Ireland (Fanning 2009; Lentin and McVeigh 2006[1]). Ultimately the capacity to exclude and 'other' derives from differences in power, which itself is embedded in structural inequalities that are related not only to race, but also to gender and social class. During a period of economic boom, relative inequalities increased in Irish society, giving rise to a heightened sense of vulnerability and intensification of racist practices (Garner 2004). These are likely to be compounded during a period of economic decline. Racism is intimately tied with the exercise of power by a privileged majority that structure society in terms of their worldview. A key mechanism for this structuring is the school system, because of its formative influence on young people and its role in communicating the dominant 'message systems' of the society (Bernstein 1975). The work of Michel Foucault (1979, 1980) is especially useful in highlighting the dynamics of power and control that underpin identity making and belonging, and the significant role of schools in this process. He draws attention to how identities are constructed in line with 'regimes of truth' which signify, classify and govern. For Foucault, the establishment of schools, along with hospitals and prisons, both derived from and gave rise to new modes of governance by the state. This enabled more systematic regulation of key sections of the population. Such regulation (governmentality) was especially effective because of its capacity to both *subject* and *create subjects* through a series of disciplinary practices in these institutions. This process of subjectification focused on creating distinctions between those who were normal and 'other', a form of 'bio-power' which centred especially on efficiency, rationality and the maximal utility of the body. For Foucault, racism must be understood in terms of this attempt to shield the state from abnormalcy – from those defined as 'other' (through inferior blood lines that also connected with class and sexuality) who threatened the normalcy and productive capacities of modern nations centred on bio-power:

> It is a racism against the abnormal, against individuals who as carriers of a condition, a stigmata, or any defect whatsoever, may more or less randomly transmit to their heirs the unpredictable consequences of evil, or rather of the non-normal, that they carry with them. It ... is the internal means of defence of a society against its abnormal individuals. (Foucault 2003: 316–317)

Rather than being coercive, disciplinary power is especially effective because of the emphasis on the individual working on their own 'selves', a governing of the soul (Rose 2001) that embodies ways of seeing and acting that are informed by dominant circulating discourses. Constructs of whiteness as normal and blackness as 'other', of sedentarism as normal and nomadism as deviant sets the parameters for identity making which includes some and excludes others through practices at an institutional level. These define such exclusion as normal and common sense. However the exercise of power is neither linear nor hierarchical, nor ever complete and can have both intended as well as unintended outcomes. This is the capillary effect that allows for the possibility of resistance and accommodation to dominant discourse and norms:

> We must make allowance for the complex and unstable process whereby discourse can be both an instrument and an effect of power, but also a hindrance, a stumbling block, a point of resistance and a starting point for an opposing strategy. (Foucault 1979: 94)

Through interaction, especially in institutions such as schools, individuals become both defined and classified as 'normal' or 'other', as well as feel themselves to be 'norm' and 'other'. Power is exercised, not through beliefs or thoughts but through institutionalised *practices* – it is not a question of imposition but normalisation through everyday practices that become embedded as taken for granted 'truths' of the way 'we' are, or the way 'things are done around here'. The presence of 'others', of what is not 'normal' (e.g. increasing presence of minorities) can rupture this 'taken for grantedness'. This leads to cycles of production and reproduction, of resistance, accommodation and change, as new discourses merge, become accommodated and subsumed, in the knowledge/power/knowledge circuit that is constantly evolving.

> Power must be analysed as something which circulates, or rather as something which only functions in the form of a chain. It is never localised here or there, never in any body's hands, never appropriated as a commodity or piece of wealth … And not only do individuals circulate between its threads, they are always in the position of simultaneously undergoing and exercising this power. (Foucault 1980: 98)

In looking at power in schools we need to consider how dominant discourses of norm and other become instantiated in practice (Giddens 1984). This occurs through the dividing and classifying practices that permeate schools as organisation, but also the spaces and locales of resistance which develop arising from these disciplinary practices. In Ireland, we can ask what norms around cultural and ethnic identity permeated education and how were these signified and legitimated through the dividing and classificatory systems in schools. What were the implications for the creation of subjects who came to know and define themselves as norm or other? How did this set the context for patterns of belonging, inclusion and exclusion in an increasingly multi-ethnic Ireland?

Culture, power and identity in Irish education

I have highlighted previously the significance of the exercise of power in Irish schools to how childhood is constructed and how children come to see and define themselves (Devine 2003). Given its wider impact, it is no co-incidence that struggles over who controls education have been key to the construction of certain forms of identity, belonging and meaning making in Irish society. The very establishment of a formal state primary school system in Ireland as early as 1831 (in advance of such moves in any other part of the UK) derived from a desire by the British government that 'schools [would] serve politicising and socialising goals, cultivating attitudes of political loyalty and cultural assimilation' (Coolahan 1981: 4). A defining feature of education from that period right up until the end of the nineteenth century, was the struggle over the control of schools, especially denominational control. Following concerted action by each of the main Christian denominations (Roman Catholics, Protestants and Anglicans) by 1900 the system became 'de facto' denominational,[2] endorsed through state funding for separate Protestant and Catholic schools and teacher training colleges.

Just as the English government sought through the curriculum to engage in processes of cultural assimilation in line with English norms (especially with reference to the neglect of Irish studies), so too did the education system become a key instrument in the transition from a colonial to a post-colonial society and attempts to consolidate the position of the new Republic from 1922 in a relatively unstable and war torn Europe (Garvin 2004). Understood in terms of the exercise of power, what is of interest are the constructs of identity which came to be shaped and how this constructed who belonged and who/what was defined as 'normal' within the emerging nation state. This set the context for regulatory mechanisms within both education and the broader society that are prevalent up to the present day. Reflected in the 'defensive ethnocentrism' based on resistance to imposition from the outside (MacGreil 1996) a 'hyper Catholicism' (Allen and Loyal 2006) became prevalent in state policy. Irishness was constructed in relatively essentialist and homogenous terms. The associated 'shaping of the nation' in line with Gaelic, nationalistic and Catholic ideals typified the homogenising thrust of modern and emerging nation states (Goldberg 2002; Green 1997; Lentin and McVeigh 2002) intent on consolidating a distinctive national identity. This had negative implications for the albeit small but established minority ethnic communities (indigenous Travellers, immigrant Jewish, Italian and Chinese communities) whose history differed from the majority, but who had been part of Irish society for a considerable length of time (Fanning 2007; Lentin and McVeigh 2006). Significantly, minority traditions where recognised, were only conceived of in religious terms (Fanning 2002). Ethnic minorities were relatively invisible in Irish society, reinforced through carefully regulated patterns of immigration and a defensive legislative framework (Aliens Act 1936) that foreclosed entry by those who were ethnically and culturally different.

Education in the new Republic became redefined in terms of adherence to Catholic teaching and the re-establishment of a Gaelic civilisation (Coolahan 1981; Hyland and Milne 1992). Inspired by the ideology of cultural nationalism and a heightened patriotic fervour (Farren 1995), a central role was accorded to the Irish language with an emphasis on courses in Irish literature, history, geography, mythology, games, music and dancing. Through schooling, a cultural revolution was envisaged that would provide a solid grounding in nationhood, conceptualised in terms of Gaelic rituals and ideals. Underpinning such practice was the pervasive and accepted influence of the Catholic Church, the circular and capillary nature of power giving rise to a school system which:

Produced successive generations of laymen imbued with loyalty to the church ... in their turn these new generations of national school educated adults approved the education of their own children in the same religious atmosphere in which they themselves had been educated. (Akenson 1975: 98).

Educational policy up until the 1960s reflected a *laissez faire* attitude by the state, content to play a subsidiary role to the Churches in the organisation and maintenance of schooling. 'Governmentality' was invested by the state in the Churches through a symbiotic relationship that mutually benefited both (Drudy and Lynch 1993). This is perhaps best reflected in the infamous comment of the Minister for Education (Richard Mulcahy) in 1957 who defined the role of Minister in the Department of Education as 'a kind of dungaree man, the plumber who will make the satisfactory communications' rather than one who would 'philosophise on educational matters' (O'Connor 1986:1). This subsidiary role by the state mirrored a similar approach to social policy generally in Irish society (Fanning 2002/2009) and specifically policy related to the welfare of children (Devine 2008). A segregationist mindset prevailed, the partitioning of the child population denominationally (classic of Foucault's dividing practices as technologies of normalisation and control), mirrored by further separation on the basis of gender, as well as physical and mental disabilities, and classified 'deviance'. Given the state's subsidiary role in matters of child and family welfare, the care of these marginalised 'others' was devolved to the voluntary sectors, constructed as a matter of charity and Christian empathy rather than rights and social justice. The pursuit and indeed assumption of cultural homogeneity ensured that little attention was paid to the needs and position of those who were also culturally different. While this clearly included religious minorities, as detailed, it was also reflected in the denial of the distinctiveness of Traveller culture, the latter classified as a subculture of poverty. The 'problem of Itinerants' (Report of the Commission on Itinerancy 1963) was to be addressed through processes of assimilation and absorption into sedentary norms (Fanning 2009/2002; Lentin and McVeigh 2006; O'Connell 2002).

The predominance of what O'Sullivan (2005) refers to as a theocentric paradigm in Irish education up to the 1960s, coupled with the reluctance of the state to be actively involved in the formulation of educational policy (save with the exception of the revival of the Irish language) had important implications and consequences for patterns of inclusion and exclusion in the education system. This mirrored broader processes of social closure in the wider society. In a climate of assumed consensus on values and goals, and a general indifference to difference (Devine 2008), the education system was characterised by significant inequalities in both participation and achievement and a highly conservative approach to any form of social innovation and change. Religious and moral socialisation in line with

Catholic teaching formed the backdrop to provision in the majority of primary and post-primary schools.

However as Foucault (1979: 101) notes 'the field of force relations' is never 'completely stable'. Running parallel to the Catholic school system was a relatively small number of Protestant schools which catered for the declining Protestant community and which the Protestant Churches were keen to uphold. Akenson (1975) argues that while the state demonstrated a high degree of religious tolerance for this minority – supporting the right of Protestant children to attend separate Protestant schools – it was especially insensitive to Protestants as a 'cultural' minority. Their affili- ations to English culture and language were at odds with the dominant Gaelic nationalism the state pursued with vigour through its compulsory programmes of instruction in the Irish language. It was only in the 1960s that the 'ghetto' mentality (ibid.: 119) of the Protestant community began to lift, as a new assertiveness of themselves as Irish nationals (ibid.: 134) emerged in negotiations over the provision of significant financial support to Protestant children to attend Protestant post-primary schools.[3] Akenson notes that supporting the Protestant community in this manner was indicative of a tolerance demonstrated by the state to a religious minority in a manner which did not threaten Catholic hegemony. On the contrary it supported and upheld Catholic educational orthodoxy in that all education was perceived to be essentially religious education and that children should be segregated religiously for their schooling (ibid.: 118). However the space for challenge was created by the circulation of discourses from abroad. This was itself spearheaded by a recognition within the state that social and economic closure was now a threat to the its very survival in a rapidly changing European and international context (Garvin 2004).

Discourse and counter discourse in educational governance and practice

A radical shift in policy took place in the 1960s, mirroring broader moves to modernisation and recognition by the state of the significance of education to economic development. Policy now became framed in terms of a human capital paradigm, with a new focus on the need to maximise individual talent to the betterment of the economy. Policy to widen participation in the education system, through for example the provision of free post-primary education in 1967 and extending the school leaving age was framed in terms of a liberal concept of equality (Baker et al. 2009; Lynch 1999). This derived from a desire to make education more widely available to those who were perceived to have the ability and motivation to do well in the system. This dovetailed with the wishes of parents, who, in a society characterised by an increasing propertyless middle class viewed education as the primary means through which the life-chances of their children could be secured.

O'Sullivan (2005) argues that the modernist agenda pursued elsewhere, characterised by a rationalist approach to issues such as equality, difference and democratic participation was not pursued ideologically in Ireland. Rather it was subsumed in a gradual and pragmatic manner into a mercantile paradigm. With its undertones of new public management characteristic of educational reform in Anglo Saxon societies, education as a consumptive good (rather than solely a moral good), essential for individual progress and the fostering of economic development came to the fore. Significantly such an orientation was not realised through concerted and overt advocacy, but rather through a 'cautious and staggered' approach that positioned the state as neutral mediator between competing stakeholders. This paved the way for change which was reactive rather than proactive. New discourses were incorporated and merged without the need for radical overhaul and change. Little was offered by way of analysis or policy making to tackle the structural causes of inequality or to explain poverty, exclusion and marginalisation in terms of imbalances of power in the wider society.

Significantly during a period of rapid educational expansion, the Catholic Church negotiated new zones of influence within the rapidly expanding post-primary sector through its representation on the boards of community schools and colleges – established with the aim of providing a more vocationally oriented curriculum that would be in tune with the modernising economy. While the national school system was de jure non-denominational (allowing children to withdraw for separate religious instruction where this was required owing to the absence of a choice of schools in the local area) it was de facto denominational. It became even more so in the 1960s with the removal of any obligation for teachers to be 'careful in the presence of children of different religious beliefs not to touch on matters of controversy' in the new rule for national schools produced in 1965 (Alvey 1991: 37; Hyland 1989: 94). Combined with the introduction of a primary curriculum in 1971 that endorsed the principle of an integrated educational experience with cross linkages across all curricular subjects, this resulted in religious education (as faith formation) permeating many aspects of teaching and learning across the entire curriculum. Epitomising bio-power in practice through the embodiment of certain constructions of self in schools, the primary curriculum of the time states:

> Each human being is created in God's image. He has a life to lead and a soul to be saved. Education is therefore concerned not only with life but with the purpose of life. (Dept of Education 1971: 3)

The principle of mixed education, where the state would not interfere with the 'religious tenets of any pupils' (Dept of Education 1947) was abandoned. This situation made it impossible for parents of children whose religion was not Catholic to experience a secular education in state funded primary schools (Hyland 1989), or indeed to gain right of admission to schools in their local areas. A precedent was established which as we will see later had considerable consequences for the rights of admission by immigrant children newly arrived into Ireland, especially in areas where there was intense competition for school places. Exemplifying the circulatory and unstable processes in the exercise of power, counter discourses which challenged Catholic hegemony in education gained new voice. The establishment of the first multi-denominational school in Dalkey (later to become known as 'Educate Together') in Dublin in 1978 derived from the frustration of a group of parents to the absence of choice in the primary school sector for those who did not want a denominational schooling for their children (Hyland 1989). Its development co-incided with an increasingly educated population (itself a by-product of increasing state investment in education), who were more interested in having an integrated and inter-denomi-national educational experience for their children. Following protracted negotiations, substantial private fundraising and the eventual garnishing of political support (including from the Taoiseach [Irish prime minister]), the Dalkey project national school was opened in temporary accommodation, finally securing permanent buildings in 1984. The subsequent relatively ad hoc expansion of the sector in the earlier years (owing to the absence of structured financial support from the Dept of Education, itself perhaps an indicator of counter-resistance to the change that was occurring) was predicated on perseverance of parents and the intervention on a personal basis, ironically, of individual ministers for education.

A notable change was also evident from the 1980s in government policy toward the recognition of other minority groups – notably Travellers, derived in part from the activation of the voices of Travellers themselves through finding their own 'ethnic voice' (Liégeois 1994). Key state initiatives to emerge included the establishment of the Task Force for Travellers (1995) and the publication in 2002 of guidelines on Traveller education. This signalled at the level of discourse a willingness to engage with and recognise the distinctiveness of Traveller identity and culture. Yet at the level of practice, Travellers continued to occupy a marginalised position in Irish society, subjected to institutional racism and the enactment of legislation that forestalled a nomadic way of life (Fanning 2009; Lentin and McVeigh 2006). While there were positive developments through for example the establishment of a network of resource teachers and the integration of some Traveller children into mainstream education, the focus remained at the level of enrolment and participation rather than mainstreaming Traveller culture and improving learning outcomes for Traveller children in schools (Lodge and Lynch 2004; McDonagh 2004). Significantly the absence of a discourse of racism in policy initiatives with respect to Travellers is testament to a broader resistance to confronting issues of power, misrecognition and structural inequalities in Irish society. The broader pattern of cultural misrecognition mirrored the experiences of other minority ethnic groups (including those who were allowed immigrate through designated Refugee programs) who were expected to assimilate into Irish society and into the education system. McGovern (1993) speaking of the experiences of Vietnamese refugees, identifies the total absence of cultural supports and recognition. Subsequently, as will be highlighted in Chapter 7, second-generation Vietnamese students almost twenty years later, continue to speak of their 'othered' status in Irish society and their relative invisibility in the school system.

A significant degree of discussion and debate took place over the future direction of Irish Education in the 1990s, culminating in the Education Act 1998. Yet little changed by way of status hierarchies in education, nor patterns of power and control. The language of deficit changed to that of difference, but in practice gross inequalities in the system in both participation and outcome prevailed, with piecemeal approaches to policy intervention. As Bryan (2009/2010) notes, the language of diversity in policy or indeed legislative provisions does not imply its recognition or implementation in a meaningful manner in curricular or pedagogical practices. The absence of critical reflection on institutional barriers in education, dovetailed with social policy initiatives in the broader society. These eschewed overly active interventions by a 'welfare' state (Fanning 2007) in favour of a form of Christian communitarianism (O'Sullivan 2005) that left structures of power and privilege intact. The Education Act (1998) was especially significant, not only because it was the first piece of legislation to be introduced in the field in ninety years, but also because it set the context for shaping discourse and policy at a time of significant social and economic change. How equality and indeed diversity was construed within the Act was important then, and is significant in terms of the absence of any specific reference to cultural/ethnic diversity. Equality of access and participation are to be promoted (rather than guaranteed) irrespective of 'diversity of values, beliefs, languages and traditions'. In so doing the Act merely affirms the rights of children to access and participate in education as required by obligations under the United Nations Convention on the Rights of the Child (1989). Ethnic diversity is subsumed under religious diversity, and here contradictions in the legislation abound, which, as we will see later, have real consequences for the rights of children from minority traditions to access education in their local schools. Specifically, the Act upholds the rights of Patrons to establish, maintain and uphold the ethos of schools (Section 15 (2)), to ensure that 'reasonable instruction time [is allowed] for subjects relating to the characteristic spirit of the school (Section 30 (2) (d)).

The legislation so defined has considerable implications for the policies of enrolment and admission, especially among primary schools – given that so many of these, as noted in Chapter 1, are already Roman Catholic and the only school open to children living in the locality. By endorsing the rights of Patrons to establish and maintain schools in line with a specific ethos, dividing practices (Foucault 1979) on the grounds of belief systems is built into the system. This is reflected in state support not only for Catholic and Protestant schools, but also for example for Muslim schools and a Jewish school. While pluralist in intent, tensions arise in practice in the availability of sufficient choices locally to allow for the range of belief systems which may prevail (Lodge 2004). Significantly, the rights of parents to a school of their choice is conditional on 'having regard to the rights of patrons and the effective use of resources'. These provisions are currently coming into play in negotiations over the future governance and establishment of new primary schools. In the event that children attend a school not of their belief, they are guaranteed the right to withdraw from instruction that is 'contrary to the conscience of the parent or [for a student aged 18 years] the student (Section 30 (2) (e)). Subsequent legislation (Equal Status Act 2000 and the Equality Act 2004) expanded provision for diversity under nine grounds, while simultaneously maintaining the rights of schools to exclude children from admission who are not of the denomination of the school. Thus it states in Section 7 (2) (c):

> Where the establishment is a school providing primary or post-primary education to students and the objective of the school is to provide education in an environment which promotes certain religious values, it admits persons of a particular religious denomination in preference to others or it refuses to admit as a student a person who is not of that denomination and in the case of a refusal, it is proved that the refusal is essential to maintain the ethos of the school.

Not surprisingly, the state has been subjected to some criticism for its failure to pro-actively cater for the needs of minorities. Current concerns reported by the OECD (2009a) come against a backdrop of criticism from the United Nations (2008) in its reports on the implementation of the UNCRC, as well as the elimination of racial discrimination (UN 2005). While the legislation sets the context, itself derived from significant representations by the Churches on consolidating patterns of governance in education, criticisms have been made about the slowness of the Catholic Church to respond to the rate of social change (O'Sullivan 2005). More recently, the bishop of Cork, Cloyne and Ross, notes that as a matter of 'justice' the predominance of a 'few interest groups' in positions of patronage, should be an issue of concern for those patrons themselves (Colton 2009: 258). This is especially the case in relation to the protection of the rights of other minorities, including the rights of non religious and those who do not wish to have a denominationally based education. As we will see, current moves to address the situation are bringing to the fore the tensions, contradictions and dynamics of power which permeate education but also the continued positioning of the state as neutral mediator, as it seeks to divest patronage of existing Catholic schools. The recent report from the Department of Education and Skills (2010) on possible divesting of Patronage for Primary schools highlights urban centres where there is an identifiable need for school reform in light of demographic change. While it is appropriate to raise questions about school choice (and therefore patronage) in such centres, questions remain about minorities in areas not included in the review.

Making a difference?
Policy and educational practice today

The absence of critical engagement and reflection on matters of social policy, the resistance to name issues of racism and racialisation in the experiences of existing cultural and ethnic minorities and the consolidation of traditional patterns of control in education set the context for state responses to the rapid and intensive immigration that was to occur in the following years. Essentialising and homogenous constructs of 'the Irish' in policy statements neutralise and indeed foreshadow any critical engagement with issues around race and marginalisation. We will see in Chapter 5 how teachers themselves draw on such constructs in explaining their own orientations to migrant children in the classroom. Two key texts : Migration Nation (Office of Minister for Integration 2008) and the NESC Report (2006), invoke a positive and open discourse in relation to 'Irishness' drawing on past experiences of emigration to convey a sympathetic and open response to the experiences of immigrants coming to Ireland:

> A history of emigration has made the Irish people and government sensitive to the discrimination encountered by newcomers, so migrants are arriving in a country with a strong commitment to social justice. (NESC 2006: 93)

> Our identity as a friendly and welcoming people demands that we continue to manage immigration issues with sensitivity. (Office of the Minister for Integration 2008: 7–10)

Immigration itself and indeed cultural/ethnic diversity is positioned as something 'new'. This forestalls recognition of the overtly defensive approach to immigration and the admission of refugees characteristic of state policy in the previous fifty years. Intolerance, where evident is construed as an 'aberration' and due to ignorance (Know Racism 2005), rather than any inherent structural resistance to those who differ substantially from the norm. Yet immigrant policy itself has been overtly directed towards the minimisation of social and cultural change (Haywood and Howard 2007). While the discourse presents immigration in positive terms, as promoting the interests and future well-being of Irish society, it is clear that tolerance is equated with having a 'particular type of immigration' (NESC 2006: 160). This is characterised by those who are most productive through their higher human and social capital and who will prove less likely to draw on the state for support.

Labour recruitment policies have been underpinned by the classification of immigrants themselves in economic terms, serving and prioritising the needs of capital in a globalised economy (Allen and Loyal 2006). Reflecting bio-power in practice, systems of classification and signifi-cation evolved which divided immigrant groups into those on the 'outside' (illegal – asylum seekers) and those on the inside (legal), further sub-divided into those on work visas and those on work permits, with significant consequences for their capacity to settle and integrate into Irish society. Signifiers reflected the dehumanised discourse which revolved around immigration and immigrants, as those positioned as 'asylum seekers', 'illegals', 'guestworkers', 'deportees' – non-Europeans, were defined as 'the other' (Lentin and McVeigh 2006), mirroring broader processes of exclusion in an increasingly 'Fortress Europe' (Geddes 2008). Mechanisms of inclusion such as citizenship, became refashioned in exclusionary terms. Significant changes were introduced to citizenship rights, following constitutional change in 2004, as previously noted, and the subsequent denial of access to welfare entitlements by certain groups depending on their immigrant history and status.

Discourses which signal contradictory tendencies are evident in state policy, welcome and inclusion of immigrants underpinned by the need to 'manage' migration and immigrants' capacities to integrate economically and socially (Bryan 2008). In Foucault's terms the 'subject' of immigration is one who approximates to the neo-liberal ideal – mobile, responsible, 'subjects of choice and aspirations to self actualisation and self fulfilment' (Rose 1996: 41). They should be enterprising, autonomous, individuals, contributing productively as active consumers to the Irish economy. Simultaneously considerable policy work has taken place with respect to anti-racism, culminating in the publication of the National Action Plan Against Racism in 2008 and a comprehensive analysis of the measures required to tackle racism against minority groups, including Travellers.

With respect to the latter, there was an acknowledgement of the absence of monitoring of progress in relation to Traveller well-being (witness the very low levels of progression of Traveller children through the education system identified in Table 1.4, Chapter 1). Yet it is this issue of monitoring the effectiveness of strategies which underpins the seriousness with which policy recommendations are taken.

In both Migration Nation and the NESC report references to education are relatively minimalist, geared toward language support in English, (since significantly cut back due to the economic downturn), the improvement of teacher training and a more inclusive and intercultural school environment and curriculum. Bryan (2008) provides a cogent critique of such policies in terms of their 'additive' status to the existing ethno centric curriculum and of the consequences for the positioning of immigrant students as 'objectified others' outside of dominant constructions of national belonging (ibid.: 305). Kitching (2010) also notes the superfluous importing of policies from elsewhere, conveyed in 'inclusionary niceties' (ibid.: 223) that articulate the challenges and opportunities that arise for schools, without addressing substantively structural racisms and prejudice in the system. Neither Migration Nation nor the NESC report make any reference to in/ equalities of outcome among minority ethnic groups in education, which as in the case of Traveller children in Ireland (Kenny 1997) or African Caribbean children in the UK (Gillborn 2010) provides a stark indicator of recognition/marginalisation in any system. Significantly it is only in the NESC report (ibid.: 140) that any mention is made of the predominance of Catholic schools in primary school provision – a factor noted of concern in the report by the 'NGO', rather than for example the state, or indeed the Churches, sectors. Yet it is in the education sector that the gaps in state policy and practice have converged to highlight in a very explicit manner the potential for segregation and racialisation in Irish society with respect to (certain) immigrant communities.

Racialisation and segregation: the case of Balbriggan

The narrow focus of government policy on labour recruitment and the absence of co-ordinated planning and integration of services and policy in relation to immigration, had considerable consequences for services that dealt with the reality of the expanding population on the ground. Within education the broader legislative context, which in orientation was pluralist but in practice endorsed the continuance of state funded religious run (the vast majority Catholic) schools, created a legal minefield for school principals in regulating patterns of enrolment in local primary schools. This was especially the case in centres of intense immigration and rapid demographic change and was signalled in our own earlier research in 2002 during the initial phase of immigration (Devine et al. 2002) and by O'Gorman and Sugrue (2007) in their report on Dublin 15. It crystallised in this latter community, in a series of events in Balbriggan in September 2007 that came to national media prominence. The intersection of poor urban planning, an insufficient number of school places and a system that upheld the rights of children (in this instance Catholic children) to gain preference in enrolment in local schools resulted in eighty children, mostly of African descent, and religious backgrounds other than Catholic (and therefore outside of the dominant ethnic norm) being unable to enrol in any of the local schools. This required the establishment of new schools to cater for these children, as well as the need to 'bus' some to schools outside of the local area. It provided an example of how enrolment policies in schools, in *practice* if not intent, could operate in a racialised manner, deriving from gaps in policy and planning during a period of significant social and cultural change. This mirrored in many ways the indifference to difference that charactersied state policy in earlier decades (Devine 2008). It also provided a telling example of how *practices* are key to signifying dynamics of power, and of the inter-woven capillary nature of this power across key institutions which govern, classify and shape in line with deeply embedded and 'taken-for-granted' norms. While the events in Balbriggan spurred state authorities to action because of the clustered numbers involved, what happened in Balbriggan merely crystallised the difficulties that were being faced individually by other immigrant parents in accessing local schools for their children in other urban areas (detailed in Chapter 6).

Media headlines at the time reflect the range of discourses and counter discourses which came into play, Church authorities critical of the state's lack of provision of a sufficient range of schools: 'Archbishop says state to blame for school crisis' (*Irish Times*, 4 September 2007). The state sought to distance itself from any racialised intent: 'Hanafin [minister for education at the time] proposes inclusive school model' (*Irish Times*, 7 September 2007). The minister's response was revealing not only in terms of the deracialised discourse which was evident in her remark that 'It might be a skin-colour issue, but it's not necessarily a race issue' (*Irish Times*, 8 September 2007) but also her attempts to isolate the events to a single community, rather than as a signifier of broader dynamics of power and inequalities in Irish society. The construction of the 'problem' of access to schools as a local/individual rather than a national/societal matter (derived from 'people' making choices to 'gravitate to areas'), devoid of political responsibility ('it is not desireable'.) was further reiterated by the Minister's response to questioning in the Dáil [national parliament] when she stated:

> While it is not desirable that a school would only have children from an ethnic

background, the position is reflective of the area and the new communities which have been established in Balbriggan. A similar situation arose in areas to which Irish people emigrated because people gravitate to areas where members of their own communities live. (*Dáil Eireann*, 2 October 2007)

What is interesting from this excerpt is how it also brings to the fore overlapping discourses related to school choice, integration (and what this might mean in a multi-ethnic Ireland), segregation and exclusion. It also calls upon prior experiences of Irish emigration to signal understanding/ similarity to/embracing of the immigrant community and the difficulties 'they' are encountering. The simultaneous construction of the children of immigrants as 'other' by defining them as from an 'ethnic' background highlights the normalcy of Irish ethnicity, which does not need to be named or defined. It also indicates the 'polite' discourse which governs rhetoric in the field, delimiting the racialised dynamics at play given that most of these children 'from an ethnic background' were black.

O'Gorman and Sugrue (2007) outlined the diversity of enrolment policies in Dublin 15 and of the guilt facing primary school principals as they turned away anxious parents who may not have the resources or 'know how' to find a place locally for their child. Similarly, Devine et al. (2002) suggested that schools, even at that initial phase of immigration could be using religious denomination as a method for 'screening' out immigrant applicants. A report by the Department of Education (2007) subsequently confirmed highly selective practices by certain schools in relation to the intake of children. This was creating considerable imbalances in the numbers of children with additional needs in school enrolments, including immigrant students. This was more recently confirmed by Smyth et al. (2009) in their identification of disadvantages facing immigrants in accessing local schools. These included the giving of priority enrolment to siblings and children of past-pupils, the capacity of the school to secure additional funding for the support of immigrant students (especially for those who arrived in the middle of the year) and the levels of competition between schools for students in a local area. These will be dealt with in more detail in Chapter 4.

Power, governance and the language of 'choice'

Debates over enrolment are not simply concerned however with access to a place in a local school. They are also part of a broader script of parental choice and the increasing significance of social class (this will be elaborated upon in Chapter 3) in influencing the decisions parents make about schooling for their children. Indeed the legitimacy of the churches controlling influence in education has always been grounded on the subsidiary role of the state, underpinned by the Irish Constitution, in family matters.[4] Education is firmly construed as being within the 'family domain' – the church acting *in loco parentis* in taking responsibility for children's faith formation and broader education in schools. Significantly recent announcements by the Catholic bishops in relation to future changes in patterns of governance reiterate their view of the central role of Catholic education in Irish society (Irish Catholic Bishops' Conference 2008) and draw on this discourse of parental choice and rights of preference for their children's education (O'Mahony 2008). For the Catholic Church, problems of enrolment are a matter for the state, in terms of sufficient provision of choice and school places, where this is requested or warranted by parents. At the Parnell Summer School in 2008, for example, Bishop Leo O'Reilly indicated that:

> Irish society is pluralist in make-up and accordingly the Irish education system must reflect this pluralism in its provision ... The Church has no desire to be the sole provider of education and, where the wishes of parents dictate, will play its part to assure the type of school that most appropriately meets the needs of parents and children

Problems arise however in the implementation of this policy in practice, especially where one group is clearly in the majority and has the capacity to 'draw upon sufficient resources of power and demographic prevalence' to ensure the provision of schools across all geographic areas (Daly 2009: 249). Further in a recent submission to the DES Technical group on the establishment of new primary schools (DES 2010), a joint submission by the CPSMA (Catholic Primary Schools Management Association) and the Episcopal Commission, indicated that the provision of new schools should be viewed as 'additional' to existing (Catholic) schools, rather than as a replacement of them. This is of key importance in terms of the future direction of state funding of new schools (which type and for whom) and the possible divesting of Church control in existing primary schools. Indeed in its submission to the Technical working group, both issues are intertwined as an act of 'reciprocation of goodwill' i.e that the Catholic church would be prepared to transfer ownership of certain schools if recognition (i.e. funding) of new Catholic primary schools was met with favourably by the state. Submissions by the Church of Ireland were also clear in their preference for a diversity of school provision that would include recognition of Church of Ireland schools, even where they fall below the minimum requirement for enrolment. It is clear that tentative negotiations are taking place over the governance of primary schools, as the state nudges toward introducing change.

Contradiction closing cases:
change to maintain the status quo?

In response to the 'demographic' crisis a new school governance model is currently being 'piloted'. What occurred in relation to the Balbriggan crisis is an example of a 'contradiction closing case' (Gillborn 2008) in that accommodation is made to the interests of a minority when an 'inequity becomes so visible that the present situation threatens to become unsustainable' (ibid.: 32). It does so without altering the overall structure or system which continues with its 'business' as usual. Known as 'community national schools', these schools (of which there are currently two located in the Dublin 15 area) prioritise geographic location rather than denominational affiliation in the right to enrolment. While multi-denominational, a guiding principle in these schools is that of faith formation, and in the words of the then Minister for Education, to provide 'an additional choice that can accommodate the diverse preferences of parents for varying forms of religious education and faith formation during the school day' (Press Release, 13 December 2007).

Sociologically a number of questions arise in the development of this new layer of governance for primary schooling. There is already a patron structure for multi-denominational schooling at primary level through the 'Educate Together' system, which caters for children of all social, cultural and religious backgrounds. What distinguishes both school types however is the emphasis on and responsibility for faith formation. While a core ethical curriculum and religious education (education about religions) is provided in Educate Together schools, faith formation is deemed to be the explicit responsibility of parents, to be conducted outside of school hours. In the community national school model, morality education and faith formation are identified as a core element of the curriculum, provided to children, in accordance with parental wishes, during the school day. As a new model, research on the delivery of religious education in these schools is currently taking place, facilitated by Dublin Vocational Education Committee (VEC). The move by the state toward a new model of schooling that provides for a diversity of beliefs, while safeguarding religious socialisation, could signal the continued emphasis in the state toward 'shaping the nation' in religious based values, however the latter is defined. At a broader European level, there is a renewed interest in religious education in promoting social cohesion and civic values, as advanced capitalist societies struggle with migration, globalisation and secular individualism (Bauman 2001; Coulby 2008). It also dovetails with the neo-liberal thrust of state policies, the education 'market' enhanced through competition and the provision of greater diversity of choice for parents as 'consumers' from a menu of school types.

It must also be considered as the negotiation of a new zone of influence by the Catholic Church in the area of state funded education (in much the same way as was done in relation to Community Schools at post-primary level in the 1970s). This consolidates the principle of faith formation as central to education and of the Church's right, on behalf of Catholic parents, to engage in such formation for children of the Catholic religion. Support by the Catholic church for the community school model at primary level, and its rejection of a model with a 'neutral religious common education syllabus' (such as for example what takes place in Educate Together schools) is specifically indicated in its submission to the DES Technical working group (2010) on the establishment of new primary schools mentioned earlier.

A further question arises, however, as to the composition of these schools that connects with broader questions of integration/segregation (in Foucault's terms dividing practices) and the creation of an inclusive education system. The new community primary schools have a minority of Catholic enrolments,[5] a majority of those enrolled coming from immigrant communities and minority faith traditions. The diversity of school patronage that now exists at primary level (to include Catholic, Church of Ireland, Muslim, Jewish, Educate Together, An Foras Patrúnachta, and the community school model under the Vocational Education Committee (VEC)) provides more choice (in a minority of geographic areas) to parents, but in a manner which also copper-fastens a segregated approach to education. This is no-where more evident, than in rapidly expanding urban areas, where a pattern may be established of schools (Educate Together and/or the new Community schools) that serve immigrant, mainly black African, Muslim and Asian communities, and schools which serve the [mainly white] Catholic communities. The demarcation of school types and parental 'choices' by ethnic/immigrant status, is an issue which is absent from the submissions of most patron bodies to the Technical group, with the exception of the Dublin 15 community council. Their reference to the need to avoid ghettoisation in the recognition of new schools highlights not only their own specific experiences (see for example Chapter 5), but also how diversity of provision by parental choice alone, can result in inclusion by exclusion. As we will see in Chapter 3, the exercise of choice and what parents 'want' (especially with respect to schools) is not a neutral phenomenon, independent of class, raced and gendered dynamics. It must also be recognised however that while in structural terms denominational status of a school can operate as a mechanism of both exclusion and segregation, a majority of migrant children in Ireland currently attend Catholic primary schools (DES 2007) and many of these schools, as we will see in Chapters 4 and 5, assert their inclusive focus by referring specifically to their Catholic mission. This highlights the capillary nature of the exercise of power, which can simultaneously operate in both inclusionary and exclusionary terms. Structurally, faith based schools may [legitimately] exclude on the basis of religious belief, which can lead to racialised patterns of segregation, yet practically such schools may be highly supportive of faith minorities which are enrolled in the school.

The state continues to position itself as neutral mediator (O'Sullivan 2005) in the field of governance relations. Such positioning sees it drawing on a range of often competing and contradictory discourses (e.g. support for inclusion while endorsing segregation), and, with the exigiencies of the current economic crisis, an emphasis on the need to gain 'value for money' in the establishment and maintenance of schools (DES 2010). Evident are subtle shifts in the discourse, as the principle of parental 'input' and choice is considered alongside the need to balance this with 'the optimal use of resources.' Concerns over the need to promote social inclusion and equality are also indicated (ibid.: 5) yet there is no indication of what these concepts actually mean, or how inclusion and equality is envisaged. By taking a pragmatic approach, the state risks undermining its own policy that 'there is an absolute need for an overarching mainstreaming approach for integrated services ... failure to adopt such an approach will lead to segregated services and in turn segregated communities' (Office of the Minister for Integration 2008: 16).

Concluding discussion

This chapter has outlined the patterns of power and control in Irish education and the central role of education in 'shaping the nation'. Drawing on the work of Foucault it was shown how dominant discourses in relation to ethnic and cultural 'normalcy' provided the backdrop for state policy in relation to immigration as well as educational practice. In more recent years these have been reshaped to align with a modern neo-liberal fashioning of Irishness in line with consumer capitalism (Inglis 2008). This situates migration firmly as serving the needs of the (then) rapidly expanding economy and migrants as economic actors, defined predominantly in human capital terms. Migration is constructed as a process that needs to be 'managed'. While the discourse draws upon the language of inclusion and recognition of diversity, contradictions in the implementation of policy in practice are clearly evident at the inter-face of poor urban/social planning, lack of investment in diversity training across the public sector and the endorsement of a segregated policy on education through the establishment of further 'layers' of schooling. In urban centres especially, this risks demarcating 'immigrant' schools from those which are the 'norm' for the mainly white, Catholic, population.

While the past ten years has witnessed extensive change in the demographic make up of many schools in Ireland, such change has occurred in a context of broader social shifts in Irish society. This was itself spearheaded by rising educational levels and a consolidation of the role of education in shaping life chances in a global market economy. A central criticism to emerge from the analysis has been the absence of a coherent vision by the state with a clear social justice agenda underpinning policy formation, with respect to social policy in general and educational policy in particular. As Bloemraad (2006) notes the signalling power of the state is profound, and how immigrant communities experience their interaction with the state in the short term sets the groundwork for processes of integration in the long-term. The changing nature of migration is also important. Transnational mobility alters traditional constructions in terms of both class and ethnicity, as well as multiple experiences of identity and belonging. The following chapter considers these processes in more detail, and how social class intersects with race/ethnicity in facilitating immigrant experiences of education.

Notes

1 Lentin and McVeigh (2006) emphasise the key role of the racial state in promoting racism, drawing on the work of Goldberg (2002) on the nation state as essentially racialised. This occurs through the denial of heterogeneity and the active suppression of those deemed historically inferior, who do not 'belong'. Fanning (2009) argues that racism in the Irish context cannot be reduced to the role of the state alone, but rather should be understood in the context of ethnic nepotism in the society at large – a desire by members of an ethnic group through shared bonds of belonging and identification, to favour those who are similar ethnically and culturally.

2 This was in spite of a distinct desire on the part of the British government to instigate an integrated system 'to unite in one system children of different creeds' (Akenson 1975; Hyland 1989).

3 This issue has recently emerged in national media debates as part of a reaction to the broader state subvention of fee-paying schools, with the protestant churches vigorously defending such subvention on the grounds of protecting the rights of protestant children to attend protestant schools.

4 While these provisions are reflective of Catholic social teaching, other churches have also continuously sought to retain control of the education of children in their faith.

5 Confirmed through personal correspondence with Dublin Vocational Education Committee (VEC).

3

Capitals, markets and positioning in the education of migrant children

This chapter provides an analysis of the intersection between ethnic/racial dynamics, immigration and experiences and outcomes in education. With economic boom and success, Ireland mirrored the trajectory of other developed nations in terms of supplanting labour shortages with immigration and deliberately targeted immigrants with high educational skills. Such policy has been developed against a wider international context of increasing competition between western developed states, vying for position and advantage at the 'high end' research and innovation spheres. The recent emphasis by the Irish government on creating a 'smart' economy epitomises this trend, building on its relatively successful track record of multi-national investment in the areas of IT and pharmaceutical industries since the late 1960s. Education is centrally involved in such processes, the success of multinational investment itself attributed to state policy in the 1960s in expanding post primary and third level provision that began to reap benefits in terms of a high graduate youth population from the 1980s. The link between opportunity and outcome is not clear cut however and involves a complex inter-play between structural and individual level factors that derive from classed, gendered and ethnic identities. Drawing especially on the work of Bourdieu, this chapter considers the significant role of capitals in mediating educational opportunities and life chances in a society marked by significant inequalities. It begins however with an overview of the broader international context, especially the work of the OECD given its increasing impact on policy at national level.

Outcomes and trends in immigrant education: the role of the OECD

How national policy in immigration is devised, and with it policies in education, cannot be divorced from the broader global context within which immigration, and by implication education, is situated. With the advent of advanced market capitalism, competition states (Ball 2009) seek to harness the best talent among citizens, but also boost the supply of labour through targeted immigration which adds to the 'talent' pool. This 'global war for talent' (Brown and Tannock 2009) is underpinned by meritocratic assumptions about the operation of labour markets (those with ability and who make the effort will reap the rewards) as well as assumptions about a linear relationship between 'learning' and 'earning' (ibid.: 377). It is also characterised by attempts to crackdown on 'illegal' and low skilled immigration and restrictions on refugee and family reunification programmes. Irish migration policy has followed this trajectory, reflected in the profile and general education levels of migrants to Ireland, as outlined in Chapter 1. However, given the central role of education to processes of 'human capital' enhancement and development, states compete not only on the attraction of 'high end' immigrants, but simultaneously on positioning themselves competitively with other states in terms of national education outcomes. These latter become a signifier of present as well as future economic and social capacities – all important in the sustained attraction of inward high end investment. This is where the discourse of migration as contributor to national prosperity becomes a double edge sword however. Tensions arise between the 'use value' of migrants as economic labour and threats to long term economic and social stability if migrants do not integrate into the broader social and cultural fabric of the society. Concerns over the lack of immigrant integration have given rise to a substantive focus in European policy in this area in recent years, with education targeted as a key mechanism through which integration is to be realised. The European Directive on the education of children of migrant 'workers' (EU Directive 77/46/CEE) is one example as is the evolution of policy through the work of the OECD, IMF, EU, UNESCO and the World Bank.

What is especially important is to consider the language that is used in such policy documents, as well as the manner in which policy is implemented. Most noteworthy is the framing of discourse in a distinct human capital paradigm that collapses integration and education with the creation of 'productive citizens' (OECD 2008a: 3). This economically instrumentalist discourse advocates sustained investment in immigrant education, not as a 'good' in and of itself, but almost as a firewall against the negative social and economic impact of the lack of immigrant integration. Social justice concerns in terms of inclusion, participation, recognition and rights as valued members of society are reframed in terms of the need for the acquisition of social capital and shared responsibility through community bonds and enhanced civic participation (Rizvi and Lingard 2006). Citizenship is to be 'earned' through productive technologies of self that includes for example demonstrable willingness to integrate via the acquisition of the host country language,[1] with education having a key role to play in this. Green (1997) notes at a broader level the increasingly 'porous' nature of national education systems, as governments are influenced by what takes place elsewhere. Nowhere is this more evident than in the operation and functioning of the OECD as it shapes and monitors economic policy informed by a neo-liberal agenda of market capitalism, free trade and competition. The significance given to education in this respect is evident from the establishment of a Directorate of Education in 2002, toward the goal of promoting a global knowledge economy. The impact of this 'global policy space in education' on national policy is fundamental (Rizvi and Lingard 2006: 247), as member states compare, contrast and measure the effectiveness of their own national policies in light of what takes place elsewhere. The production of thematic policy reviews as well as comparative indicators of education performance (PISA) is a key element in this process of policy influence and implementation.

Such measures constitute new technologies of control in education generally, a form of 'governing by numbers' (Grek 2009) that parallels the increasing emphasis on performativity and audit cultures in education systems characterised by new managerial reform (Apple 2006; Ball 2003; Gleeson and O'Donnabháin 2009; Grummell et al. 2009a). In such a scenario, the under-performance of migrant children – especially the persistent long-term underperformance of second and third generation immigrants (Schnepf 2006) becomes a matter of concern in the competition stakes for global positioning as educated, high skill economies. Policy reports highlight differences and mark out countries that are doing 'well' (Niessen and Huddleston 2009) but offer little by way of analyses of the complex factors which we know contribute to the differences themselves (Crul 2007; Crul and Holdaway 2009; Cummins 2001; Teddlie and Reynolds 2002). Children's under performance are defined as 'inequities' that arise from barriers to participation in a system that is assumed to be meritocratic. These elements are evident in the Green Paper on migration (OECD 2008a) where education is construed as a mechanism through which individuals can 'chose' to make the best use of the opportunities open to them, irrespective of their immigrant status. In this functionalist framework, underlying structural causes of inequality (through for example unequal distribution of resources, misrecognition, racism and discrimination) and their impact on capacity to 'use' and 'chose' are not part of the script. Policy suggestions draw primarily on maximising outputs in education. This is to be achieved through school and class level processes which of course are important. There is not however an equivalent focus on state level redistributive and recognitive initiatives that have been shown to yield significant benefits for minority groups, as well as to the society as a whole (Wilkinson and Pickett 2009).

Such trends are evident in the most recent OECD (2009a) review report on Ireland which makes some telling observations on both the strengths as well as 'challenges' that currently prevail in the Irish education system. The review is praiseworthy of the 'strong political commitment on successful integration of immigrants in schools' (ibid.: 4), and frames this in terms of quality assurance, standards, accountability and transparency. What emerges from the final report (OECD 2009b) is clear support for the state's (host) language acquisition policy (and recommendations regarding mother tongue support – an important aspect of cultural recognition) but some concern about the absence of sustained investment in teacher training and in the evaluation of practice with migrant children in schools. Specific queries are also raised in relation to early childhood care and education, to engaging migrant parents and in leadership for whole school and community planning for immigrant integration. Inequities in school choice through 'inadequate information' and the need for 'fairer and inclusive' enrolment policies are also referred to.

The comparative 'peer pressure' deriving from OECD reviews undoubtedly provides an imperative for governments at national level to monitor and 'take note' of immigrant patterns in education. In this sense the identification of how migrant children are doing in the education system is important in signalling relative differences and inequalities in practice and experience. Cognitive outcomes are an important element of children's overall educational well-being[2] (see Chapter 7) and crucial to patterns of transfer through the education system, including higher education. Where it becomes problematic however is in the crude interpretation of such outcomes on a narrow range of indicators, leading to standardised testing regimes which reduce education to the 'basics'. Further, if the patterns themselves are not interpreted in the broader social, economic and cultural contexts in which they emerge, deficit constructions of children who do not do well are reinforced, especially with respect to working class children (MacRuairc 2009) and those from (certain) immigrant groups. In the absence of meaningful engagement with patterns in terms of systemic/ structural as well as local/school level influences, policy responses can be a form of 'surface dressing' that has little impact on everyday practices in schools and ultimately on the educational well-being of minoritised children. Chapter 7 details aspects of migrant children's social and cultural experience and their attempts to maximise their educational well-being through their relations with teachers and peers. Teachers' and principals' struggles to cater for the range of needs of migrant children in classrooms and schools are also documented in subsequent chapters. Below I outline patterns on children's academic performance in schools.

Immigrant achievement in Irish education

There is very little data nationally available on patterns of immigrant achievement in Irish education. At post-primary level, the OECD (2006) data provides the only currently available information on the cognitive performance of immigrant students relative to their peers in Ireland. While drawing on a small pool of data,[3] findings confirm the higher than average performance of immigrants who come from English speaking backgrounds across all three areas of performance. Those whose mother tongue is other than Irish or English, considerably under perform relative to their native peers. The findings also suggest that [first generation] immigrant students performed higher on average in Ireland than the OECD norm (for all students), and performances for this cohort were markedly similar to those recorded in Canada and Australia – countries noted for their policy of recruitment of immigrants with already existing high human capital. Smyth et al. (2009) also confirm high/average estimations by school principals of the achievement of immigrant students, as well as high rates of motivation, but confirm concerns of sustained academic difficulties among approximately 10% of such students. Subsequent analysis in the OECD 2009(b) report highlights the impact of social class on immigrant student's performance, with a greater effect than among indigenous Irish students. As we will see in Chapter 5, these overall patterns have important implications for teacher perceptions of immigrant students and their practices with them in schools.

Patterns in relation to socio-economic background, ethnic profile and immigrant status appear more pronounced in data that is emerging in the primary school sector, where there are a higher overall proportion of immigrant students. Smyth et al. (2009) for example highlight a smaller proportion of immigrant students perceived by school principals to be in the 'above average' category. National evidence of reading achievement (Eivers et al. 2010) highlights evidence of lower reading performance among children whose home language is other than English or Irish, a difference that was significant for children in second and sixth class. While differences in maths were also evident, these were not found to be significant for older children but were significant for children in second class. Our own analysis of evidence[4] from a national study of DEIS schools provides patterns based on teacher estimations, as well as how these are attributable to certain minority ethnic groups, including Traveller children. Comprising a nationally representative sample of responses from 675 teachers in grades 3 and 5 in DEIS schools (band 1 and 2), teachers were asked to rank each minority ethnic child in their class in terms of general ability/performance (above average, average and below average). A majority of such children were classified by teachers as of average ability (41.4%), a substantial minority below average (31.5%) and a further minority above average (23.0%). Table 3.1 provides an indication of teacher estimates of ability by ethnicity, where the numbers recorded are greater than twenty.

Table 3.1   *Teacher estimates of ability across minority ethnic categories*

Ethnic identity	N	% of total	Above average	Average	Below average
Irish Traveller	38	2.6	0.0	8.1	92.0
Polish	342	23.4	26.6	49.5	23.9
Nigerian	259	17.8	24.0	44.8	31.2
Romanian	114	7.8	22.4	37.4	40.2
Lithuanian	99	6.8	16.7	53.1	30.2
Filipino	64	4.4	41.5	37.7	20.8
Latvian	43	2.9	29.3	51.2	19.5
Indian	43	2.9	38.1	45.2	16.7
Slovakian	44	3.1	13.6	38.6	47.7
Brazilian	27	1.9	3.7	25.9	70.4
Pakistani	34	2.3	29.4	38.2	32.4
Czech	25	1.7	8.0	16.0	76.0
Russian	20	1.4	40.0	40.0	20.0
Chinese	20	1.4	40.0	40.0	20.0

A number of patterns are immediately evident from this data set which provides outline indicators of patterns, supplementing that of Smyth et al. 2009 and Eivers et al. 2010. First, the prevalence of certain immigrant groups is indicated through the larger numbers of Polish, Nigerian and other Eastern European groupings (Romania, Lithuania, Slovakia and Latvia), as well as immigrants from Asia (Philippines, India and Pakistan). With respect to teacher estimates of ability/performance, what immediately strikes is the number of Traveller children in the 'below average' category. That 92% of such children are estimated by teachers to be in this category is a clear indicator of structurally embedded patterns of inequality with respect to this indigenous minority noted in Chapter 2 and is a matter of concern. These lower estimations are also supported by the data from Eiver et al. (2010) which confirmed the significantly lower performance of Traveller children relative to their peers.[5] Third, the patterns suggest that teachers identify children of Asian background (Filipino, Indian, Chinese) and children from certain East European countries[6] (Russia) as having generally higher estimates of ability (as 'above average') while children from Romania, Slovakia, Brazil and the Czech Republic were more likely to be identified as in the 'below average' categories. Children from Nigeria and Poland (the two largest groups) were more likely to be identified as in the 'average' category. Subsequent analysis highlights how teacher estimations of the children's ability appears to be significantly linked to whether or not the child attends English language support as indicated in Table 3.2. This lends some support to the findings of Eivers et al. (2010) of the relative underperformance of children whose language at home was other than English.

Table 3.2   *Teacher estimates of ability and whether or not child attends English language support*

	Above average		Average		Below average		Totals	
	N	%	N	%	N	%	N	%
Attends English support	142	42.5	315	52.6	347	75.8	804	57.8
Does not attend	335	57.6	599	47.4	458	24.2	588	42.2

Note: Level of significance: $p < 0.01$.

Knowing how 'well' children are doing relative to their peers is important in framing policy in a way which caters to the needs of different groups. Migrant children are not an undifferentiated 'whole' and we know from research elsewhere that there are substantial differences across immigrant and minority ethnic groups in how they fare in education (Archer and Francis 2007; Crul 2007; Crul and Holdaway 2009; Gillborn 2008). Such research points to classed and racialised practices in schools which contribute to such effects. In this sense, teacher estimations are not unproblematic and can be informed by teacher's own constructs of normalcy and 'otherness'. Gillborn's (2010) work in England clearly indicates the devastating impact of teacher estimates on subsequent performance of black children in standardised assessments because it is these estimates that determine placement in lower tracks. In Ireland, teachers have consistently been identified as holding 'deficit' assumptions of the abilities of migrant children who are not fluent in English (Devine 2005; Devine et al. 2010b; Lyons 2010; McDaid 2009), a perception that is reinforced by the almost unique focus by the state on immigrant integration through (English) language acquisition. Education in the language of the host country is of course important and something which migrant children (and their parents) want in school. However identifying language acquisition as the central goal of educational policy, to the neglect of the social and cultural dynamics in children's lives will only consolidate and reinforce existing patterns, as has been shown with respect to working-class children (MacRuairc 2009). This has also certainly been the case with respect to Traveller children. What must also be borne in mind interpreting these patterns is the location of the children in DEIS schools, which by national standards tend to have lower than average academic attainment, given the socio-economic profile of children's home background (Eivers et al. 2010). Yet we know that many of these migrant children come from families with higher educational capital than their indigenous peers in DEIS schools (Devine 2009) and existing research suggests that migrant children do less well when they are in such schools (Shapira 2010). More in-depth analysis of how these estimations dovetail with the social classification of the children is required to identify the intersection between ethnic and social class variables in teacher estimates of the children's ability. Subsequent chapters provide a qualitative overview of the influence of both class and ethnicity on teacher constructs, as well as on immigrant parent orientations to school. The fact that the OECD highlights social class as having an even stronger effect on achievement for immigrant children in Ireland (ibid.: 2009a), than for indigenous groups, also suggests a compounding of negative effects (ethnic and class) for immigrant children who are poor. It also points to the structurally embedded nature of class inequalities in Irish education, upon which further layers of inequality may now being built.

In policy reports, however, including those of the OECD, social background tends to be presented as a 'neutral category', rather than a marker of prestige, or conversely marginalisation, underpinned by networks of power that operate to safeguard and protect position and prestige. The work of Bourdieu provides a useful conceptual lens in which to explain how social, cultural and economic factors work in and through education to consolidate patterns of power and privilege among those who already 'have' in society. This is especially important in any analysis of the experiences of migrant children in the school system. In many ways the very decision to migrate reflects a desire to improve life chances and mobilise opportunities for advancement into the next generation. Questions arise as to the extent to which education enhances these opportunities or consolidates and reproduces inequalities that are already embedded in the society.

Bourdieu and the mobilisation of capitals in education

While education may be considered both a public and social good, who benefits from education and what is valued as and in education varies by social group. Bourdieu's work is important as it provides a set of conceptual tools (capitals, habitus and field) which allow us to draw links between everyday practices in families and schools, with broader processes of production and reproduction in the society at large. His work challenges assumed perceptions that connect education achievement with natural aptitude and intelligence, directing our focus to strategies and investments that are made in and through education. These consolidate and (re) produce privilege among those who are advantaged and dominant in society. Three concepts are central to his work: habitus, capital and field.

The concept of *habitus* draws attention to identity in its embodied form: 'systems of durable, transposable dispositions' (Bourdieu and Passeron 1977: 72), durable ways of 'speaking, walking, and thereby of feeling and thinking' (Bourdieu 1990: 70) which integrate 'past experiences' [and] 'functions at every moment as a matrix of perceptions, appreciations and actions' (Bourdieu and Passeron 1977: 83). Linking to Foucault, we can say that discourse becomes embodied in practice through the formation of the habitus. For Bourdieu, habitus is acquired through social interactions that give rise to collective dispositions attributable to social groups. This is not to suggest that individuals are determined by the habitus into which they are socialised, but that habitus provides the 'logic of practice' (Bourdieu 1990), dispositions which are 'durable but not eternal' (ibid.: 133), that orient individuals to act in different settings. Habitus provides the common sense understanding of everyday life ('le sens pratique' ibid.: 52) and the actions and interactions that take place within it. In education, habitus is typically referred to in class terms – as in a middle class 'habitus' or disposition to learning (Lareau 2003). It provides children from more affluent homes with the dispositions necessary to do well in school. Bourdieu has been subjected to some criticism for not fully taking account of either race or gender (and indeed age) in his analysis of habitus, yet as a concept it is equally useful in exploring perceptions, actions and mediations that are embedded in race, gendered, aged and abled relations (McNay 1999b).

The concept of habitus is closely linked to that of capital in that both the production and (re)production of the habitus contributes to and depends upon the acquisition/generation of capitals. Central to the concept of capital is its exchange value and the capacity for both social and cultural capital, through solid investment of time and effort (Bourdieu 1986: 253) to be converted into economic capital:

> Capital can present itself in three different guises: as economic capital, which is immediately and directly convertible into money and may be institutionalised in the form of property rights; as cultural capital, which is convertible on certain conditions into economic capital and may be institutionalised in the form of educational qualifications; and as social capital, made up of social obligations ('connections') which is convertible, in certain conditions, into economic capital. (ibid.: 243)

Cultural capital has considerable currency in the field of education comprising embodied (dispositions, sets of meaning and modes of thinking), objectified (access to cultural goods such as art, literature) and institutionalised forms (educational/academic qualifications). These are given recognition by those who are already dominant within the field. Those with the 'recognised' cultural capital are competent in their knowledge and 'feel' for the 'game' (Lamaison and Bourdieu 1986: 111), and play accordingly, confident in their capacity to generate long term benefit from their investment in education. More recent analyses has stressed the affective dimensions of cultural capital – connected with the sense of entitlement, feelings of self efficacy and confidence in making the system work to one's own advantage (Skeggs 2004). Such work ties into calls for greater attention to be paid to the affective domain (connectedness, care and love relations) in both the experience and reproduction of inequalities (Lynch et al. 2009), including in schools. While the exchange value of cultural capital derives from the ultimate conversion of educational qualifications into economic reward, social capital underpins this process through being:

> Consciously or unconsciously aimed at establishing or reproducing social relationships that are directly usable in the short or the long term … implying durable obligations subjectively felt (feelings of gratitude, respect, friendship) or institutionally guaranteed. (Bourdieu 1986: 249)

Recognition is central to the mobilisation of social and cultural capital – endlessly 'affirmed and reaffirmed' through everyday inter-change between social actors with mutual dispositions in a given field. Of course the capacity to recognise and be recognised is itself subject to the distribution of power. There are significant differences across social groups both in the volume of capital (economic, social and cultural) individuals hold and the relative weighting of different types of capital in each field (Bourdieu 1989: 17).

Finally, the concept of *field* for Bourdieu relates to the contexts in which different types of capital are mobilised or struggled over. All fields are characterised by tension between different groups in the struggle for the field's capital (McNay 1999b). Field for Bourdieu is characterised by its own dynamics of power, which is conceptualised as multiple and varied. As such his conceptualisation mirrors that of Foucault in terms of power as diffuse, with intended and unintended consequences. Fields are in essence 'social spaces' characterised by varied configurations of power and control:

> A field is a structured social space, a field of forces, a force field. It contains people who dominate and people who are dominated. Constant permanent relationships of inequality operate inside this space, which at the same time, becomes a space in which the various actors struggle for the transformation or preservation of the field. All the individuals in this universe bring to the competition all the (relative) power at their disposal. It is this power that

defines their position in the field, and as a result, their strategies. (Bourdieu 1998: 40–41)

This is key in highlighting both the role of education in the broader 'field' of power relations in society, but also in the relative autonomy of education, which must be perceived as a space in and for itself. It has its own dynamics of power, competition, transformation and/or preservation operating within it. This suggests the need for a nuanced analysis of both processes and practices in education. There are a myriad of fields, as there are social relations but field, habitus and capital are inextricably linked in shaping our orientations and *practices* in the world, as well as individual's positioning within it:

> Social reality exists, so to speak, twice, in things and in minds, in fields and in habitus, outside and inside social agents. And when habitus encounters a social world of which it is the product, it is like a 'fish in water': it does not feel the weight of the water and it takes the world about itself for granted. (Bourdieu and Wacquant 1992: 127)

Again there are parallels with Foucault, in terms of the discourses that position individuals along a continuum of acceptance and/or rejection based on their affiliation to and embodiment of norms. However unlike Foucault's (1979) 'docile bodies', Bourdieu emphasises the active (rather than mechanical) and reflexive nature of agent's 'doing', in which they orient themselves, depending on their access to capitals, to the preservation or subversion of the field (Bourdieu and Wacquant 1992: 109). It is this very agency which lends a dynamic quality to the concept of field, which can be construed as a field of struggle and/or force as agents compete with one another for recognition and position. 'Being a fish in water' or alternatively 'out of water' depends not only on one's own prior experience that has shaped meanings, perceptions and orientations (habitus), but also on the dynamics of power which operate within and across fields, and one's access to the capitals which are valued in those fields. Education as a field can be understood as a social space in which agents are positioned according to their access to capitals, and according to the habitus which shapes their action. The gap in/between positions is core to understanding the dynamics of interaction in a field as agents define themselves in terms of their 'mutual exteriority' (Bourdieu 1998: 6) and orient themselves to maximum exchange within the field. Bourdieu uses the analogy of a game of cards, the dynamics of the game constitute the 'field', the forms of capital brought by players are equivalent to 'trump cards' – what is considered 'trump' will vary from one game to another, just as the forms of capital that are valued will vary from one field to another:

> Those who have lots of red tokens and few yellow ones, that is, lots of

economic capital and little cultural capital, will not play in the same way as those who have many yellow tokens and few red ones. (Bourdieu 1993: 34)

Such analyses highlight the pivotal role of economic capital in social positioning in and through education. They also highlight how education itself, through practices of cultural representation and recognition position winners and losers in the education 'game'. Where there is lack of cultural recognition, pedagogy can represent a form of 'symbolic violence' (Bourdieu and Passeron 1977:5) in which alternative cultural knowledge is subjugated and misrecognised. An example of this is the misrecognition of migrant children's mother tongue in school, or an interpretation of children whose first language is not English as 'deficient'. There is a considerable amount of research in the sociology of education which highlights the selective tradition in school curricula (Apple 1979, 1986; Young 1971) and how priority is given to ways of 'doing' and 'being' of those who are dominant. We saw this for example in Chapter 2 in the very specific forms of national identity and belonging that permeated the primary school curriculum from the foundation of the state, and the marginalisation of those who speak with a different voice. For Bernstein (1996), there is a direct link between these processes of pedagogical/curricular misrecognition and children's learning, which 'drain the very springs of affirmation, motivation and imagination' (ibid.: 5) of those who are misrecognised. Travellers as a group are one very explicit example. Other pedagogical practices such as tracking and streaming have consistently been shown to reproduce inequalities by the placement of immigrant children in lower streams (Crul 2007; Gillborn 2008), a pattern that is also evident in Ireland (Devine 2005; Smyth et al. 2009). There is also a substantial body of research which suggests a surface treatment of cultural diversity in schools, and an absence of deep engagement with the perspectives of and values of minority ethnic and immigrant children and youth (Archer and Francis 2007; Chan 2007; Peck et al. 2008). These will be more substantively outlined in Chapter 5.

Markets and school choice in Ireland: survival of the fittest?

Education then is a competitive field, in which the achievement of qualifications can be exchanged in the labour market for power and privilege. What takes place at international level (in terms of competition between nation states in the global knowledge economy) is replicated at local level as individuals seek competitive advantage through success in education. As educational levels rise, the stakes in education rise (Collins 1979), as parents, dependent on the resources available to them, try to maximise their children's life chances. Lareau's (2003) research in the United States provides a clear account of the differences in strategies and practices engaged in across social groups, especially of the 'concerted cultivation' of children in middle class families toward success in and through education. The impact of social class on educational trajectories is especially evident at key transition points in children's lives – where choices are made about the school children will attend and the courses they will follow. It is these transition points which become the sites of differentiation between social groups on the basis of gender, social class and ethnicity (Hatcher 1998). Key transition points identified include from primary to post-primary because of the sorting of students into vocational and academic tracks, and the subsequent effect on access to higher education (Kloosterman and de Graff 2010; McCoy et al. 2010).

Research internationally draws attention to the stress parents increasingly feel to pick the 'best' school for their child, as well as the range of criteria they draw upon (Ball and Bowe 1995; Poupeau 2007). Ball's work especially highlights the strategies employed by different groups of parents in selecting schools for their children and of the significant role of the 'grapevine' (Ball and Vincent 1998) as a source of knowledge of both the reputation and formal achievement results of schools. While overall the system is assumed to be fair, Bourdieu's analysis points to the institutionalisation of class power through the networks of relationships that are supported and developed, recognised and validated in the education system. This preserves the status of some groups, while excluding and marginalising others. Issues of social, cultural and economic capital are at play, not only in the access to social networks who 'know' the rules of the 'game' (criteria for entry, enrolment dates, subject requirements, tracking processes). They have the self efficacy and confidence to negotiate the system. Also important however is the capacity to live in a 'socially ranked geographic space' that brings a whole series of benefits through access to further social and cultural capitals:

> To account more fully for the differences in lifestyle between different fractions – especially as regards culture – one would have to take account of their distribution in a socially ranked geographical space. A group's chances of appropriating any given class of rare assets (as measured by the mathematical probability of access) depend partly on its capacity for the specific appropriation, defined by the economic, cultural and social capital it can deploy in order to appropriate materially or symbolically the assets in question, that is, its position in social space, and partly on the relation between its distribution in geographical space and the distribution of the scarce assets in that space. (Bourdieu 1984: 124)

Geographical space is thus relational as much as physical, itself embedded in social, cultural and material dynamics (Rizvi 2010). This ties in directly to the patterns of racialisation and segregation that were identified in

Chapter 2 with respect to one community in Dublin. It also connects more broadly not only to the impact of state policies in urban planning, but also in regulating 'the market' of education (or not) through the provision of schools in local areas. Internationally the phenomenon of 'white flight' has been identified in areas of high concentration of immigrant communities (Poupeau 2007). Migrant children are consistently clustered in marginalised communities and vocationally oriented schools (Crul 2007; Gillborn 2008; PISA 2006; Smyth et al. 2009). Social (and ethnic) segregation becomes mirrored in the selection of different types of schools, as those 'in the know' and who have the resources make their choices strategically and seek out schools with children most like themselves. Parental choice then is not simply a matter of personal preference for schools with a defining curricular or religious ethos, but is also embedded in classed and racialised patterns of sorting and selecting (Blackmore 2006).

These dynamics are of relevance to debates over school enrolment and access to choice of schools in Ireland that were highlighted in Chapter 2. Traditionally parents in Ireland have exercised considerable choice in relation to the post-primary schools their children attend (Smyth et al. 1999), with over 50% of such choices outside of the 'local' school area. Class segregation is clearly evident in the vocational and traditional secondary school sector. It is also evident within the latter in terms of differences in status and positioning between religious run schools (Lynch and Lodge 2002; Lynch and Moran 2006). Choices made are dependent on knowledge and understanding of how the school system works and what different schools provide. They are dependent on the resources (economic, social, cultural) which parents can draw upon to facilitate the choices they wish to make. Some are more in the 'know' than others and exercise their choices strategically. The significance of the choice of school for transition not only to higher education, but more and less prestigious forms of higher education is also quite marked in Ireland (Lynch and Moran 2006). Schools have also been identified as playing an active role in the sorting and selecting process, excluding certain groups on the basis of fees, 'high' voluntary subscriptions, expensive uniforms and elite sports cultures. Selective/screening practices by certain schools have also been identified by the DES in their audit of school enrolment policies (DES 2007). Applied to ethnic background, where Traveller children have remained in secondary education, this has tended to be within the vocational/community/comprehensive sector, with correspondingly few members of the Travelling community transferring to the higher education sector (CSO 2006; DES 2007). With respect to immigrant communities, we see clear inter-connections between the spatial as well as social aspect to school choice, as immigrant communities in urban centres especially, become concentrated in working class areas, which also have a higher concentration of vocational/community/comprehensive schools. In a denominationally structured system, choices open to parents will also be influenced by their faith background which can operate as a mechanism of exclusion or inclusion (people 'like' us or not 'like' us), depending on the faith background of the migrant children themselves. We will see this emerging in the interviews with immigrant parents in Chapter 6. In an increasingly competitive school system, 'faith' can also be used as a resource to gain access to what is perceived as 'the best' and more prestigious schools and schools which are 'more like us'.

The operation of markets and choice mechanisms in education highlight in a very real way the structural dynamics that are play with respect to race, ethnicity and immigration in society. Ultimately this gives rise to different patterns of participation, representation and achievement in education. Such analyses helps our understanding of the experiences of immigrant groups in negotiating the education system, as well as the trajectories of achievement and integration that are followed on the basis of the capitals/resources they bring with them to education. It highlights the extent to which such capitals have currency in the field of Irish education. Differences will exist both within and between immigrant groups in their negotiation of education, based on their access to capitals and corresponding sense of entitlement/ confidence of what is possible in and through education.

It would be simplistic however to suggest a one way correspondence between structure and outcome – a more nuanced analysis is required that focuses on the complexity of the formation of identities (ethnic, gender, classed) and how these intersect with structural characteristics of the school system and society at large. For Bourdieu, the habitus is not determining, but generative – a lived category (McNay 1999a:100). Everyday experience and orientation derives from past experience and an imagined future of what is both practical and desirable based not only on that past experience but also present context and reality. Social practices both generate and reproduce the habitus, and by implication patterns of inequality and difference between social groups. Concepts of agency and processes of identity formation are central to the instantiation (Giddens 1984) of the habitus in practice.

Agency, identity and the mobilisation of capitals in education

A central tension in social theory is that between structure and agency. One of the criticisms to emerge from overly structural analyses of education is the inadequate account provided of individual differences in negotiating identity and belonging. Not all members of pre-defined groups will act in the same way. With respect to Bourdieu for example, criticism has been levelled at the insufficient attention given to within group differences in working class responses to education (Hatcher 1998). In the work of Foucault, criticism has been levelled at the overemphasis on processes of normalisation to the exclusion of transformation and resistances in the exercise of power (McNay 1999b). Central to such critiques is the impact of identity on action and behaviour – how we think about, feel about and define ourselves influences how we interact with others.

The formation and construction of identity is itself a complex and often contradictory process. This is especially so in modern societies that are characterised by risk, flexibility and uncertainty (Bauman 2001; Beck 2010). How we come to think about, define and 'know' ourselves is an active, reflective process (Giddens 1991/1984). Identities are something we 'do', not something we 'are' (West and Zimmerman 1987). Identities are a form of situated social practice in which individuals perform roles that are relational and embedded in norms and expectations related to self and 'other' (McNay 1999a; Pullen and Simpson 2009). Conflicts and contradictions abound, multiple identities merge and overlap giving rise to a crafted self (Devine et al. 2010a) that is at once fragile and versatile, depending on the context of interaction and the resources individuals bring. It is the act of 'doing' (gender, race, class) which reproduces the identity in a cyclical process of action, reaction and social positioning. This becomes embodied in taken for granted ways of 'doing' and 'being' (akin to Bourdieu's habitus) that becomes the 'script' of our everyday world. Identities then are not fixed, but evolve, taking on hybrid forms depending on context and interaction. This is especially relevant in considering the hybridity of ethnic identities in an era of mass globalisation and mobilisation – what Anthias (2010) refers to as translocational positionality. Moving between spaces and places that each connect with different parts of our 'selves' gives rise to contradictory processes of positioning. These can destabilise and indeed invert more linear patterns of class, nationality and ethnic identity. What is the class position of an immigrant woman working as a cleaner in the local primary school, but who holds a teaching degree from her home country? What is the ethnic/ national identity of an immigrant boy who has lived in three countries, as his parents move across continents securing employment in the health care sector? However, while identity can take hybrid forms, shifting and evolving in time and space, identity making always takes place in contexts of power that validate and recognise some forms of presentation and positioning over others (Anthias 2010; Gillborn and Youdell 2009; May 2009). Struggles over identity occur both within ethnic groups inter-generationally (Archer et al. 2010), as well as across ethnic groups influenced by and inter-secting with structures which are also classed and gendered.

Migrant children also actively manage their ethnic identities. Evergeti and Zontini (2006) for example speak of ethnicity as a 'flexible' social property, mobilised in different ways according to context and need and by the multiple experiences of children and young people in the homeland and the host society. A minority ethnic child may react and present herself differently with her majority ethnic peers in school, than with her minority ethnic peers outside of school or in the home, or when she returns on a visit to her families' country of origin. She may shift between multiple identities as she negotiates her positioning across different spheres. Schools are especially important as sites for identity meaning making for migrant children, not only because of the routes of entry education provides to the dominant host culture, but also because of the disjuncture that is created between the 'known' and the 'unknown', as taken for granted norms are inverted and destabilised (Youdell 2006). In schools structure and agency merge and collide (Devine 2009), as questions of: 'who am I?' and 'who do I want to be?' (agency) are framed by, and frame the structuring of their experience in school: 'What do I learn?' 'How am I defined and understood?' (structure). It is *how* the intersection between structure and agency takes place that governs how children 'do' in education, and ultimately contributes to the differences in patterns identified earlier in this chapter.

In previous work I have drawn together these strands of thinking about the inter-relationship between structure and agency in a model which demonstrates the circular and interactive nature of processes of production and reproduction with respect to childhood and education (Devine 2003, 2002). Applying this to our understanding of immigration and schooling, the model foregrounds the significance of habitus (by placing it in the centre) as both an outcome of and contributor to (re)productive practices in schools. The habitus is shaped by structures (access to valued capitals which have currency in the field and which derives from structurally embedded patterns related to class, gender, race etc. in the society), as well as agency (the capacity to reflect, orient oneself and generate exchange possibilities in the field). Habitus is at the intersection of relations of power (structure/agency) and practice. It is part of the process as well as outcomes of these relations. Dominant discourses and policies, as well as structurally embedded patterns related to, for example, class and ethnicity, set the context for practices in schools. This is done through the type of curriculum which is taught, the pedagogical practices which ensue as well as the nature of social relationships developed between principals, teachers, parents and students. These frame activity, perception and being, which in turn is mediated by the specific characteristics each of these individuals bring to the educational encounter. They can resist, accommodate or assimilate into school norms, (re) producing existing discourses or developing counter-discourses which challenge the status quo. Power is conceived as something which is exercised through social interaction, rather than as possessed by the parties to that interaction. It is nonetheless always present in a continual flow between agentic and structural influence. These influences, actions and reactions are not linear but circular and capillary like embedded in relations and dynamics of power which seek to restrain, constrain, resist and transform (see Figure 3.1).

Figure 3.1   *Power circulates: a model of the interrelationship between structure, power, agency and habitus in shaping school practices*

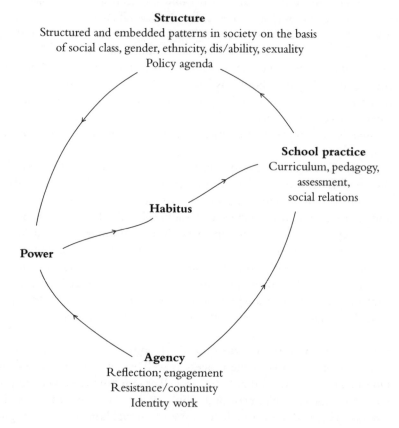

Structure
Structured and embedded patterns in society on the basis of social class, gender, ethnicity, dis/ability, sexuality
Policy agenda

School practice
Curriculum, pedagogy, assessment, social relations

Habitus

Power

Agency
Reflection; engagement
Resistance/continuity
Identity work

The positioning and practices of each of the actors in education can be understood in terms of these dynamics and forms the basis for the analysis of the subsequent chapters. Principals, teachers, parents and children come to school with a set of dispositions (habitus) which itself derives from past experiences and imagined futures that are embedded in structural patterns and practices. National and indeed international policy sets the context for local practices, mediated through the preferences, power and priorities of actors in schools. Tensions around transformation or conservation in the field are played out in the everyday accommodations, resistances and struggles in classrooms and schools. This does not take place in a linear manner, but in one which is complex and contradictory. It is nonetheless profound in terms of the impact on migrant children's opportunities in education.

Conclusion

This chapter has provided an account of the intersection between ethnic/racial dynamics, immigration and experience and outcomes in education. Macro-level processes at the level of globalised competition nation states and the increasingly significant influence of the OECD, as well as the more localised but structurally embedded dynamics of power and control sets the context within which immigrants experience education. Immigration does not occur in a vacuum but is transposed upon pre-existing systems, structures, logics of practice (Bourdieu 1990) which govern reactions to sweeping change. Such 'logics' are in turn underpinned by dynamics of power, which shape the debates, struggles and strategies that inevitably emerge in attempts to assimilate and accommodate 'newcomers' with existing 'knowns' and norms. As a competitive field, access to valued social, cultural and economic capitals is vital to educational success, yet such capitals are dispersed differently among immigrant groups. This gives rise to differing orientations, motivations and capacities to engage with the school system. How schools adapt to increasing diversity, as well as how immigrants themselves experience schooling provides a key lens through which to understand broader processes of inclusion/exclusion in the society at large. The following chapters will apply some of these ideas by exploring the perspectives and experiences of key actors in the education field – principals, teachers, parents and children.

Notes

1 Such a requirement is not essential for those who migrate within the EU, as they enjoy a 'fundamental right to move freely within the European Union, without any particular integration requirement for their residence in another Member State. Fanning (2007) provides an excellent outline of how the very concept of citizenship can become an exclusionary mechanism especially with respect to immigrants, given the exclusionary processes which are now legitimated through the category of non-citizen.

2 When used in reports (e.g. UNICEF 2007), educational well-being refers to achievement as well as transition through levels of education that ultimately influences labour market participation. When I refer to it I am also speaking

about the development of the 'whole personality' of the child, in line with the spirit of Article 29 on the Convention on the Rights of the Child.

3 The data set for Ireland only refers to first generation immigrants, given that second generation students were difficult to identify, and where identified only comprised 1.1% of the total cohort (OECD 2009a). The total sample size of first-generation students in the study is still small, at 4.5%.

4 This data derives from a nationally represented sample of DEIS schools, that is part of current doctoral research by Deirdre McGillicuddy into patterns of ability grouping by teachers in primary schools. I am grateful to Deirdre for allowing me to add some additional questions to the questionnaire in order to identify more in-depth data on the ethnic profile of children in these schools.

5 Eivers et al. (2010) also indicate that such data should be interpreted with caution owing to the small sample (2% of the overall cohort) of Traveller children in their study.

6 Analyses of smaller groups of children (< 20) indicated higher estimates also for children from Hungary and Ukraine.

4

Leading *for* diversity:
moving beyond practical tolerance in schools

This chapter identifies how school principals have adapted to the challenge of change as a result of immigration. Principals are key actors in the field of education, positioned at the inter-section between state policy and practice. It is in the principal's 'office' that an immigrant parent often has the first contact with his/her child's school. In primary schools especially, it is the principal who is the 'face' of the school, setting the tone and defining the culture of the school. The chapter documents the experiences and perceptions of a sample of primary and secondary school principals and how they have coped with increasing ethnic diversity in their schools. Not all schools are the same however and differ in terms of social context, ethos and gender and social profile of their students. The chapter highlights the significance of the social context of the school to the leadership practices of principals, their own evolving 'habitus' and the impact of both social class and ethnicity on their approach to the change. School ethos is also explored, as is the competing tension between 'managing' and 'leading' for diversity in newly multi-ethnic schools. The chapter begins with an overview of national and international research in the area.

Leadership and diversity in schools

Broader shifts to neo-liberalism and new managerialism across the Anglo Saxon world, documented in Chapter 3, has led to significant changes in both the workload and roles of both teachers and principals in schools, including schools in Ireland (Devine et al. 2010a; Sugrue 2005). Such roles have become more intense, characterised by struggles to maintain a balance between care for students, with the time that is required to cope with curriculum change and calls for accountability in an era of increasing emphasis on performance and outcomes in education (Ball 2003; Day et al. 2005; Grummell et al. 2009a). Perhaps not surprisingly, the OECD has turned its attention to the role principals can play in bringing about effective educational change (OECD 2008b). While we know that principals can make a difference, it is important to understand *how* they make this difference (Leo and Barton 2006). In this respect we can consider principals and school leaders as having a strong mediating effect on what takes place in the classroom. They set the broader context and conditions within which teachers and students interact in schools. Not surprisingly the idea of 'leadership' in schools itself has changed. Principals are no longer defined as 'managers' but as 'transformational leaders', engaging in a form of 'super leadership' that realises both the broader visionary elements of education, with the practical accountability demands for money well spent (Creemers and Kyriakides 2010; Day 2005). Increasingly leadership is also defined as a distributed process, the effective principal one who can draw on school colleagues to support and initiate change through teaching leadership (Gunter and Fitzgerald 2008; Moller 2009; Spillane and Diamond 2007). Lingard et al. (2003) speak of the need for dispersed and productive leadership, the principal positioned at the centre (rather than the top) of the school generating debate, discussion and strategic action with diverse members of the school community. For these authors a productive leader is one who is critically reflective, and whose practice is underpinned by strong commitment to social justice. Such *leaderful* practice (Perumal 2009), it is argued should combine with that of teachers, to create a collective approach to student learning, that involves debate, extended professional development and alignment with curricular goals and standards.

Schools today are more complex demanding spaces, not only because of increasing diversity brought about through immigration (as well as the mainstreaming of children with dis/abilities), but also by a greater awareness of equality and rights issues in education. In leadership theory, ethical and moral leadership are now viewed as central to the principal's role, s/he expected to engage reflectively and authentically with diversity in all its forms (Leo and Barton 2006; Lingard et al. 2003; Stefkovich and Begley 2007). This is a difficult challenge that involves stepping out of the comfort zone, especially during periods of rapid social and cultural change (Bottery 2004; Lumby 2006). It involves moving beyond 'a practical tolerance' (Blackmore 2006), working with the continual 'flux' of school life in an open way, encouraging new approaches to learning and building relationships, both inside and outside of the school (Walker and Shuangye 2007: 186). Such practices have been shown to be especially important in multi-ethnic schools, yet differences exist in the type of leadership which principals display. Some are highly pro-active, fostering curriculum change, supporting bilinqual education, reaching out to minority parents and monitoring student progress with an eye to realising an inclusive rights based approach to education (Gaetane 2008; Walker and Dimmock 2005). Other principals are 'hard to reach' (Crozier and Davies 2007), lacking the commitment and/or experience to bring about effective change (Blair 2002; Perumal 2009). Realising an ethical vision of leadership founded on principles of social justice is not an easy task, especially if we consider the 'messiness' of school life and the myriad of power plays and positionings which are played out on a daily basis. Emotions are embedded in ethics – especially if we define ethics in Rose's (2001) terms as 'acting' upon oneself. The feelings we derive from our interactions with others are underpinned by a range of normative dispositions. These relate not only to how we understand and 'define' ourselves but also our expectations, perceptions and 'definitions' of others. Returning to the work of Bourdieu outlined in Chapter 3, schools are 'fields' of power in their own right and how principals position themselves will be influenced by their own prior dispositions and 'habitus' as well as the 'logics of practice' which govern the field. These will vary from one school to another, dependent on local community dynamics and national policy frameworks. It will also be influenced by the levels of support and training that is provided to principals, as well as recognition being given to diversity in leadership. This includes a decoupling of embedded taken for granted associations of leadership with 'whiteness' and management positions deemed to be the preserve of the dominant ethnic group in society (Cambpell–Stephens 2009).

Leadership in newly multi-ethnic schools in Ireland

In Ireland, recent research on the work and role of school principals mirrors findings elsewhere, especially the considerable pressure experienced by principals as they accommodate to the increasing demands of their role (Devine et al. 2010a; Grummell et al. 2009b; Sugrue 2005). Prominent in such research is the commitment of principals to the care of their students, and their desire to provide a holistic education that emphasises personal, social as well as academic development. Sugrue (2005) for example speaks of principals as being 'passionate' about their roles and viewed as important role models and community leaders, especially in rural towns and communities. Simultaneously principals are subjected to the time bind of record keeping and accountability, arising from the range of legislative changes in recent years (Education Act 1998; Special Needs Act 2004; Education Welfare Act 2000; Equality Act 2004). They are also under pressure to source additional funding (both voluntary and state) to support on-going activitities in the school. Such pressures are acutely felt by principals working in schools with a higher proportion of educationally disadvantaged children and those with special needs, schools we know where there are also more likely to be a higher number of students of immigrant background. These changes have occurred in a period of rapid social change in Irish society that is also characterised by an increasing attention by parents (and the media) to differences between schools. As we saw in Chapter 3, in competitive societies, education is a key regulator of life chances and opportunity and making the 'right' choice of school is viewed as an important element in securing advantage in the education market (Lynch and Moran 2006). Devine et al. (2010a) speak of the crafting of an 'elastic self' that is now required of principals, as they seek to marry not only their pastoral, administrative and academic roles, but also secure and safeguard the 'reputation' of their schools in an increasingly competitive context.

Research that has focused specifically on the perceptions of principals in schools with high immigrant enrolment paints a mixed picture. Smyth et al. (2009) for example point to the generally positive disposition by principals to immigrant students, who suggested that most students integrated well into

Table 4.1   *Profile of school principals*

School	Ethos	Principal	Length of time as principal	School type
Oakleaf Primary	Roman Catholic	Mr Dempsey	> 10 years	Suburban (DEIS) co-ed
Beechwood Primary	'Educate' Together	Ms Hannigan	4 years	Suburban (DEIS) co-ed
Silverwood Primary	Catholic	Ms O'Sullivan	1 year	Suburban co-ed
Maryville Primary	Roman Catholic	Sr Bríd	7 years	Urban (DEIS) girls
Riverside Primary	Roman Catholic	Mr Martin	> 10 years	Suburban co-ed
Newdale Primary	Roman Catholic	Ms Curran	8 years	Rural girls
Redford Comm. Coll.	Inter-denominational	Mr O'Loughlin	> 10 years	Suburban co-ed
Bellview Secondary	Roman Catholic	Mr Hickey	> 10 years	Urban (DEIS) boys
Parkway Comm. Coll.	Inter-denominational	Ms Moran	4 years	Suburban (DEIS) co-ed
Spireview Secondary	Roman Catholic	Ms Murphy	5 years	Urban girls
Brookvale Secondary	Roman Catholic	Mr O'Connor	> 10 years	Rural boys

the Irish system. This it was felt was significantly helped by the increasing allocation of language support services in the previous three years. However an absence of sufficient in-service training for teachers, combined with appropriate curricular resource material, as well as difficulties communicating with immigrant parents, cut across the intercultural work principals sought to encourage in their schools. Similar challenges are pointed to in O'Gorman and Sugrue (2007) who also noted principal's concerns with the enrolment of immigrant students of other faiths in Catholic schools and the risk of 'white flight' in communities characterised by intensive levels of immigration.

This chapter presents findings related to interviews with principals across eleven schools. As indicated in Table 4.1, the principals are drawn from both secondary and primary levels, and differ in their length of time in the leadership role. The analysis explores the leadership habitus of these principals, as this is reflected in their work in newly multi-ethnic schools. It highlights the personal and professional struggles they encountered in their roles with respect to four inter-linked areas – the significance of 'field' to leadership practices, habitus and authenticity in the leadership role, managing for diversity and finally leadership for diversity.

The significance of 'field' and social context to leadership practices

We saw in Chapter 3 how the concept of 'field' is an important one in understanding the dynamics of power and control in social interaction, each field characterised by its own structures, history and ways of 'being' and 'doing'. We can consider schools as 'structured social spaces' (Bourdieu 1998: 40), characterised by configurations of power and patterns of representation and participation that have evolved over time. Each of the schools that I have been involved in doing research with over the past ten years had their own unique histories or 'narratives'. These influenced the way they are today and how they have responded to the rapidity of social change in the school community. This is very evident for example in the description provided by Mr Dempsey, in Oakleaf Primary, where he locates the school's openness to diversity in the context of prior experience of working with an already marginalised community:

> 100% of the children were Irish and we were very conscious of that you know, working with people who are less empowered or less well off, it brings out something in staff. So what I am saying really there were certain conditions already in existence in the school that was suitable for children coming from other countries.

The 'field' of Oakleaf Primary then was one in which the school staff had a relatively long history of engagement with issues of social and cultural diversity – not with respect to ethnic diversity *per se* (although this school had a tradition of Traveller children attending also), but with respect to working in a context of relative educational disadvantage and familiarity with the struggles of those who are marginalised in society. Given the level of low-cost private rental accommodation that existed in the area, it became a magnet for immigrant families. While Oakleaf was a relatively well established school, Beechwood Primary in contrast has only recently been built in response to intensive demographic growth during the 'boom' years:

> We started off with just 53 children and 3 teachers. Now, we have 360 children and 23 teachers so it has been quite a big explosion. So right from the word 'go' we have always had the majority of pupils really would be migrant families. (Ms Hannigan, Principal)

Ms Hannigan bemoaned the absence of 'proper' planning in terms of the provision of sufficient social supports and resources in such a new community:

> I could see areas like this end up being complete ghettos in the future because there are no resources for the people. Yes there are shops, off licences, bookies, but there is nothing for the community except the school thank goodness.

Similarly, Silverwood Primary in another area of high urban growth, has changed from being a small school, within a very tight knit community, to one that has seen intensive immigration:

> We have a whole new staff. There were 73 children in June and everybody knew everybody else, it was like a big family; Now we have 212; of the 212 probably 75% would be immigrant. (Ms O'Sullivan, Principal)

Newdale primary is located in a rural town. The school had some prior experience of social change by hosting refugees from a state sponsored programme a number of years previously. Responses however to the 'newer arrivals' were much more mixed, many housed in a reception centre, with evidence of some tension in the town:

> It was a totally different situation [with the programme refugees]. They were all the one nationality as well. It's not the same [with those arriving now] because they come from many situations, there is an attitude in the town that some people are 'on the make'. Whereas with the [programme refugees] there was a genuine welcoming feeling of sadness. (Ms Curran Principal)

In Riverside Primary, change has occurred gradually ('*it didn't all land on us one day*'), but nonetheless, the estate while still comprising privately owned housing, has seen an increase in rental housing being sub-let to the State [the Health Board]. This has led to some change in the socio-economic profile of those living there:

> The make up of the area has changed. It was all families and then in the last number of years a lot of people bought houses for investment, so you ended up with a whole lot of single fellas or girls which was one thing, but then the single parents came in and then there was lots of foreign nationals. (Mr Martin, Principal)

In general, the intense change was not experienced as dramatically among secondary schools, partially due to their larger size, but also the age profile of immigrants into the country (see Chapter 1). Mr O'Connor, principal of a boys' secondary school in Newdale for example, in contrast to his colleague in the primary school, spoke of having a 'small number of non-nationals' and of the benefits of prior experiences with programme refugees. Mr O'Loughlin, the principal of Redford Community College states the local area in which Redford is located has always attracted some international students, by virtue of its location near a hospital.

> We have always had a number of international students. ... that was because there was a lot of doctors in this area ... mostly Indian, Arabic and Pakistani doctors and because they are moving around ... but the numbers here haven't grown hugely in comparison to other schools, we have had at most 9, 10 or 11%.

In contrast, Mr Hickey, of Bellview Boys, speaks of the change as an 'explosion' and the lack of preparedness within the school and the local community:

> It's a problem that has mushroomed ... there's been an explosion in recent years. So as a school, or a country, I don't think we were prepared for what was happening ... the type of people coming or the variety of needs.

The rapidity of change, coupled with the intensity and type of immigration had an important influence in shaping local community reactions on the ground. Given that immigrants are most often located in areas of low rental cost, as well as where there is a high degree of social housing (Byrne et al. 2010; CSO 2008) this could create 'friction' in the local community over competition for scarce resources. While undoubtedly mitigated by the economic boom, as well as the contribution of immigrants to human capital within their local communities (Fahey and Fanning 2010), school principals were aware of these community tensions and how this could 'spill over' into perceptions of policies with immigrants in schools:

> This is a poor area and the people were coming and housed [by the health board] in the new apartments. So that caused a little bit of friction at the beginning. (Sr Bríd, Maryville Primary)

> A number of parents said straight out that I shouldn't be nominating these foreigners [for the community award] and that I seemed to be encouraging them. (Mr Martin, Riverside Primary)

Such comments indicate the tension within the broader 'field' of community and locality and the configurations of power and competition for resources and recognition within it. Principals were conscious of the dynamics within this field, and the need to maintain the school's reputation and connections with the local community, especially in an increasingly competitive education market place (Lynch and Moran 2006). Furthermore they also had to be conscious of the dynamics of reaction and interaction *within* the school (in terms of staff and students). Mapped onto this broader context however were the visions, values and 'habitus' each of the principals brought to their leadership roles. This influenced how they managed reactions and interaction *within* the school.

Habitus and authenticity in the leadership role

Effective principals tend to be passionate about their roles (Sugrue 2005), bringing a level of personal commitment in time and energy that derives from a vision of the kind of school they wish to create. It is an emotional role in which there is a huge investment of self. Principals spoke consistently about their strong commitment of care to the children and young people in their schools. This was equally evident in their narratives about their work with migrant children. There was a strong sense that principals often viewed themselves as 'protectors' for the children, arguing on their behalf, irrespective of their legal status or background. This was grounded in their construction of the school as a safe space, and one of care and learning:

> I have come across some families that are absolutely destitute. All we can do is our best for the child in the school setting. I would have mentioned them to Social Services and Vincent De Paul[1] have been great. (Mr Dempsey, Oakleaf Primary)

> The girl from social services asked me yesterday if I ask what status they have? I don't. She asked me why not and I said because my job is here, this is a school. (Sr Bríd, Maryville Primary)

We will see later how such views were also framed within Christian/ Catholic perspectives of community. A number of the principals spoke of how they had helped the parents of migrant children by writing references, seeking out additional social supports, or in one case nominating a parent for a local community award. What is perhaps especially interesting is how these school principals view themselves as a 'buttress' against state polices of non-recognition where these immigrant parents were 'illegal':

We have written letters plenty of times to either the courts or social welfare or any of these other places. (Sr Bríd, Maryville Primary)

We had a very bright boy in his Leaving Cert, problem is he doesn't have [legal] status so he may not be able to go to the University. I've given him a letter of support for status, his father is a very nice man, had been a teacher in Romania. (Mr O'Connor, Brookvale Secondary)

The Ukranian boy that we had in the school I nominated him for person of the year award a number of years ago. I knew the father very well and he was looking to become legal. The President was presenting the awards and I said this might be helpful. (Mr Martin, Riverside Primary)

Such leaderful practices (Perumal 2009) are embedded within the principals' construction of their role as leaders within the community, and of the schools they lead as central to, and embedded within community. This is especially reflected in the comment of Mr Dempsey:

The one institution of the State where children from other countries and parents can have very positive experiences, where they can be made feel welcome and where they can be given self confidence, and encouraged to participate is the primary school. (Oakleaf Primary)

The construction of the principal as a community leader, and the centrality of care and concern for children and their families, was part of the 'logic' of practice (Bourdieu 1990) of most principals studied. These dispositions were in turn influenced by the principals' own histories, including past experiences of Irish emigration within their own families:

It's appalling for them ... *I mean people like ourselves* [emphasis added] coming into a position of beggary – it's – look in somebody else's eyes and think this could be me ... and it was us, the Irish in America. (Ms Curran, Newdale Primary)

Principals' habitus was also framed in the context of their own class position, and a tendency to empathise with immigrant families who clearly came from a middle class background (*'people like ourselves'*). While this will be dealt with more fully in Chapter 5, classed perceptions inter-sected with ethnic status as distinctions were also drawn between different immigrant groups:

For instance there's a doctor who is now scrubbing floors – there's professionals, absolutely everything, teachers down there [in the reception centre]. (Ms Curran, Newdale Primary)

Our international students are specifically from particular areas of Afghanistan and they were all professional people; we have scatters of those from India and Pakistan. (Mr O'Loughlin, Redford Community School)

Similarly there was a noted tendency to comment more circumspectly about those who were culturally very different, especially when this cut across the running of the school. While many of the migrant children attending Catholic schools were from another religious denomination (Protestant, Hindu, Buddhist), it was those who were from a Muslim culture that were referred to in more problematic terms. What is significant is that principals who spoke more negatively about certain groups, did so only where there were a large number of that community in the school. This seemed to provide a threat to the underpinning culture of the school which principals found challenging to address. It raised questions about their own priorities, dispositions and values – what they considered as 'normal'. This was especially evident in Oakleaf Primary where there were a large number of Muslim community members (albeit from a diverse range of countries), but was also mentioned by principals in other schools where there were Muslims present:

> When we have been dealing with Nigerian children or Nepalese children or Indian children of a faith other than the Muslim faith, they are very anxious to participate and do whatever they can do, but integration in relation to the Muslim community is something that is not as straight forward and not as easy because of the culture and particularly the religious and dress and all of that. (Mr Dempsey, Oakleaf Primary)

Interestingly because of the inclusionary policies being pursued by Mr Dempsey, especially related to the provision of Muslim faith instruction during school hours, Oakleaf primary was developing a reputation among the broader Muslim community of being a school suitable for Muslim children. This in turn led to an increase in enrolment from a broader geographical area. This was not without its problems, in terms of managing concerns within the teaching staff, as well as the local community giving rise to Mr Dempsey's conditional response. It highlights the broader field of power relations in which Mr Dempsey must position himself, negotiating the reputation and profile of the school both within and outside of the school.

In Silverwood primary, conflict arose over adherence to everyday 'rules' (related to parking, collecting children and waiting in the corridor) and styles of communication, among different ethnic groups. Ms O'Sullivan struggled with her own sense of identity and values as she sought to manage inter-ethnic hostilities between parents in the school, as well as complaints that were arising from teacher concerns. The rapidity and intensity of change in the school and local community has unsettled 'hegemonic meanings' (Gillborn and Youdell 2009) related to how Silverwood primary both defines and seeks to present itself. It is significant that in expressing her concerns, 'African' and 'black' are conflated in negative terms in

Ms O'Sullivan's narratives, giving rise to a potential legitimation of racism. This latter also challenges Ms O'Sullivan's sense of herself:

> But I have become more anti- … well not anti- … well maybe a bit, but I can see big problems and not only in this school but I can see big problems and it tends to be Africans. That's an awful thing to say isn't it? … I would never have been racist, but when you are trying all the time and you don't seem to be getting any sort of communication back.

Ms O'Sullivan is a newly appointed principal and struggling with the demands of her role. This may have derived not only from the recent nature of her appointment but also the contextual factors that related to the 'field' of the school. This was undergoing a significant shift in 'habitus' by virtue of the rapid demographic change. The cultural dissonance she is experiencing in terms of her own expectations and dispositions is reflected in her comment that the school is a 'normal' school. Yet the patterns of enrolment and demographic profile indicates that it has gone through a profound shift. This is reflected in her own drawing on a classificatory discourse of 'white' and 'black' in discussing the school profile. In the quote below we see her conflation of 'white' with both 'normal' and positive:

> We are just trying to follow the rules, it is a normal school, they are normal rules and we are not asking you to do anything out of the ordinary … I mean our Board of management is fantastic but I mean like they are all white.

Ms O'Sullivan's comments also reflect the assertion by Langlois and Lapointe (2007) that less experienced principals tend to base their practice on an ethic of justice grounded in rules and procedural norms rather than reflexive engagement when conflict arises.

Nonetheless it would be a mistake to suggest school principals in general do not struggle with their roles in this changing environment. All principals spoke about the uncertainty of their roles and of their own struggles to be authentic and true to what they believed in, in pursuing change. This required an inevitable degree of risk taking, in relationships with staff as well as with parents (both immigrant and indigenous Irish) and self questioning about what was the correct course of action:

> People can be quite demanding and quite fervent when they themselves feel threatened. It really does require to try and articulate where you are coming from and not to be afraid. And to be sure of what you are meant to do. (Mr Dempsey, Oakleaf Primary)

> One of my fears, well not fears but it is in the back of my mind … I'd be careful to be seen to be fair. There was one particular man and he wanted to start his child in school and he wasn't four … And then he said 'is it because I am black?' I was shocked. (Mr Martin, Riverside Primary)

Principals are clearly influenced in their leadership practices by their own prior experiences and histories. Much of their practice is habituated, taken for granted 'logics' that have stood them well in working within a community framework which they knew. Immigration has changed this, especially in those schools where change has been rapid and intense. Mr Dempsey's more confident stance in relation to embracing change derives from years of experience working 'against the odds' in a marginalised working class community, but also with Traveller children in the school. Ms Curran is also highly experienced, yet struggles with the radical change in her school from being a Catholic girls' school in a rural town to one that is now populated with a range of cultural and religious diversities. Mr O'Loughlin experiences the shift as adding to the profile of the school, given that many of the immigrant students come from families of professional background. While the principals worked within broader (and changing) community contexts, as well as their own personal 'habitus', the space of each school was also structured by the defining 'ethos' of that school that contributed to certain dispositions in their leadership practices.

The significance of ethos to school leadership

School culture is often referred to as 'the way we do things around here' indicating deeply embedded and habituated practices that are taken for granted as the 'normal' way of doing things. In general principals spoke about the culture of their schools in terms of being a place of welcome, care and learning for children and young people. Most spoke of the positive contribution immigrants were making to the school culture, using words such as 'richness', 'openness' and the benefits for all from embracing cultural diversity. This latter, with the exception of a number of the schools, tended to be conceptualised however in relatively limited terms, surface engagements with cultural diversity that did not radically change practice in the schools (see Chapter 5). In some instances it was clear that the principals viewed themselves as important role models, consciously putting themselves forward as the 'friendly face':

> You try and do lots of smiling, body language to try and get across this message 'you are very welcome, come in, cup of tea'. (Ms Hannigan, Beechwood Primary)

Each school had its own mission statement that emphasised issues around the importance of respect and recognition for each member of the school community. In some cases principals spoke very clearly about the defining ethos of the school and how this framed their response to migrant children as a group. In the case of Beechwood Primary, for example, Ms Hannigan related the openness of the school to the 'Educate Together' ethos which underpinned all its work and was framed very much in terms of a human rights perspective:

> Within 'Educate Together', we have our core ethical curriculum which is very human rights based. So, we would try and use a lot of human rights and development education resources with the kids.

In other schools the Christian and especially the Catholic dimension to school culture was emphasised with respect to a concern for community (Grace and O'Keefe 2007), the poor and welcome of diversity as a core element of the school 'mission':

> The original function of the school was to look after the needy and I think that's where we go back to our roots and the vision of what was then the Christian brothers. (Mr Hickey, Bellview Secondary)

> Just because they're not Christian ... you have to make them very aware that everyone is God's children. To celebrate the differences ... it's wonderful we have all these beautiful children from all over the world in our Catholic school. (Principal, Newdale Primary)

> The mission statement is that every child is part of a community and a child-friendly school. (Ms O'Sullivan, Silverwood Primary)

A defining school 'ethos' then provided a framework for school principals to shape their practice with immigrant students. The role of patron and management bodies (e.g. Educate Together, Catholic religious orders) in guiding this philosophy was an important reference point. Of note however, is the distinction between a 'human rights' perspective, and a more charitable based approach that derives from a core philosophy of working with the poor and under-privileged. While both are underpinned by an ethic of justice (although one is framed in terms of rights, the other in terms of charity), there was evidence that school ethos could also be used as an exclusionary mechanism, especially with respect to immigrant groups. The comments of Ms Hannigan and Mr Dempsey below are instructive in pointing to the anomalies that exist in the education system and of how 'ethos' (in terms of denominational status) may intersect with factors such as social class, as well as ethnic status to influence the number of immigrants in a school:

> The 'Educate Together' ethos would be one of equal access, so our enrolment policy is first come, first served so there would be no criteria like how long you have been in Ireland, your religion, ... none of those things matter, it's good and bad. (Ms Hannigan, Beechwood Primary)

> Now there are anomalies and there are difficulties ... you know you could

effectively use an enrolment policy to exclude people and I know this has happened. (Mr Dempsey, Oakleaf Primary)

This points to the competing logics of practice (Bourdieu 1990) which can exist in the educational field, and of the contradictory exercise of power through institutionalised practices (Foucault 1979). In this sense, school 'ethos' can simultaneously promote inclusion and exclusion, depending on the broader 'field' in which the school is situated. We saw in Chapter 2 (and later in Chapter 6) the difficulties which were encountered by some immigrant parents from minority faiths in accessing a school in their local area. Simultaneously principals drew on a discourse of inclusion when talking about migrant children. It was clear that they frequently extended themselves personally in facilitating immigrant families to settle into the local community. However such discourse was rarely framed in terms of a rights or social justice perspective. While the pressure to enrol caused considerable distress to principals if they had to refuse entry to some immigrant families, a pragmatic response to assimilation into the Catholic ethos of the school was also evident in their responses. Principals felt that the majority of immigrants once enrolled into the school, did not have a difficulty with religious ethos and sought to be the 'same' as their Irish peers. In one example, this could include parents converting the children to Catholicism:[2]

> When I would speak to parents coming in I would point out that it is a *Catholic* national school. But if they wanted the children moved [during religion instruction] good and well. The vast majority of people chose to have the children staying in the class. I have noticed if the Irish children are having confirmation, they want whatever the Irish children have. I do know the priest recently baptised a number of them and it wasn't him going out searching for them … most of them would be *wanting to conform to whatever is normal in society* [emphasis added]. Again the Latvians and the Lithuanians. (Mr Martin, Riverside Primary)

'Inclusion' for Mr Martin is defined in terms of immigrant parents accommodating to the ethos/culture of the school – requiring a form of 'practical tolerance' (Blackmore 2006) on his part such as facilitating parents who wish to have their non-Catholic children moved during religion instruction. It does not involve a fundamental questioning of how the system is or what children (and their parents) are being asked to be included into. In contrast, for Mr Dempsey, the inclusive culture of the school was not linked directly to the Catholic ethos of the school, but rather to a discourse of empowerment and a tradition within the school in working with more marginalised communities. However this knowledge of the community gave rise to a sense of place and purpose that was fundamentally challenged by the arrival of immigrant communities, from a diverse and unknown range of backgrounds, histories and cultures:

> We had an unarticulated understanding about where they were coming from, their background and culture and that made it very free and easy to deal with parents ... now we have people coming from different cultures, different experiences and maybe different expectations ... their experiences are quite alien to us.

Furthermore the increasing Muslim population in the school caused serious questioning about the core Catholic ethos of the school and the extent to which the current system could function effectively in this changed social and ethnic context. It was clear that Mr Dempsey felt ethically conflicted. He struggled to maintain his core principle of being inclusive of and working with all parents, while also satisfying core obligations to maintain the Catholic ethos of the school:

> Can we have a Catholic multi-denominational multi-cultural school? I would say we probably can even though it is a contradiction in terms ... there's a whole legal aspect to it, and I don't mean to be pejorative when I say this but it is sectarian in its structure, by and large.

An ethos that is embedded in a core philosophy of care and concern for members of the school community can also be one, which, albeit unintentionally, structures the school space as an exclusionary one. This was especially so with respect to immigrant parents who come from religious traditions which differ from the dominant Catholic norm. In essence this is about state policy, rather than religious belief *per se,* and the absence of provision of sufficient school choices at local level to accommodate the range of diversities that exist. More fundamentally, and as noted in Chapter 2, it raises questions about what is community (Bauman 2001), who belongs to the community (who 'is' community and 'whose' community is it?). Is it to be defined in terms of religious belief and/or sense of belonging to the local physical space within a geographical area? This latter is especially important with respect to children, in terms of diverse and separate affiliations in time and space (Zeiher et al. 2007) which influence and intersect with their own sense of belonging and 'otherness'. Connections and friendships in school consolidate through shared after-school and playtime activities making the school an important bridging space in the local geographical community. These are not solely philosophical or ethical challenges related to the meaning of integration and belonging in Irish society, but are practically experienced by school leaders on the ground, as they seek to manage diversity in their schools.

'Managing diversity' in school

Blackmore (2006) points to the tendency for diversity within schools to be treated as a 'managerial problem' and diversity itself to be construed as an individual attribute (ibid.: 189) that needs to be 'managed' and 'contained'. Nonetheless an examination of the day to day realities of managing increasing ethnic diversity highlights the structural (systemic) factors which shape and constrain how principals work with immigrant communities, as well as the 'habitus' that informs their work. Two key themes consistently emerged in this respect that related to managing enrolments, classroom placement and allocations; and the negotiation and access to financial and support services to cater for the specific needs of immigrant groups.

Planning for diversity:
enrolment, placement and classroom allocation

The management of student numbers is always a difficult, yet important challenge for school principals. While immigrant students were broadly welcomed across all of the schools for their positive contribution to the academic and learning climate (see Chapter 5), their arrival also contributed in some cases to the survival and growth of the school. This was especially the case in four of the schools (Riverside and Maryville Primary, Brookvale and Bellview Secondary) whose 'numbers' had been in decline and who had now had an injection of life, as a result of the immigrant wave:

> As regards our numbers it has been a great thing as the population was dropping here and we'd have lost a teacher, probably two teachers less. (Mr Martin, Riverside Primary)

Problems regarding enrolment arose when schools were already 'full' and when the demand for places exceeded the existing capacity of the school. In such instances the school had to resort to a list of criteria in terms of the right to a place, which could legitimately exclude migrant children (depending on the denominational status of the school) and/or which proved challenging for immigrant parents to understand. This was a difficult and often traumatic issue for principals to resolve

> You see, this is a Catholic school, and the Patron of the school is Archbishop of Dublin so our boundary is a parish and we are bound first of all to take Catholic children into the school first. (Mr Dempsey, Oakleaf Primary)

For intensive 'growth' schools, such as Beechwood and Silverwood Primary, the challenge lay in securing adequate resources in good time, including additional classrooms and teachers. While their levels of immigrant enrolment is unusual (Smyth et al. 2009), managing the 'flux' in numbers, created specific difficulties for principals. In both Silverwood primary and Beechwood, but also in other schools, the situation was aggravated by the tendency for immigrant parents to place their children on the enrolment lists of a number of schools, uncertain of where they would finally gain access.

A further difficulty for principals was the transitory nature of many immigrants' lives (increasing with the economic recession) and the arrival of immigrants throughout the school year. This created practical problems in terms of teacher recruitment, which by DES regulations will only be determined by the numbers enrolled in the earlier part of the school year. It could act as a disincentive to schools to enrol students after that time, creating further difficulties for immigrants in accessing local schools. There were also challenges around the placement of migrant children in appropriate classes and a lack of knowledge about the prior educational history of the children. At second level especially this led to decisions often to place such students in the lower streams, primarily because of difficulties over language and lack of certainty over the ability of the child. This of course could have serious consequences for such children in terms of their subject selection and general academic progress, as well as teacher expectations (Crul 2007; Gillborn 2008):

> We put them [two immigrant children] in the lower stream and teachers were saying how bright they were but the language was such a barrier. And they did quite well. They both passed the Junior Cert at foundation level, but they still passed it. (Ms Moran, Parkway College)

Resourcing schools for diversity

State responses were important in setting the ground work for how migrant children would be received in schools. The lack of immediacy of response by the state to changed circumstances that require an immediate response by schools was frequently commented upon by school principals. In respect of Silverwood Primary for example, the rapidly changing profile of the school should have placed it within the DEIS[3] category, with implications for the level of resources the school could apply for.

> Last year when the [DES] questionnaires went around ... this wasn't a DEIS school but now it would definitely be DEIS ... now we are a totally different kettle of fish, and not even a hope in the future [of getting DEIS status] with the budget cut backs.

Mr Dempsey of Oakleaf Primary critiqued the absence of co-ordination across state services in response to immigrant needs. While individual personnel in such services were helpful, principals recounted the time they spent lobbying local politicians, writing letters to state bodies, negotiating with DES officials and welfare officers. This was in an attempt to secure not only practical supports such as books and school uniforms, but also language support services, psychological support, assessment and cultural mediation services. Significant improvements were made in state provision for language support from 2006, and this made a substantial and positive difference to planning and co-ordination in schools (see Chapter 5). These were rescinded however in the budget of April 2009. As a result there were real concerns that the cut backs in education would adversely affect the hard won progress which had been made in the area:

> We have three language support teachers but now we will only have two from next September onwards and that will make a big difference because we immerse kids in English and that will all now be cut back. (Sr Bríd, Maryville Primary)

> Between all the schools [in this area] we stand to lose 86 teachers and €250,000 worth of grants and that's in one area. It affects morale among teachers ... it's like going back in time. (Ms Hannigan, Beechwood Primary)

Where state support was insufficient, principals relied on voluntary contributions and help from the voluntary sector, including for example Catholic charitable run organisations. Furthermore serious difficulties could also arise with respect to the distribution of resources within the school. Oakleaf Primary has a strong record of working to empower all marginalised groups, yet felt challenged by the fairest way to distribute extra supports to all children in the school. Given the general model of allocation of support to schools, principals juggled the provision of such supports, especially difficult when they were faced with relatively large groups of children (both migrant and indigenous Irish) with support needs. This could create, dichotomies between 'them' (our international students) and 'us' (our Irish children) in teachers' minds, a situation that is likely to worsen with the reduction in language support provision:

> Because many of our international students fall short on the Micra T (reading test) they need learning support, so then other children who wouldn't be as low on the reading scale won't be able to attend the learning support whereas they probably would in another school. It's not about creating a difference between our Irish child and our international child but it's very much about losing out when they all need the extra support. (Ms Macken, Deputy Principal, Oakleaf Primary)

There were also substantial differences across the schools in the extent to which principals had systems in place which monitored the progress and participation of migrant children. This was especially evident as a researcher going into the different schools and the ease with which information could be provided related to the actual number of migrant children, their progress, subject choices etc. While this reflects the extent to which principals may be overwhelmed by the changes (Goddard and Hart 2007), it reflects core issues related to school and educational effectiveness (Creemers and Kyriakides 2010; Teddlie and Reynolds 2002). It also reflects the need for training and support for school principals to set up appropriate monitoring systems at whole school level (Blair 2002; OECD 2009a). One example is Redford College, where the principal has put in place a tracking system with respect to migrant students. This detailed not only their academic achievement from year to year, but also broader processes of inclusion related to participation in school events, the awarding of class prizes etc. In spite of these practical challenges, it was clear that principals were committed to effecting change, albeit to differing degrees. What is at issue here is the extent to which principals were reactive to the change, or whether the change itself led to an 'awakening of consciousness' (Bourdieu 1990:116). This latter involved moving the school beyond a practical tolerance (Blackmore 2006) of the immigrant community, resulting in significant change in the way in which 'we do things around here'.

Leadership for diversity: moving beyond practical tolerance

A major challenge for principals is to move beyond the management of diversity with all of its practical challenges, to *leaderful* practices (Perumal 2009) that inspire learning and real change in the culture and effective operation of the school. This is perhaps best reflected in Mr Dempsey's vision of integration, akin to Lingard et al.'s (2003/2007) portrayal of a productive leadership habitus that is predicated on openness and cycles of learning:

> I would strongly feel that any initiative should be done not with the purpose of integration but with the purpose of learning but that learning should embrace the Irish and the non-Irish. I don't think necessarily setting up an initiative purely targeting non-Irish parents, personally I don't think that works, I think it's almost insulting really. (Mr Dempsey, Oakleaf Primary)

Such learning suggests moving beyond the 'comfort zone' (Lumby 2006) and side stepping uncomfortable issues, to real and meaningful engagement with those from minority ethnic communities. There were two aspects to this leaderful practice evident across the comments of school principals. The first related to leadership work with teachers, while the second to that with parents. A third related to leading students is significant in that it did not feature strongly in principals' discourse.

Leading teachers for diversity

While there was generally a culture of welcome across the participating schools with respect to immigrant students, principals were mindful of the increasing pressures on teachers and their need to be prepared for the change.

> I know teachers were somewhat reluctant because they are saying am I going to be taking on a problem? (Mr Martin, Riverside Primary)

> At the beginning there were some comments like: what are going to have to put up with inside our classrooms? ... very quickly the teachers got used to it and allowed the inclusion policy to do its own work. (Mr O'Connor, Brookvale Secondary)

This is not to suggest that all teachers willingly took to the change. Mr O'Connor struggled with the overtly racist comments by a member of staff in the staffroom, while Ms Curran tried to avoid placing migrant children in one teacher's class because of her unwelcoming stance:

> That [immigrant child] spends most of her time between the two resource teachers because we have one member of staff who is not welcoming ... these things are said out and through the child didn't understand the language she did get the vibes.

> Once or twice I did have to say to a member of staff 'that comment is racist whether you like it or not'. (Mr O'Connor, Brookvale Secondary)

There was evidence of principals actively working toward the professional development of staff, organising courses, seminars and information sessions that would encourage them to reflect on their classroom practices. In such instances, the challenge of working with migrant children was constructed as part of the learning within the organisation, providing opportunities for staff members to extend themselves, taking on new types of teaching activities or sharing knowledge and understanding among colleagues:

> I'd like more staff to become involved in teaching English on a one-to-one basis [with migrant children], understanding them and their needs. I think that helps the teachers then in their own subject areas. (Mr O'Connor, Brookvale Secondary)

> I asked the local Education Centre Director to organise a course. It was on multicultural education ... We had 9 weeks; 7–9pm, usually lasted until 10pm because we found it so interesting. (Mr Curran, Newdale Primary)

Differences were evident across the schools however in the extent to which specific policies were targeted at particular groups of children, including minority ethnic children, rather than at the generality of children in the school. Oakleaf primary for example developed a supplementary education team (SET) that focused very specifically on addressing the needs of migrant children with respect to language, cultural recognition and pastoral care. Redford College tracked and monitored the progress of immigrant students on a range of indicators of well-being and has worked solidly on the development of a whole school policy toward immigrant students. In Beechwood Primary, involvement with the yellow flag programme[4] provided a very tangible mechanism for the whole school community to become involved in the development of a diversity code. This was centred on respect, recognition and mutual accommodation of all members of the school community:

> It's all to do with inclusion and setting up a committee that involves staff, parents and children. So we are really trying hard to come up with ways of including people. (Ms Hannigan, Beechwood Primary).

Such approaches are in direct contrast to the views expressed by Ms O'Sullivan, who had very specific challenges that arose from the nature of change in her school. In this sense a whole school policy on integration was spoken of reactively rather than pro-actively, as part of a culture of critical reflection in the school:

> In terms of integration policy, we are just starting, we don't have one … but then every child is supposed to be integrated in every school. I mean I don't have to say that.

This last comment points to a difference that was evident among schools in the extent to which and in what manner principals led for diversity. In some instances, inclusion and integration was perceived as a taken for granted and natural everyday aspect of school life, because that is what schools are *supposed to do*. This reflects the 'comfort zone' and practical 'tolerance' approach and the assumption that with good intentions, inclusion happens. It is reflected in Sr Bríd's comment in Maryville Primary that *'we have a policy on bullying and that kind of thing. We don't have specific policies because the school is a place of welcome. It doesn't matter what country you come from'*. In contrast, principals who worked with the whole school community on the development of policies, dealing directly with more uncomfortable issues (Lumby 2006), struggled with the concept: *'It is really hard'*. These ethical and moral leadership practices (Stefkovich and Begley 2007) were routed in self reflection and engagement, that required profound identity work for both principals and teaching staff:

> It's really hard … I suppose initially we are all afraid of change, we are all challenged … we all have our built in prejudices and it is only when we come face to face and deal with it that you know, we would really see that change is worth the challenge. (Mr Dempsey, Oakleaf Primary)

Such leadership was generally not practised by the principal on his/her own, but was more often a distributed effort, with designated areas of responsibility for individual staff members. Language support teachers were especially important as were home/school liaison teachers. They provided an integrating thread to the work of the classroom teacher and principal in the school, as well as to the experiences of parents in the wider community. This was evident in Parkway college, for example, where following the employment on a part-time basis of a designated staff member with responsibility for working with immigrant students, a more co-ordinated approach to practice ensued. This included visits by this teacher to the homes of the immigrant students. Ms Moran outlines:

> She made such a difference because it made me more aware of problems the students were experiencing at home. We changed the annual end of year commemoration to an inter-denominational (rather than Catholic mass) ceremony so that all immigrant parents would feel welcome.

A further aspect of leading teachers for diversity, but which can be noted for its absence in the narratives of principals, is the need for representation of minority ethnic groups on school staff (Blackmore 2006; Campbell-Stephens 2009). Leading for diversity should also include diversity *in* leadership, not at a tokenistic level but in recognition of the diversity of cultures that are part of the school community. The deep embeddedness of 'whiteness' to constructs of both teacher and principal in Ireland is reflected in the fact that the absence of minority ethnic teaching staff was not 'named ' or defined as problematic by principals in their attempts to create culturally inclusive schools. Again there are structural patterns at systemic level (e.g. the requirement of fluency in the Irish language at primary level) which precludes many immigrants from applying for teaching posts in the primary school system. In only one school was the issue specifically raised by a principal, although as we will see in Chapter 7, the absence of teacher role models from minority ethnic communities is something which migrant children are aware of, and alluded to in Ms Hannigan's comment below:

> A big barrier is the fact that there is no diversity in teaching staff ... so from the children's and the parent's point of view you would look at the school and it's all white Irish teachers, and even the children would say: 'how come there are no teachers from other countries who speak different languages?' (Beechwood Primary)

Leading parents for diversity

There were also significant differences in the extent to which principals actively promoted parental involvement in the school and in the promotion of activities which would support the inclusion of immigrant parents in the broader community. While these are dealt with more fully in Chapter 6, most primary schools initiated events such as open days and cultural fairs. Schools such as Maryville primary acted as a link for parents to attend out-reach activities organised by local religious run organisations. These provided valued counselling and support, as well as English language tuition. Oakleaf Primary, with its strong history of parental involvement, extended and adapted their policy to include immigrant parents. A series of initiatives were put in place to provide recognition to the diversity of cultures in the school, as well as encourage parents to visit and feel a sense of 'belonging' in the space of the school:

> We had a strong culture of encouraging parents to get involved and that proved a very big challenge when we had people coming from other countries, first of all for language reasons and then for cultural reasons many were slow coming to the school. So one of the first initiatives we did was to work with some of the adults doing English class … it created the message that they were very much seen as being partners of the school. Since then we have weekly coffee mornings, art classes, an Arts festival, an inter-faith week, a launch of our own international cookery book (that came from an Irish parent and an immigrant parent)

At second level the focus on parental involvement was not as marked, and where it did happen this derived in the main from initiatives by language support teachers and school chaplains.

Leading parents for diversity however is more than simply involving parents in cultural and learning activities in the school. Unless supported by concerted efforts to involve parents in decision making at a formal level, such practices can be additive extras to school life, that do little to bring about real change (Crozier and Davies 2007). Principals spoke however about the difficulties of getting such parents to become formally involved through participation in Parent Associations and directly on the Board of Management. The voluntary aspect of school Boards of Management, in a context of the intensification of many parent's working/family lives has put strains generally on voluntary participation nationally across schools. This has also placed greater strains on the workload that is carried by school principals (Grummell et al. 2009a). This is especially the case in schools serving marginalised communities where rates of parental participation can be low. Nonetheless, both classed and racialised patterns to parental involvement were evident across schools. These cut across and in many ways underpinned issues around leading parents for diversity. This will be dealt with more substantively in Chapter 6.

Leading children for diversity?

The issue of children's role in contributing to a socially just and inclusive school was noticeable by its absence in principals' narratives. This in some respects is not surprising in light of dominant constructions of children in paternalistic terms (Devine 2002, 2003). There may also be a tendency, especially at primary level to consider children as immune to many of the racialised processes and tendencies that may exist among the adult community. Racism among children for example was not seen to be a major problem by principals in any of the schools, and all were very clear about their intolerance if any was identified:

> Whenever a race issue comes up I have always gone immediately to the teacher. You take a strong line immediately because you would want to be seen to be doing the right thing as well ... You deal with it as it arises. (Sr Bríd, Maryville Primary)

However principals were also unclear about the level of racism that existed (confirmed also by Smyth et al. 2009), or indeed the social world of migrant children generally, and assumptions were made based on casual observations in the school yard:

> I wonder if we are fooling ourselves ... I was standing in the yard and we were watching kids playing – ordinary stuff that you see everyday with kids piling on top of each other. At the bottom there was an African boy, there was a Cuban girl and an Eastern European ... when you watched it there were all newcomer children playing together. (Mr Martin, Riverside Primary).

Similarly at second level, there was an uncertainty if students were genuinely mixing and of the degree to which racism may be part of their everyday experiences in school:

> It would be interesting to have a chat with them about it ... I am just not aware of it and maybe I should be. (Ms Moran, Parkway Community College)

Even in Redford, which had a proactive stance on monitoring the progress of immigrant students, racial incidents were not part of the tracking process, a pattern noted in other research (Walker and Dimmock 2005). By not naming children's racialised perceptions/practices as an issue, it remains within the 'comfort zone' of school culture. It is based on assumptions that because the school values inclusion, therefore it *realises* inclusion and exclusionary practices are perceived as aberrations from the norm.

While there was evidence of class level initiatives across the schools to work with children in relation to diversity (see Chapters 5–7) children as a group were rarely consulted on policy in this area at a whole school level. An exception was evident in Beechwood primary, where through the yellow flags programme; children were actively involved as one of the stakeholders in developing the school's diversity code. This is important in terms of an underpinning culture of inclusion that seeks to give voice, respect and recognition to all as members of the school community. As we will see, children are active negotiators of both culture and identity and have much to contribute to policy formation in schools (Devine 2002/2003).

Concluding discussion

This chapter has considered the impact of immigration on the leadership practices of school principals, and how they are positioned in their role at the inter-section between state policy and practice. Schools are 'structured social spaces' with their own logics of practice that foreground how immigrant communities are both received and accommodated in the every day life of the school. Factors related to social class and school ethos especially mediate both the access of immigrants to schools, as well as responses by the school community to them. Principals are responsible for negotiating between competing logics of practice, and this is especially challenging when large scale immigration occurs in the local community. The cultural discontinuity which can ensue and the consequent 'threat' to the school's sense of itself and community, provide a difficult and at times overwhelming challenge for principals to accommodate to. Some were more skilled and confident at doing so than others, their leadership 'habitus' dependent on their prior management experience, educational and personal histories, as well as the level and intensity of change. Principals had their own sense of place, as well as a sense of place of others (Bourdieu 1990: 131) in the school community. Most principals were passionate about their work, strongly committed to the care and well-being of their students. In this sense their leadership practices were underpinned by a strong ethical dimension. The extent to which this ethical leadership was framed in terms of a distinct rights and social justice perspective, or one based on charity and concern influenced the manner and depth of engagement with immigrant communities and cultures. Principals who fore-grounded social justice concerns in a critically reflective and engaged manner spoke about how difficult and challenging the process was, but rewarding in terms of facilitating change. Systems of distributed leadership were evident across most schools, and where there were teacher leaders in the area (most often teams organised for English language support) this made a substantive difference to planning and co-ordination of work with immigrant students (and parents) in the school. Strong concerns were expressed about the impending impact of budgetary cuts on the progress that had been made in the past three years. While there were day to day challenges in the 'management' of diversity in each school (related to enrolment, class placement and securing additional resources for learning, language and psychological supports), significant differences were evident across schools in terms of actively working toward an inclusive school culture that sought to critically reflect upon and engage in and with cultural change.

While principal's leadership practices may be localised to their school and community, they must also be considered at systemic level in terms of embedded patterns of power, positioning and identity making. In this sense, their practices are part of the capillary like feedback loop that connects macro level patterns with micro level processes and outcomes in schools. Figure 4.1 below highlights the factors which contribute to the framing of principals' responses to ethnic diversity:

Figure 4.1   *Habitus and the framing of principals' responses to diversity*

Structure
Patterns related to class, race;
funding and policy decisions vis-a-vis immigrant education
Local community dynamics; systems of governance

Leadership practice
Constitutive, distributive, recognitive
Ethical/authentic/productive?
Distributed?
Charity? Justice?

Principal habitus

Power

Agency
Reflection; engagement
Resistance/continuity
Identity work

Applied to our model, their practices are constitutive (in terms of defining the school culture), distributive (in terms of decisions about how to use resources) and recognitive (in terms of the level of mis/recognition towards those who are different to the 'norm') – each of which has a profound influence on how schools are experienced by parents, teachers and students. Principals do not work in a vacuum, however. Their leadership habitus is itself embedded in prior experiences, including classed and racialised understandings of identity and belonging. These are both reinforced and supported by system level practices and influences. Power is exercised by these principals in a complex and sometimes contradictory manner. Principals can demonstrate deep care and concern for immigrant children, without radically altering embedded patterns of belonging to the school. As active agents they can reflect and position themselves based on their own prior experience as well as in response to the 'unsettling' of assumptions about 'normality' and 'otherness'. In some instances profound identity work was evident, as principals struggled with what they valued and what they sought to achieve. In others, the emphasis was on a limiting of inclusion to tolerance and an individualised approach to managing diversity. Principals are similarly constrained in what they can do. Broader dynamics in the field, at state level related to governance, funding and policy decisions, as well as at local level in terms of tensions in safe-guarding the school's 'reputation' highlighted the inter-play of both classed as well as racialised dynamics in the negotiation of their roles. These latter issues will also emerge in our analysis of teacher, parent and children's perspectives.

Notes

1 This is a Catholic charitable organisation that has a long tradition of service to poor and marginalised communities in Ireland.
2 We will see in Chapter 7 how dynamics of inclusion and exclusion among the children centred very much upon this experience of being different or the same as peers, including differences around religious identity.
3 DEIS (Delivering Equality of opportunity In Schools) is a targeted programme of investment that was specifically geared for schools in economically disadvantaged communities.
4 This is a programme designed by the Irish Traveller Movement to promote and foster interculturalism among primary school children: www.itmtrav.com/ yellowflag.

5

Who'(se) normal?
Teaching for diversity
in newly multi-ethnic schools

This chapter considers the perspectives and views of a cross sample of teachers working in newly multi-ethnic schools and of the discourses that frame their narratives about their work. It situates the analysis in the context of critical perspectives on race and pedagogy in the classroom as well as research on teaching and learning in multi-ethnic schools. When asked about their work with migrant children, teachers usually speak positively about the experience and there is often a prevalence of the 'no problem here' approach in their responses that belies more complex patterns and processes. In this chapter I identify two central areas of concern. The first relates to the conditional acceptance of migrant children in the classroom based on the productive and added value they bring. Such constructions I argue mirrors broader constructs of migrants as 'useful' that has both classed and racialised dimensions to the ascription of value, as well as problematic implications when migrants are no longer 'of use', especially during times of economic decline. The title of the chapter relates to the second major theme which plays on the concept of 'normality' and whose normality becomes reflected in teaching and learning practices in schools. Pedagogy for diversity involves profound identity work for teachers where they need to step out of their known 'self', in order to meaningfully engage with those who are different.

Critical perspectives on race and curriculum
in education

As we saw in Chapter 2, education is a key mechanism through which the state 'imagines the nation' and how teachers work with children in classrooms is central to this process. As Bernstein (1975) notes schools are the primary vehicle through which the dominant 'message' systems in society are communicated, including those related to the formation of a national consciousness. For this reason, both the nature of the message (curriculum) as well as the manner of transmission (pedagogies) has important consequences for how migrant children are received and included into the host society. What is taught, how it is taught and to whom, are political and sociological questions, as much as educational ones, as decisions are made as to what is selected in or out of programmes in schools (Apple 1979, 1986; Young 1971). In this respect, debates over how cultural and ethnic diversity should be catered for in schools are contentious, ranging from assimilationist models which view multiculturalism as an 'additive extra' to the 'normal' curriculum, to more critical multicultural approaches which foregrounds pedagogy as the practice of respect, recognition and voice for minoritised groups (Banks 2009). It is no coincidence that with the rise of neo-liberalism in recent years, coupled with mass migration as a result of globalisation, there has been a retreat from more critical multi-cultural approaches to curriculum design and implementation. Spearheaded by Islamophobia and the threat of terrorism following 9/11, as well as evidence of inter-generational marginalisation of (in particular) non-European immigrants in education (OECD 2006), countries with a long history of immigration are moving towards 'watered' down versions of multiculturalism in order to curtail 'ethnic separatism' and threats to the 'nation state' (Castles 2009; Rijkschroeff et al. 2005). Conversely those who seek to embed cultural diversity more deeply into school practice, critique much of what is labelled as multi-cultural education for its tendency to 'museumize' and essentialise minority cultures (May 2009; Modood 2007), rendering them 'exotic; and 'other'.

It is also argued that acritical approaches to multiculturalism (re) create hierarchies and boundaries between majority and minority ethnic groups, without challenging differences in power and status /recognition between them. Kowalczyk and Popkewitz (2005: 424) refer to such forms of multiculturalism as 'border making', creating 'ghettoes of difference' in terms of those who belong to the imagined nation of the past, and those who do not. This resonates with Bryan's (2009) analysis in the Irish context of the additive status of intercultural guidelines (NCCA 2005) intended for mapping onto existing curriculum structures, but also the repeated endorsement of a distinctive Irish 'we' that marks out immigrants as 'other', to be 'granted' inclusion and welcome. Similar tendencies were noted in our discussion in Chapter 2 related to national policy documents such as Migration Nation (2008) and the NESC report (2006). Power is at the heart of such processes in terms of who has the power to define, to regulate, to govern and whose voice is included in such forms of governmentality. Of course this is not new and has a long history with respect to the absence of the voice of Travellers in curricular design and practice (Lodge and Lynch 2004; McDonagh 2004). In spite of the development of intercultural guidelines (NCCA 2005) issues related to the minoritised status of Travellers relative to the settled community is rarely highlighted and Traveller education in practice is perceived to be very much *about and for* Travellers, rather than also about and for the settled community (DES 2002a, 2000b). The question arises if multicultural education is about minority cultures or about challenging constructs of national, cultural and ethnic identities for all living in more complex, cosmopolitan societies?

Critical race theory [CRT] adds a further dimension by seeking to foreground the issue of race in studies of inequality and has been usefully applied to the study of education. With its origins in US legal scholarship and the work of Ladson billings and Tate (1995) in education, CRT queries the tendency by white people to assume that racism is an attribute of errant individuals rather than a structural feature of everyday social life. An interrogation of white racism is central to such an approach, bringing with it an increasing focus on 'white' studies in research in education (Gillborn 2008; Leonardo 2009/2002; Reay 2007) and how 'white' confers advantages and benefits in a society which valorises 'white' as both superior and norm. Policy documents on ethnicity and migration in Ireland when viewed through this lens, do not problematise the notion of 'white Irishness', (or indeed white, settled Irishness), instead conferring as Bryan (2009) notes this positive 'we', which is assumed to be inclusive and 'normal'. While Foucault (1979) outlines the concept of 'otherness' as key to the exercise of power in terms of processes of domination and meaning making, Butler (1990: 133) speaks of the 'abjected other' that is subjected to exclusionary practices by those who have the capacity to define what is 'true'. This is where both curriculum content and teacher practice is so *powerful,* carrying with it the potential to 'empower' or 'disempower' by virtue of the modes of meaning making that inform what goes on in the classroom (Adams et al. 2007; Freire 1993).

As May (2009) notes, even accepting the fluid and contingent nature of identities both within and between ethnic groups in cosmopolitan societies (Beck 2006), individuals are always located within specific classed, raced, gendered and historical boundaries that shape who they are. Teachers, as much as their students, are classed, aged, raced, gendered beings that are shaped also by the discourses which are embedded in their social worlds. Their habitus permeates their practice in both visible and less visible ways. Knowing what teachers think, how they construct difference, integration and immigration is important in order to understand what shapes their practice in school and influences their effectiveness, broadly defined, as teachers. It is also important to bear in mind, as Youdell (2006), notes that while discursive practices are not always intentional they are nonetheless just as profound in their effect. Often what is not spoken about, addressed or confronted (discourses of silence) is as significant in its impact as what is said and discussed. The absent presence of race for example in principal's narratives (or indeed policy documents) about patterns of representation in leadership (and indeed teaching) positions in schools in Ireland is one example. Further, just as we saw with principals in Chapter 4, teachers' work is embedded in their emotional lives, espoused not only in their commitment to care for their students but also in dealing with the fear and uncertainty in coping with the complexity and multiple demands that increasingly pervades classroom life. The intensification of the working lives of teachers has been well documented internationally, as they struggle to adapt to demands for transparency, accountability and improved productivity in their work in schools (Ball 2003; Hargreaves 1994). Intensive cultural change alters the emotional geographies of school and classroom life (Hargreaves 2001) as old certainties and ways of being and doing may be undermined by feelings of closeness and distance with different groups of students. Building trust, real engagement and emotional understanding between teachers and students is essential for effective practice, yet requires considerable confidence and fortitude, as teachers may feel overwhelmed and lacking in the skills and competence to cope with the change. This can also be influenced by the length of experience teaching and life stage in the teaching career (Sammons et al. 2007).

Teachers and teaching in multi-ethnic schools

Much of the research on teacher practices in multi-ethnic classrooms highlights their practical, pragmatic approach that involves occasional 'ad hoc' attention to diversity, along with a tendency to 'exoticise' the culture of minority ethnic children (Chan 2006; Connolly 1998). Studies of refugee and migrant children identify teachers' deficit assumptions about the learning capacities of students whose mother tongue is not English (Pinson and Arnot 2007; Rutter 2006). This is in spite of findings which highlight the positives of multilingualism and of adapting learning to incorporate the mother tongue of the child (Cummins 2001). Such patterns are mirrored elsewhere in Europe (Faas 2008; Holm and Londen 2010; Horst and Gitz-Johansen 2010; Moree et al. 2008) with direct implications for the 'othering' of those who do not belong to the national norm. In the USA similar findings have been noted related to the colour-blindness of teachers in their narratives about schooling (Lensmire 2010; Picower 2009) and a dysconscious racism that precludes a critical awareness of the influence of race and ethnicity on school life (King 2004; Vaught and Castagno 2008). The 'no problem here' viewpoint predominates (Gaine 1995), with teachers tending to individualise racist incidents as aberrations from the norm, expressing reluctance to involve pupils in discussions about race-related issues. However, the prevalence of a racialised discourse in teacher practice in times of stress has also been noted as has the racialised, gendered and classed constructions which teachers draw upon in explaining patterns of achievement in school (Archer 2008; Archer and Francis 2007; Bell McKenzie and Sheurich 2008; Walters 2007; Zembylas 2010).

While such research critiques teacher practice, this should not imply an absence of care by teachers in relation to their pedagogical practice. What is at issue however is the extent to which teachers may lower their expectations for minority ethnic children because they are different to teacher 'norms' (culturally, ethnically, socially). In such instances there is a risk that the discourse of 'care' translates in practice into a benevolent sympathy arising from assumed 'deficiencies' in the minority ethnic child. Lingard (2007) highlights the 'pedagogies of indifference' which permeated the practice of Australian teachers that was characterised by a lowering of expectations and demands for those who were 'different' in school. Such patterns have consistently been identified with respect to children from poor and working class backgrounds in schools (Lynch and Lodge 2002; MacRuairc 2009; Reay 1998/2005) and specifically with immigrant and minority ethnic groups (Blair 2002; Crul and Holdaway 2009; Warikoo and Carter 2010). While teachers themselves may view their work with minoritised groups as positive and often 'heroic' especially in challenging circumstances (Bell MacKenzie et al. 2008), their resistance to changing the 'tried and tested' and lack of overt recognition of racialised practices in schools can undermine progress and outcomes with respect to minority ethnic groups.

In Ireland, members of the teaching profession tend to be white, Catholic and settled and very much embedded in the lifeworld of the dominant social group in Irish society (Drudy et al. 2005). At primary level, a majority of entrants come from professional, managerial and farming backgrounds, a pattern that has remained persistent over the years. Recent research of recruitment into second level teaching indicates greater diversity in terms of socio-economic profile, although still with a predominance of those who come from farming and professional and managerial backgrounds[1] (Clarke 2010). Further the ethnic homogeneity of entrants is also evident in the 98% who identify themselves as having Irish nationality (Heinz 2008). Teachers' social and cultural background is important in defining their 'habitus' and sense of what is 'normal', leading to deficit perspectives of those who differ from this norm. This is evident for example in the consistently held deficit constructions of Traveller children among teachers identified by Kenny (1997) and Ryan (1996), as well as in the curriculum (Bryan 2007). A lack of sensitivity by teachers to identity differences on the basis of sexuality, gender, culture and religion has also been noted in research (Lynch and Lodge 2002; Mayock et al. 2009). There is also an emerging body of research in Ireland on teacher practices in ethnically diverse classrooms which highlights the lack of attention to cultural diversity in classroom practices (Bryan 2010; Devine 2005; Lyons 2010) reiterating earlier findings in relation to the marginalisation of children from the Travelling community, as well as the Vietnamese communities in the 1980s (McGovern 1993). Our own most recent research that included observing teacher practices in primary and post-primary classrooms (Devine et al. 2010b) identified worrying trends related to less challenging teaching in classrooms as the number of immigrant children present increased, along with lower levels of observed engagement in learning among such children. The clustering of these students in DEIS schools is an additional cause for concern, given what we know about lower expectations for learning in such schools.

The remainder of this chapter considers research with respect to teachers at primary and post-primary level in a cross sample of schools. While much of the data comes from the six schools in the most recent research, it also draws upon interviews with 73 teachers in the ISTOF project (Devine et al. 2010b), as well as earlier research (Devine et al. 2002) and subsequent visits by me to some of these latter schools in the intervening years. The benefit of drawing on data collected over an extended period of time is the ability to track changes in perceptions as well as consistencies of patterns that remain, in spite of the intervening period. These are referred to as appropriate in the text. The analysis is presented in terms of two interrelated themes that connect with broader dynamics of power and positioning in the field of education. The first considers the construction of migrant children in 'productive' terms and the conditionality of their acceptance based on the added value they bring to the classroom through their working and learning. The second theme explores teacher constructs of integration and the practical and emotional challenge of stepping out of 'self' if meaningful pedagogical change is to occur in working in multi-ethnic classrooms.

Constructing the 'productive child': the 'added value' of migrant children

The analysis of state responses to immigration in Chapter 2 highlighted how these were consistently framed in terms of the productive value of immigrants as a group to Irish society. Drawing on the work of Rose (1996), we can say that the 'subject' of immigration in such discourse is one who approximates to the neo liberal ideal of self actualisation and self fulfilment through hard work and effort. Children no less than adults are 'subjected' to these norms and expectations, no more so than through schooling practices (Devine 2003, 2002). We can explore this by considering the extent to which teacher discourse reflects this emphasis on productivity and self actualisation in their narratives about migrant children.[2] Consistently throughout my research with teachers generally positive views were expressed about migrant children that directly related to the *added value* these children brought to the classroom environment. In this sense teachers' construction of migrant students as productive, model members of the school, mirrors state discourse with respect to the welcoming of immigrants *where* they provide an added value to the society through their productivity and work ethic. It is not surprising that such values would be appreciated and commented upon by teachers given that working hard and viewing schooling as a productive activity in which one engages one's self and identity is central to teacher habitus. This discourse of productivity and self-actualisation was evident in teachers' repeated commentary that migrant children were positively disposed to learning, contributed to an enriched learning environment for all (including for teachers themselves) and served as positive role models for children especially in working-class schools.

> I guess that the first generation migrants have the manners and the gratitude ... so my experience has been phenomenally positive. (Ms O'Mahony, Redford Community College)

> They have a fantastic kind of spirit about them . I've seen [Irish] students who were initially kind of anti social towards teachers and because they see the ethnic minorities being very mannerly, they suddenly change. (Mr Collins, St Anthony's Secondary)

For Ms Macken in Oakleaf Primary, the presence of migrant children was a source of enrichment for the whole school as it added to the diversity of learning that could now take place for children, teachers and parents:

> Well for me it has been a very positive experience, very enriching for the school ... I think it's great that the children go home with stories from other countries I mean it's a geography lesson in itself, it's a history lesson, it's a religious lesson.

Underpinning this construction of migrant children were both classed and racialised perceptions that positioned such children simultaneously as 'other' and 'norm' depending on their classed and ethnic affiliations. In many of the schools it was the 'middle classness' of the migrant children that marked their productivity and more positive acceptance:

> Very quickly we discovered that the children coming in were by and large I'd say that most of the people coming from abroad here, probably came from a very ambitious set of people and very middle class, very positive. (Mr Martin, Riverside Primary)

> They are mostly professional people ... we would have very few in the low IQ bracket. (Mr O'Loughlin, Redford Community College)

This is not to suggest that immigrants were all perceived to be middle class, as clearly they were not, and teachers recognised that there could be substantial differences in the educational and work profiles of immigrant parents. While teachers were often unclear as to the economic status and background of immigrant children ('we don't like to ask') there was evidence of a discourse of Christian charity and concern, in light of the trauma some immigrant children were perceived to have experienced both in their country of origins as well as their arrival to Ireland. However teachers also drew on racialised perceptions of immigrant groups that intersected with their views on social class. This gave rise to subtle distinctions in how they spoke about and constructed different immigrant groups but also the tendency to 'homogenize' ethnic identity as something that was fixed and essentialist (Modood 2007). Teacher narratives were most positive when migrant children dovetailed with their own habitus in terms of both culture and class. With respect to immigrants from Eastern Europe, especially those from Poland, Russia, Romania and the Ukraine words like 'bright', 'diligent', 'nice', 'interested' 'good at languages' and 'willing to learn' occurred repeatedly in teachers' narratives, yet more circumspect views were expressed about Latvian and Lithuanian groups:

> East Europeans on the whole come with a good basic education. They are very eager to learn and they work so hard at the homework. (Sr Martha, Maryville Primary)

> One example is a Polish child whose parents are very eager, he get lots of reading at weekends and holidays. (Ms Murphy, Silverwood Primary)

> I would say the Latvian and Lithuanians would be very much poorer and they would work at very menial jobs in their own countries and they are working at menial jobs here. (Ms Glacken, Language Support Teacher, Riverside Primary)

Teachers' comments about children whose families had immigrated from African countries were similarly positive, with a consistent emphasis on these children's positive orientation to school ('motivated', 'bright', 'keen to learn', 'quick'). While there was a tendency to essentialise 'Africans' as a group, subtle differences were also evident in teacher perceptions of the behaviours and personality traits of children from different countries in Africa. For example, 'boisterous', 'lively, 'demanding' and 'exuberant' were comments evident in narratives about Nigerian children, both boys and girls, but attributed to boys only in the context of children from Angola and the Congo. Furthermore, racialised constructions of African children drew on discourses related to bodily movement and the natural 'rhythm' of Africans in general:

African children will be a lot more forward you know and the Irish children are kind of looking and wondering what's going on! (Ms Ryan, Silverwood Primary)

Some of the Africans are very good and some are not ... some of them like Zimbabwe is a fantastic place where we had great students coming from in recent years, and they all have very high aspirations. (Mr Wilkinson, St Anthony's Secondary)

When the Tanzanians arrived five years ago it took quite a while to settle in ... it was a type of African manner. (Ms Logue, Parkway College)

Teachers' perceptions of the 'otherness' of African culture also emerged, including reference to differences in child-rearing and gender practices that were perceived to be contrary to the Irish norm:

Say, if you chastise a child or give out to them and we have our traffic lights system – so if they go onto orange or red they get a reminder, and if they get something wrong they go onto orange and then they continue on with more reminders and they go down to red. So you would get the [African] parent in to talk about their behaviour and they would say to me 'Oh just punish him'. And you are trying to explain to them that is not what we do here in Ireland. (Ms Flanagan, Beechwood Primary)

Mark is from the Congo ... great, exuberant personality ... but that is more a cultural thing where the boy in Africa is given a lot more power and position. (Ms Hammil, Riverside Primary)

Consistent patterns were also found with respect to teachers' narratives about children from the Far East and Asia, both boys and girls, with evidence of the 'model minorities' discourse noted elsewhere (Archer and Francis 2007). This was reflected in their quiet, diligent demeanour in the classroom, confirming these children as 'different' from the 'normal' pupils:

They are a different type of children, they are calm, there is something about the Asians. (Ms Glacken, Language Support Teacher, Riverside Primary)

So you would notice especially the Indian and Filipinos even before they come into the class room that they are better because so much work has been gone into it. (Ms Cawley, Language Support Teacher, Maryville Primary)

I find Chinese fantastic workers, the Filipinos brilliant workers. (Kevin, St Anthony's Secondary)

Teacher narratives about children from the Middle East also emphasised their hard-working and diligent manner. Predominant, however, were references to the cultural differences between what was perceived as Irish/Christian and Muslim ways of life, especially with respect to gender and religious norms. Such cultural dissonance gave rise to the construction of

Muslim children as simultaneously productive and potentially problematic, especially in instances where Muslim parents did not want their children to assimilate in with the 'Irish' norm:

> A mother came [into my classroom] and said: 'I don't want my girl sitting beside any boys' ... I said 'okay'. This is my first year teaching so I don't know how to cope with that. Next year I won't make allowances for that. (Ms Ryan, Oakleaf Primary)

The issue of cultural dissonance also emerged quite strongly in teachers' narratives about children of the Roma community. In the minority of schools where they were present these children were invariably spoken about in deficit terms, similar in many respects to constructions of indigenous Traveller children in Irish schools (Kenny, 1997; Ryan 1998). This is reflected in the comment of Mr Martin in Riverside, who directly equated his experience of recently arrived Romany children in the school with the 'problem' of Travellers in Irish society:

> The one problem that definitely arose was that we had a group of Romanian [*sic*] children ... they were very difficult, their behaviour, now they were not used to school ... *it wasn't their foreignness that was the problem, it was being Travellers in a different culture*. (Mr Martin, Riverside, emphasis added)

> Some of the Romanians [roma] would have had the worse attendance that I would have noticed from different nationalities. (Mr O'Connor, Redford Community College)

Teacher constructions of migrant students were underpinned by their own positioning in the dominant ethnic and social group in Irish society. Just as we saw with school principals in Chapter 4, there was also evidence that their increasing exposure to students from a diverse range of cultures and backgrounds unsettled not only their hegemonic constructions (Youdell 2006) of 'Irishness', but also their essentialist constructions of those who came from ethnic backgrounds which were different to their norm:

> I remember I was in a rural school with 36 children and there was only one African child and I asked 'So, where abouts are you from?' and she said 'Oh I'm Irish'. I just presumed that she was African but she was born and bred here and considered herself Irish. (Ms Rowland, Beechwood Primary)

> When I came to the school there was a husband and wife here from Egypt. *They were Muslims but a very lovely couple* [emphasis added]. (Sr Ignatius, Language Support Teacher, Maryville Primary)

Teachers' constructs of 'newcomer' children in positive terms was also shaped by the career trajectories of the teachers themselves. This was more evident among language support teachers, many of whom (at primary level especially) were teachers with a long record of service, who enjoyed the challenge of working in a new field, as well as working with children with more traditional values of respect for authority:

> I found discipline was getting worse, discipline problems are increasing and the difficulties in the mainstream classroom are really very great. (Ms O'Mahony, Language Support Teacher, Redford Community College)

> I think it's brilliant ... maybe it is just the fact that I've got into this now and am taking it on board and getting more of an insight into all of these cultures. (Ms Macken, Language Support Teacher, Oakleaf Primary)

Overall the analysis suggests that teachers' dispositions toward migrant children are framed in terms of the 'enrichment value' which they add to the experience of both teaching and learning. In this sense their positive acceptance of change is expressed in terms of what such children bring (middle-class values and positive dispositions to learning) as well as what they want to become (self actualised models of productivity and self enhancement), rather than voiced in terms of an unquestioning acceptance of who they are. Questions related to the latter are most evident with respect to children who came from African and Middle Eastern backgrounds. This is not to suggest that such children are not accepted, or indeed cared for by teachers, but that teachers' more circumspect views, when expressed, derive from an unsettling of their assumptions about what is 'normal' and 'other', and of the challenges this poses to their own sense of identities and good practice. As Youdell (2006) notes however, it is in this unsettling that the spaces and possibilities for change arise, itself mediated by the extent to which teachers are willing to embrace and work with diversity. The following section considers these issues with respect to aspects of their curricular and pedagogical practice.

Who'(se) normal? ... the challenge of stepping out of teacher 'self'

For Bernstein (1996) pedagogy is intricately bound with power, in terms of shaping classroom and school practices in line with specific norms and values. The question then arises as to who has the capacity (power/ resources/positions) to define 'normal' – whose voice is reflected and what are the implications for the experience of belonging, teaching and learning in schools. Resonating with Bourdieu's work, Bernstein speaks of the importance of making explicit 'the inner logic of pedagogic discourse and its practices' (Bernstein 1996: 18) in order to understand its significance for the regulation of identities and consciousness. Throughout my research, differences were evident across schools in terms of the degree of reflection and engagement by teachers with diversity and the extent to which difference was interpreted as a challenge to work toward mutual understanding, or as a deficit to be overcome. The perspective taken is significant in terms of the extent to which teachers feel they must reflect, engage, change and accommodate to diversity or whether the locus of action and responsibility (Bernstein 1996) is situated in the child and his/her family and community. The 'inner logic' of teachers' pedagogic practice was especially evident in their discussion around the concept of integration and what this meant to them. In the excerpts below, two contrasting yet inter-linked narratives are evident – the one which defines integration as 'being the same as us' and cultural diversity as a potential 'threat'; the other which views diversity as a positive development and integration as a fluid process, involving the melding of identities to construct new forms of 'Irishness' and 'being' in classrooms and schools:

> If I moved with my family to America today I would be expecting my children would go into an American school and receive an American education. And I provide an Irish education that is where I am employed. I would just be mindful that our culture is important and I have a big kind of strong opinion on that and I think that we shouldn't lose it. (Ms Hamilton, St Augusta's Primary)

> I think what is happening in this school, it is happening without us saying we must integrate, we must do this, that and the other. One of the days when I saw all the Muslim boys coming from their Qur'an – they have Qur'an instruction in the mornings here – *and where they were all coming from their Qur'an they had their helmets, their hurleys and their sliotars[3] with them and I said that's integration.* [emphasis added] … We would love to see international members of the staff body and that would be integration at its best. (Ms Macken, Oakleaf Primary)

In the first quote Ms Hamilton expresses the view that migrant children must adapt and accommodate to 'Irish' education, indicating her belief in 'Irish' ways of being and doing, that she defines as 'our culture'. She draws then on a normative based idea of integration which is embedded on notions of preservation of something that is at risk of being lost. In the second excerpt, Ms Macken also draws on specific traits of 'Irishness' (hurling) but delights in the Muslim boys coming from their Qur'an instruction (which this Catholic school makes available to Muslim children during the school day) suggesting that it is this blending which defines integration for her. It *is* integration but *not* integration – something that she indicates happens 'naturally' yet which we know from Chapter 4 is facilitated by the very direct engagement by this school with minority ethnic communities. Significantly, integration is not defined as a form of paternalistic 'acceptance' (a granting of acceptance that comes from a position of power (and relative privilege) but as belonging in terms of respect for diversity and the multiple perspectives that come with it. This latter focus was also very evident in Beechwood primary (Educate Together) and Redford community schools:

> Sometimes other teachers from other schools or even non-teachers might be quite discriminative and saying 'My god it must be really difficult working with African parents or Roma travellers or working with Irish travellers' ... it's sometimes the indigenous Irish who can be more difficult. (Ms King, Beechwood Primary)

> Our aim is that in five years time, every nationality on our school will be represented on the walls ... Redford belongs to everybody, not just the indigenous population so we have to reflect that. (Ms O'Mahony, Redford Community College)

How teachers constructed 'integration' influenced their pedagogic and curricular practice, especially in terms of the extent to which they incorporated minority perspectives and identities into the organisation of class and school life. As with principals, they were required to (re)evaluate what learning should be in the classroom and to what extent they would accommodate to the diversity that was present within it:

> So I suppose you are constantly trying to make sure you are including everyone and keeping everyone happy and trying to get that balance, *when you are brought up in a certain culture yourself and you are stepping out of that yourself* [emphasis added]. (Ms King, Beechwood Primary)

There were however specific challenges that arose for teachers at primary level centred on the teaching of religion, which is integrated throughout the curricular programme in Catholic schools. This had implications on a day to day basis for both normalising as well as exclusionary practices with respect to migrant children in schools. For example, children who were not Catholic had to choose between remaining in class during periods of religious ritual and instruction (class blessings, religious instruction, church ceremonies during school hours etc.) or exclude themselves, drawing attention to their 'difference' in front of peers and teachers. This created obvious difficulties for the children involved, but also for teachers, as they now had to question their previously taken for granted norms of appropriate curricular and pedagogical practice:

> Most of the teachers would be Catholic upbringing I suppose, and middle class backgrounds. And you would be culturally-used to saying 'God bless' and 'Thank god' ... so you would become culturally aware of saying those things when proportionately you would have a very small number of Catholics in the class. (Ms King, Beechwood Primary)

Such comments invariably arose where there were children from African and Muslim backgrounds and drew not only on differences in religious practice and belief, but also more general signifiers of cultural identity centred on language, music and dance:

> The way, even just with Christmas and we were doing letters to 'Santy' but a lot of the African children said we don't believe in 'Santy' and they don't have the same tradition so they are feeling left out in class. (Ms Wright, Silverwood Primary)

> One family said they didn't want their child to dance and dance is a huge part of the primary curriculum now but they [parents] would say no but it is a religious thing and that would have been a huge eye opener for me and the other staff then. (Ms King, Beechwood Primary)

At secondary level, the issue of religious diversity did not appear to pose a similar difficulty; schools generally responded to such diversity by the timetabling of language support to coincide with lessons in religious instruction.

Teachers were uncertain about how to proceed in terms of recognition of the cultural backgrounds of children, and engaged for the most part in a form of 'pragmatic' multiculturalism (Connolly 1998) – incorporating elements of the children's culture and ethnic identity as they felt appropriate and where they had access to resources to enable them to do so. While this 'practical tolerance' (Blackmore 2006) was sometimes embedded in a defensive concept of integration – expressed in the 'need' for migrant children to accommodate to Irish norms and customs, teachers were also concerned about not drawing attention to the 'difference' of minority ethnic children in a manner which would be embarrassing or uncomfortable for them

> My role is to make them feel part of our culture as well as understanding that they have their own ... I think you don't even know what you are doing, but little things like talking about Irish ways, our traditions, our feast ... if you don't single them out, that is how they feel part of our community. (Ms Coughlan, Riverside Primary)

> In a general classroom situation I don't think they would want their culture to be highlighted as different ... I think they would be uncomfortable with it. (Ms McGrath, Parkway College)

A notable difference existed between language support/ home school liaison teachers – who in many respects were immersed in working with immigrant communities – and classroom teachers, in terms of their level of ease at incorporating cultural difference into their teaching practices. From the time of our earlier research with schools (Devine et al. 2002), it was also clear that there was an increasing move across schools toward the 'celebration' of cultural diversity through intercultural days and festivals.

There was however less evidence of a critically reflective and structured approach to drawing on the children's diversities across the curriculum at local class level. This in part related to lack of knowledge about how best to proceed, but also a tendency to compartmentalise diversity as an 'additive extra' to the work of the classroom teacher, rather than an underpinning ethos of classroom practice. While the expansion of the language support service greatly facilitated the work of integration in schools, it could also have the (unintended) effect of compartmentalising integration work away from the mainstream classroom (and teacher). In some instances tensions were evident within schools as classroom teachers 'resisted' efforts by language support teachers to foreground the issue of cultural diversity across whole school practice. This is indicative not only of contrasting perceptions of how far 'integration' should go [including reputational concerns over the identification of the school as an 'immigrant school'], but also of gaps in perception and awareness that directly related to the level of intensity of focus and experience in working with immigrant communities. As we saw in Chapter 4, school cultures differed considerably here setting the framework for the level of reflection and engagement by teachers in structuring their pedagogical practice around cultural diversity and recognition.

It was also notable, however, that discussions around the management and experience of ethnic diversity rarely drew attention to issues of race and racism in school practice. Reflecting research internationally (e.g. Gaine 1995; Gillborn 2008), teachers felt racism was not a problem in their school and identified any incidences they had witnessed as isolated and individualised. While some concerns were expressed about increased racial tension in schools if the number of migrants continued to increase, racism was very much dealt with within an anti-bullying, rather than an anti-racism framework. This precluded discussion of the structural dimension to racism in society at large:

> The seeds are there. I've heard a few comments from children in second and third class – calling names. Rather than make a big issue out of it we let it go. (Ms Lucey, Newdale Primary)

> I think we all feel that there's a potential hornet's nest there. A lot of us would feel not competent, inexperienced, and we are. (Ms Jenkins, Ashleaf College)

The importance of language

Given the significance of language to learning, it is not surprising that teachers' priority focus in their work with migrant children concerned the acquisition of fluency in English. What was also noteworthy across schools however and consistently borne out in other research in Ireland (Bryan 2010; Lyons 2010; McDaid 2009) was the tendency to interpret children's linguistic competencies in deficit terms – as devoid of English rather than as multi-lingual. This had direct implications for their expectations of learning for them:

> If you have half your class who can't speak English … you are starting way back nearly like the child who is only learning to talk … *you know like a one year old.* (Ms Mathews, St Cecilia's Primary)

> Well I suppose the most obvious thing that stands out when it comes to migrant children *is if they have a language.* You know, that's the first and foremost. (Ms Lee, Oakleaf Primary)

> You wouldn't expect the same amount of work from them as the other students in the class. English would be the big thing. (Mr Behan, St Michael's Primary)

The issue of competency in English, as well as the mapping of curricular content to children's experience influenced how well migrant children could and were doing in school. The assessment of children's learning had implications at primary level in terms of class level placement and subsequent access to learning as well as language support, and at post-primary level in terms of allocation to higher level streams and subjects in the junior and leaving certificate. This can have important consequences not only for children's own self esteem and valuation of themselves as learners but also for their access to subsequent enhanced and appropriately challenging opportunities for learning. A major challenge in summative assessment is the level of accuracy in measuring a child's readiness and success in learning and research in this area consistently points to the culturally biased and selective nature of most forms of formal assessment (Elwood 1998/2006; MacRuairc 2009). At secondary level this issue arose with respect to the placement of migrant children in the 'weaker' streams, with teachers acknowledging, as research in this area has shown (Boaler et al. 2000; Crul and Holdaway 2009), that streaming may not be in the best interests of the students themselves:

> They are put in with the weaker Irish children. My English class, one half is weak Irish, the other half is foreign students. They may be weak at English but they are still very intelligent. (Ms Nevin, Spireview Secondary)

> We had a guy last year and his English was holding him back and that's why they wouldn't let him into the top stream but he was bored in the class he was in. (Ms Murphy, Parkway College)

A considerable difficulty for post primary schools was the often ad hoc nature of language support provision, which in many cases was being allocated to non specialist, mostly temporary teachers, who were trying to make up their 'teaching hours', a pattern also noted by Lyons (2010).

Not only did this result in a lack of co-ordination and development of consistent systems and practice in the provision of such support (with yearly changes of teachers working in the area common across schools), but also a lack of continuity in experience for the students. The co-ordinated approach evident in Redford secondary did not typify the general approach to language support in other second level schools:

> We had no TEFL department and one of the teachers kind of set up, really off her own back and some teachers were great at teaching it and others weren't because some teachers were short hours and they were making up their TEFL. So it wasn't always taken as seriously as it should have been. (Ms Fahy, St Cecilia's Secondary)

The challenge of working with children who did not speak English fluently was compounded by difficulties in communicating with their parents, especially where there was no access to interpreter facilities. Teachers were critical of the continued absence of sustained professional training in the area of language support and intercultural training, a need reiterated by the OECD (2009a). This absence of training ensured that they drew upon their practical knowledge and understanding, rather than an informed perspective of what is best international practice in the field. In most interviews there was little to no reference of drawing on the children's mother tongue as a learning resource (Cummins 2001; MacDaid 2009), the latter viewed typically as a cultural attribute – to be validated as an additive extra in intercultural activities and celebrations:

> It kind of makes me feel quite helpless because he [migrant child] is not getting any work done; his behaviour isn't great because he doesn't understand and I kind of feel that I am failing him and the system is failing him. (Ms Tuohy, St Michael's Primary)

Notwithstanding such patterns however, it is also evident that the significant investment by the state in the provision of language support teachers since 2006 set the groundwork for the development of a more sustained and professionally oriented language support service in schools, especially in the primary sector. This expansion facilitated the development of teams in schools who could plan effectively on the basis of the additional resources they had been provided. This was especially evident in Oakleaf Primary and Redford Secondary, where a clear and projected route toward integration that focused on language, interculturalism and building relationships with the broader immigrant community was evident:

> I suppose our school is very lucky because we are a disadvantaged school and we have a lot of learning support teachers and resource teachers. (Ms Tobin, Oakleaf Primary)

You know we have moved here from that approach in [exclusively focusing on] English to try to help children stay in touch with the L1 [first language] … I keep saying to the kids, you know some of them have two or three languages, if you build on these languages you could be a translator later on because we are now living in a multicultural world. (Ms O'Mahony, Redford Community College)

In both of these schools (and in others such as Beechwood primary) it was evident that practice was moving beyond a 'practical tolerance' (Blackmore 2006) for diversity, to one in which diversity embedded in classroom practice was increasingly part of the school culture. As we saw in Chapter 4, both schools were characterised by leadership which was defined in terms of reaching out rather than looking in. Perhaps significantly both schools also made a clear decision at whole school level to have senior and experienced teachers taking responsibility for the development of this area. Considerable anxiety and concern was expressed then over the recently announced education cutbacks:

These education cutbacks you know I think we will feel the pinch in language support especially. The teacher has 24 or 25 bodies in the class, the teacher can't get around to every one of them individually and if kids can't access the information where are you starting from? (Sr Mary, Maryville Primary)

I am profoundly upset and distressed about it … I just cannot believe it's going to happen. We simply would not be able to follow up on the policies that we are now doing. (Ms O'Mahony, Redford Community College)

In terms of performance in school, it was also evident that teachers attributed variation in student outcomes to the children's social and linguistic background rather than in terms of their own impact as teachers on student learning. It is significant in this respect that there was little attention across schools to monitoring the progress of migrant children, in spite of consistent evidence that differences can exist among teachers in their practices and expectations for learning among minority ethnic groups (Crul 2007; Devine et al. 2010b; Gilborn 2008). Where children's progress was poor, teachers struggled to identify if this was due to an underlying learning and/or language difficulty or as a result of trauma and upset due to prior experiences in the children's country of origin. Even where oral language fluency was high, many teachers felt that children struggled to gain written fluency and required sustained language support over a period of years to do so (rather than the two year allocation at present). This had real consequences for the children in terms of their performance on standardised and often culturally specific assessments and tests. There was then an inevitable sense of being stretched but also limited in what could be realistically achieved:

We could have a really intelligent child but they fall down on the Micra-T (English language assessment) ... they would fall down on the trick questions maybe like for example 'Green is to grass as white is to ——'. And it is *snow* but they wouldn't have that concept although they are hugely intelligent. They need ongoing English because all the little nuances of the language are lost on them. (Ms Macken, Oakleaf Primary)

Again, we are talking about pass-rates in the Junior Cert. here, but we had a 100% pass rate for the Junior Cert. here amongst the international students. It's a fairly high academic achieving place but at Leaving Cert., not so. You see, we work really hard with them for Junior Cert. – then for the Leaving Cert. it's really hard because they don't have their spaces on their timetables to come out to us for language support. (Ms O'Mahony, Redford Community College)

The issue of language competence in English intersects with the expectations which teachers had for the children's learning and the extent to what is considered 'acceptable' and 'normal' for these children's achievement in school. This in turn is mediated by the stresses which teachers feel in accommodating to the multiple demands of classroom life and the extent to which a 'dichotomy' emerges between 'them' and 'us' in times of stress and in the allocation of teacher time. Teaching is an emotional activity and 'stepping out of yourself' to engage in critical reflective practice requires a commitment to connect meaningfully with the lived experience and perspectives of children from minority ethnic communities.

The emotional investment of self

The challenge of 'stepping out' of oneself pedagogically mirrored the emotional investment of self that was also evident in teachers' engagement with migrant children at a personal level. Words like 'worrying about', 'reaching out', 'joy', 'soft spot' permeated their narratives, alongside concerns over the practical challenges of catering for the needs of all children in the classroom:

I would have a particular soft spot for these children. I was one of these in school myself, extremely quiet and diligent and never put the hand up. (Ms Boyle, St Attracta's Primary)

I had a student a couple of years ago who came into this country with no English at all and in fifth year he asked me 'can I please come to your higher level class even though my English isn't great'. He only came in the year before and he ended up getting a C 1 in Higher Level English ... So, I get such joy from that. (Mr O'Brien, St Michael's Secondary)

That would be one of the main problems ... the domino effect: they need learning support, you need to go at a slower pace, material isn't covered for that class level so you feel the standard of education is deteriorating in a way because children are not able to cope with the language presented to them. (Ms Howlett, Oakleaf Primary)

The importance of this emotional connection to children should not be under-estimated, and was something which was consistently referred to in a positive way by parents (See Chapter 6). At issue here however is the competition for teacher time in increasingly diversified systems as well as the appropriate allocation of resources to support diversity and inclusion for all in the classroom. I have argued elsewhere (Devine 2005) that state policy is significant in setting the conditions for teacher's work and the parameters within which migrant children are afforded real and meaningful opportunities to excel and integrate into the Irish system. However teachers also differ in terms of their own habitus and 'logics of practice' that derives from their own biographies. Expectations for learning and the investment of time and energy by teachers in individual children was also mediated by the transience of many within the immigrant community. This could give rise to teachers wondering about their level of investment of self and resources, creating a further dichotomy between 'them' and 'us' in the investment of such time:

> There is one student whose English is probably atrocious and my main problem in dealing with her is she doesn't communicate and her attendance has been dreadful and I feel it wasn't worth the investment of time when the others needed as much help as I could give them. (Ms McGovern, St Cecelia's Secondary)

> They either are a very transient population and it can be hard for teachers because they put huge effort on this child and then they move, so if you put all this and they are gone on you, you know, it can be hard. (Sr Máire, Maryville Primary)

Concluding discussion

The analysis presented highlights the multiple and often contradictory discourses which abound in relation to migrant children (as a source of 'enrichment' and 'added value' versus a 'drain on resources' and 'time'). These are mediated not only by the different resources migrant children themselves bring to their learning but also by the resources (expertise/ knowledge; language support, class size, etc.) teachers can draw upon in coping with the changing classroom environment. The challenges in 'stepping out of yourself' as a teacher do not arise in a vacuum but at the inter-section between state policies on education, teachers' own biographies (habitus) and the children's own differentiated classed, gendered and ethnic identities. This is reflected in our model below (Figure 5.1).

Figure 5.1   *Habitus and the framing of teachers' responses to diversity*

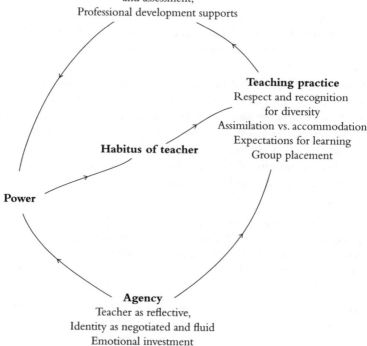

Structure
Embedded patterns related to class, gender and ethnicity;
Constructions of 'immigrants'; state policy re funding, curriculum
and assessment,
Professional development supports

Teaching practice
Respect and recognition
for diversity
Assimilation vs. accommodation
Expectations for learning
Group placement

Habitus of teacher

Power

Agency
Teacher as reflective,
Identity as negotiated and fluid
Emotional investment

The query in the title of this chapter around who'(se) normal? reflects the power dynamics that are at play in shaping practice in the classroom in terms of definitions around both *who is* considered normal, (and who is therefore in need of regulation in line with dominant expectations and goals), and secondly *what is* is taken as 'the norm'. These dynamics of both signification (who/what is normal) and legitimation (who has the power to define what is normal) become reflected in teacher narratives about migrant children, in the (often) racialised distinctions they draw between different groups of children, and subsequently in the practices they engage in at classroom level in working with migrant children and their indigenous peers. The relative homogeneity of the teaching profession in Ireland, in terms of ethnicity and to differing degrees gender and social class raises questions about pre-given assumptions and expectations around 'normality' and 'otherness' that as we have seen influences teacher perceptions, reactions and practice. While the 'unsettling of hegemonic assumptions' (Kitching 2010; Youdell 2006) can create spaces for change (e.g. learning the Qur'an can sit alongside a physical education lesson in hurling), it can also lead to a re-enforcement of norms through negative stereo-typing and labels of 'deficiency' in the 'other'. This is especially evident when we examine specific challenges that arose for teachers in working with migrant children. While issues of language instruction and gaining fluency in English were often to the forefront of teacher concerns, also evident were diverse constructs of what 'integration' should entail (who and what is 'normal' in Ireland, what does it mean to be 'Irish'), as well as differentiated practices (related to for example streaming, reduced expectations for learning) that we know have potentially negative consequences for such children's educational well-being. Furthermore, the construction of migrant children in positive terms because they conform to an 'ideal type' in terms of productivity and good behaviour, that in itself is underpinned by classed perceptions, raises questions about the conditionality of the acceptance of such children. In this sense teacher accounts mirror state policy in terms of being positively disposed towards immigrants who bring 'added value', setting a clear dichotomy between those who do and do not 'fit' such idealised norms. Teachers are not uniform however and each brings differing levels of personal commitment, values and interests to their pedagogical practice that, as with principals, is shaped by their own prior experiences and biographies. This is their 'habitus' which operates in a cyclical capillary fashion, shaping consciousness, influencing belonging and opportunity among migrant children in schools. It derives from their own positioning as classed, raced and gendered beings that influences their dispositions and orientations in their practice in schools. It is then at this inter-section – between the national, the local (and indeed the global) and the personal that both inclusionary as well as exclusionary classroom practices arise.

As we saw in Chapter 4, schools differed in their responsiveness to the level of change. This was reflected in practice at classroom level, not only in the 'emotional investment' that was involved in reaching out to migrant students, but in the level and degree of critical reflexivity that was engaged in with respect to both curricular and pedagogical practice. This latter was most evident among language support teachers (and those involved in home/school liaison work) suggesting that in the absence of deep immersion in the life-world and perspectives of migrant children and their families, coupled with teacher professional development, teacher's work with diversity remains at a relatively superficial level. The absent presence of race (Apple 2009) in most teacher's accounts reflects not only an a-critical approach to working with diversity in schools, but also perhaps a reluctance to 'step out of the comfort zone' of traditional classroom practice. The following chapters will consider these issues further with respect to the views of parents and children.

Notes

1 These findings also indicated a substantial proportion of entrants to post-primary teaching with fathers who were in receipt of social welfare (17%), although caution is advised in interpreting this latter figure, due to the range of financial supports which can be included in this category, other than unemployment benefit and assistance (Clarke 2010: 174).

2 To some extent teachers were very aware of the impact of 'discourse' on children, and this was evident in their concerns over the 'correct' terminology to use in talking about children from minority ethnic groups. Changing discourse is evident from my own visits to schools over the years and the shifting terminology from non-national, to foreign national, to international to 'newcomer' children.

3 Hurleys and sliotar are the stick and ball used in playing the Gaelic game 'hurling'.

6

Pathways to immigrant
parental involvement in schools

This chapter examines the perspectives of immigrant parents with respect to their experiences of the education of their children in Ireland, as well as their attitudes toward being involved in a meaningful manner in school activities. Contrasting perspectives are evident that signal tensions around recognition and belonging, as well as strategies that are employed by parents in negotiating their own and their children's positioning in education. We have seen from an analysis of both principals' and teachers' perspectives that fostering positive home/school relations is a key element of educational policy. It is one which is mediated however not only by structural constraints related for example to rights of access to and enrolment in schools, as well as the resourcing of school activities, but also by cultural factors related to the ethos of the school, the identities and habitus of teachers and principals, as well as the capitals (economic, social and cultural) which parents bring to the educational encounter.

'Being a fish in water':
culture, capitals and parental involvement in school

The significance of parents' role in their children's education is underpinned in Ireland not only through the constitutional recognition of parents as primary educators of their children (Article 42.1), but also increasingly at the level of policy and practice in the promotion of active parental involvement in school life, most especially in primary schools. Such practice is founded on wide ranging research, dating from the 1960s, of the significant impact of parental attitudes and values on the achievement and successful integration of children in school. Since that time there has been considerable development in understanding how parents influence children's educational life chances and of the significant role of both social class and ethnicity in mediating children's success and orientation to school. Research has followed a trajectory moving from 'deficit' perspectives prevalent in the 1960s and 1970s, which located educational failure firmly in the absence of appropriate values in the home to cultural difference perspectives. These more nuanced approaches foreground the impact of cultural discontinuities between home and school and the significance of school organisational cultures in accommodating (or not) to the diverse range of identities and cultures within which children's family lives are embedded (Lareau 2003). Such an approach also locates parental responses in the context of broader structural inequalities in society and the significant role of schools in (re) producing patterns of inequality through their everyday practices (Bernstein 1975; Bourdieu and Passeron 1977; Willis 1977), including those with parents.

Boudieu's analysis is especially helpful in understanding how parental positioning in the field of education is influenced by their access to capitals, as well as the significance of 'habitus' in shaping responses to school. Parents position themselves and are positioned differently with/by schools – those who are most aligned with the dominant school culture and ethos moving seamlessly between home and school, like a 'fish in water':

> One of the privileges of the dominant, who move in their world as fish in water, resides in the fact that they need not engage in rational computation in order to reach the goals that best suit their interests. All they have to do is follow their dispositions, which being adjusted to their positions 'naturally' generate practices adjusted to the situation. (Bourdieu 1990: 108)

There is considerable research which documents the significance of social class to the positioning of parents in education: how issues of confidence, self-esteem and absence of structured school support and recognition for the voices of marginalised parents detracts many from active involvement with schools (Crozier 2001; Lareau 1989; Parker-Jenkins et al. 2005; Reay 2005). Indeed such research points to the 'psychic damage' that results from being positioned as 'other' in a system which is embedded in middle-class ways of 'being' and 'doing'. Conversely, middle-class parents are the most likely to become involved, activating both social and cultural capitals through their focused participation in volunteering, fundraising, and collaborating in a range of school activities (Birenbaum-Carmeli 1999; Lareau 1989). This builds and fosters their positive relationships with the broader parent and teacher community in the school (Griffith and Smith 2005; Levine-Rasky 2009). Such patterns should not detract from differences within parent groups – for example middle-class parents can themselves differ in terms of values, perspectives and preferences (Vincent et al. 2004) yet what is similar is the capacity to mobilise resources when required to do so in the reproduction of the 'middle-class' child. Gender also plays a part, in that the role of middle-class mothers has been increasingly commented upon (O'Brien 2007; Reay 1998), strategically manoeuvring and confidently negotiating their position on a range of school committees. In so doing they build key networks that provide important sources of knowledge and information, enabling them to make effective educational choices and encourage effective school practices with/for their children (Reay et al. 2007; Vincent and Ball 2006). Class intersects with race, in the over-representation of white middle-class mothers in multi-ethnic schools at both a formal and informal level, and in the value that is accorded both 'whiteness' and middle classness in normative school cultures (Gilborn 2008; Reay et al. 2008). There is also evidence of majority ethnic parents engaging in exclusionary practices with respect to immigrant/minority ethnic parents through non-participation/attendance in multicultural school events, through 'white flight' in areas of intensive immigration and in seeking segregated education (through tracking) for their children in multi-ethnic schools (Levine-Rasky 2009; Poupeau et al. 2007; Reay et al. 2007).

Inside schools, research points to the 'othering' of minority ethnic parents who are often perceived by teachers as 'hard to reach' (Crozier 2001; Crozier and Davies 2007), pathologised as lacking in the cultural and dispositional attributes deemed essential to success in school (Luttrell 2003). We saw in Chapter 4 how teacher's judgements of migrant children were based on their understanding of 'an ideal type pupil'. Similarly, attitudes toward parents are informed by (implicit) assumptions about what constitutes 'good parenting' and therefore the 'good' parent. This can have consequent implications for both classed and racialised orientations by teachers toward different groups of parents in schools. They tend to express more positive orientations toward parents who are most similar to themselves – culturally and ethnically (Francis and Archer 2005; Parker Jenkins 1995; Ran 2001). The automatic conflation of 'whiteness' with middle classness means that black middle-class parents also struggle for recognition, defined first by their 'non-whiteness', leading to experiences of racist stereotyping and a doubling of effort required in order to maintain their class position (Archer 2010).

Schools also differ in the level of contact they seek with parents, ranging from what Dale (1996) terms as the 'expert' approach, where the teacher is positioned as professional expert imparting information to parents; to the 'transplant' approach, where the teacher seeks to enhance the skills of parents as co-educators and an important resource in their children's education. In both instances however as Crozier and Davies (2007) note, it is the school which sets the parameters for parental inclusion and involvement. In Bourdieu's terms it is the school which defines the 'rules' of the game, with which parents must 'choose' to comply. While schools in Crozier and Davies' (2007) research espoused the need for parental 'voice', there was little evidence of tracking minority ethnic parental involvement or indeed the educational performance of minority groups giving rise to their assertion that schools (rather than parents) could be considered as 'hard to reach'. Blackmore (2006) locates the concept of parental voice firmly in the political context in terms of the creation of a deliberative democracy that ties in with notions of social cohesion, citizenship and community. Such a conceptualisation of parental participation moves beyond tokenistic modes of representation to real engagement with the experiences of those across the entire school community. While neo-liberal reforms in education espouse greater local autonomy and participation from the bottom up, including connection with parents, the locus of responsibility for taking the initiative is placed on parents themselves, who are gifted with a range of choices (school type, curriculum, level of involvement) as consumers of education (Dahlstedt 2009). This of course ignores the structural inequalities that may be experienced by immigrant groups in the wider society and the multiple constraints that influence parent's capacities to make real choices concerning their children's education.

In Ireland increasing recognition has been given at a policy level to fostering positive home/school relationships especially with the establishment of the Home/School Liaison scheme in DEIS band schools (Conaty 2002). In practice however, deeply embedded patterns of marginalisation persist (Hanafin and Lynch 2002). With respect to Travellers, for example, while there has been an increasing attempt to incorporate the perspectives of Traveller parents into the formulation of policy (DES 2002a/2002b), patterns of prejudice and non-recognition continue to permeate the experiences of many Travellers in schools (Lodge and Lynch 2004; McDonagh 2004). Similarly Lodge (2004) identifies the difficulties of minority belief parents and their children in a denominationally structured education system that operates on the basis of 'tolerance', rather than recognition and engagement with belief difference. There has been little published research on the impact of ethnic/migrant status on home/school relations in Irish schools. Research that has been done indicates concerns among teachers regarding parenting practices among some immigrant groups, as noted in Chapter 5, as well as the classed and racialised perspectives that can be evident in teachers' views. These are exacerbated by difficulties in communicating with parents whose first language is not English, and where there is an absence of translation and other support services (McGovern 1993; OECD 2009a). O'Gorman and Sugrue (2007) documented case studies of immigrant families and the challenges immigrant parents encountered adjusting to life in one Dublin community. A diversity of needs was identified across the cases yet turbulence, challenges around language and culture as well access and enrolment to local schools emerged in most accounts.

The remainder of this chapter expands on some of these issues by drawing on data gathered with a sample of twenty five immigrant parents across five schools. Part of a wider project aimed at improving immigrant parent involvement in schools in Ireland,[1] the sample of parents involved signals the diversity of immigrant groups in Ireland, with over seventeen different nationalities presented. While not representative, a cross section of socio-economic status was also reflected in the sample, ranging from professionals in the health, IT and financial services sectors to those working in construction, catering and the cleaning sectors. Within this sample, those from India, Pakistan and Nigeria were concentrated in the former sectors, while those from Eastern European countries tended to be concentrated in the latter. A number of parents had come through the asylum process (originating from Kosovo, Iraq, Nigeria and Somalia), and two were waiting to have their applications processed. The analysis which follows is presented in terms of two major themes which emerged in the interviews: class, habitus and positioning in education and the significance of school cultures to parental experiences and expectations.

Class, habitus and parental positioning in education

Previous research has indicated the significance of the social and educational background of parents to how they position themselves in relation to their children's schools. As we saw in Chapter 3, social positioning is itself influenced by the expectations, recognition and feedback of others. While parent's positioning will be influenced by the capitals they bring to their relationships, they will also be influenced by how 'others' in school – other parents, as well as teachers, the school principal and ancillary staff interact and deal with them. These latter are governed by norms ('rules') of interaction which are classed, racialised and gendered. In this study, discernible patterns were evident in that highly educated migrant parents were most likely to be involved in some form of school activity. Among the sample, just under half had some form of graduate qualification or were pursuing graduate studies in Ireland. Five parents had attained a third-level degree (art, engineering, quantity surveying, nursing, midwifery), and three parents had a certified diploma (fine arts, radio communication, ICT). There was also considerable evidence of up-skilling among this parent group since they had arrived in Ireland, including part-time courses at higher education levels.[2] Five of the parents had also bought houses suggesting their long-term commitment to remaining in Ireland. A significant number of those interviewed had also availed of informal courses offered by their children's primary schools in the areas of English language, computer training, healthy eating and parenting, highlighting the significance, as we shall see later, of school culture in facilitating not only processes of integration, but doing so in highly normative terms. Participation in these programmes signalled their positioning as 'good parents' – mirroring the productive energies of their children in the classroom (outlined in Chapters 5 and 7) and their willingness to conform and acquire both classed/ cultural (parenting, language, diet) signifiers of normality and belongingness.

The sample, while small, mirrors findings at national level with respect to both the socio-economic and work profile of adult immigrants in Ireland (CSO 2008).[3] For our purposes what is significant is not only evidence of prior educational training through professional qualifications (e.g. engineer, nurse, accountant) among approximately one third of those interviewed, but also a desire to improve and extend life skills once arrived in Ireland. In a number of interviews it was clear that some parents in their own family backgrounds had been relatively advantaged:

> Its' really hard here especially for us because ... we are not used to do everything by yourself ... [in country of origin], you had a lot of help. You lived in a big house ... for me to do everything by myself here? (Mother, Sudan, Beechwood Primary)

> My Dad said 'If you want to do anything, I can see you as a secretary to a Minister' ... I did everything, the courses, the typing courses, he bought me a typing machine every evening after my work. (Mother, Nigerian, Silverwood Primary)

Immersed in a habitus of entitlement and embedded understanding of the 'logics of practice' (Bourdieu 1990) in the educational field, it was evident that such parents were strategic in their life choices and in making choices on behalf of their children. They actively sought to build social and cultural capital through the networks, knowledge and skills they developed in coming to Ireland:

> I haven't done an education here ... so I would go to Irish parents and I would ask them personally what things you should look for and ... then assess in my head what is best in terms of being Indian you know? I would read the newspaper, always listening to the radio or reading newspapers and anything about secondary schools. (Mother, Indian, Beechwood Primary)

> I did a series of childcare courses in Ireland so I know how to prepare [my son], and I knew I had to prepare him for a new school. (Mother, Nigerian, Silverwood Primary)

Becoming actively involved in formal school activities was also part of the mobilisation of capital employed by such parents, in terms not only of establishing bonds of trust for times in need, but also getting to know how the school worked. Such practices also enhanced the visibility of one's child with other parents and teachers in the school.

> They all know your children, they all know them by name because they do

parent reading with the children. ... so they know that this girl is your child and this boy is your child. (Mother, Ghana, Oakleaf Primary)

I want to help celebrate Pakistan week so ... I will get to know people, the teachers so I will get to know more closer. ... they know me and I am not a stranger for them. (Mother, Pakistan, Redford Secondary)

The concerted cultivation (Lareau 2003) that was part of the mind maps of these parents also ensured that they actively worked on encouraging greater mixing and socialisation of their children with other children outside of school, aware of the exchange value in terms of enhanced social capital (well-being and belonging):

My son's friends [Irish] parents they are very good to me, I call them for coffee and tea, and they call me for coffee and tea. (Mother, Pakistan, Redford Secondary)

On Saturday too we go for football ... and you can see the way they will be able to integrate with their white colleague where they know that they will be able to make friends, they can be involved in GAA.[4] (Nigerian, Father, Beechwood Primary)

This is not to suggest that all parents interviewed had come from socially advantaged backgrounds, but for those who had, they 'naturally generated practices adjusted to the situation' (Bourdieu 1990: 108) in order to maximise the chances of their children for success in the Irish school system. Their challenge was not learning how to play 'the rules' of the game, but rather discerning what the 'rules' in Ireland were and how they should find out about them. This could relate to determining what standards could/ should be expected in achievement and learning, determining the most appropriate class placement of their newly arrived children, and how this is decided, as well as adjusting to the form of education which takes place, especially in the primary school system. However, their experience of 'being on the outside' created a sense of psychic unease (Archer and Francis 2007: 89) about their children's progress, especially when the concept of education was different to what they had experienced in their own home countries (Ran 2001). Their habitus 'sought to integrate past experiences', functioning 'at every moment as a matrix of perceptions, appreciations, and actions' (Bourdieu 2000: 82–83).

An African woman would say 'I have been paying them for you to be painting!? You should be your numbers and your alphabet, not painting' but of course they are learning. (Mother, Nigerian, Silverwood Primary)

When he [my son] gets his Christmas marks I take it to my Irish friends and show them look at this and what do you think ... probably they think I am one of these parents with high expectations but I just want to know if he is lagging behind in some ways. (Mother, Indian, Beechwood Primary)

There was also evidence among the parent sample of prior poverty, war and hardship in home country experiences, that gave rise to both relief and appreciation of the opportunities to begin a new life in Ireland:

> My story is different. My country occupation Serbia so when I come here, everything is different. So they close school, may language, all people go out. Do you understand, closed school? TV station close school. So, when I come here, it's different everything, lovely people, friendly people, everything is lovely. It's different here, you understand? (Kosovan Father, Redford)

> Let me tell you in my culture we don't have something like that, it's really brilliant.

> *Interviewer*: Something like what?

> *Respondent*: Like schools in my country, like the manager or something he just ignore you not like here.

> *Interviewer*: In Iraq, are parents involved in school life?

> *Respondent*: Like they go to meeting ... Before yes. But after the war ... they ignored these things. Security. Bomb every day. (Iraqi Father, Redford Secondary)

While the move to Ireland was undertaken then for a variety of reasons (escape from war, improvement in life-chances through better work opportunities, as well as educational opportunities) the level of transience and disruption to family life was evident across all interviews. Most made reference to separation of families, as well as multiple movements from one place to another once arrived in Ireland:

> When I came into the country as an asylum seeker, I was transferred to a reception centre in Dublin and then to Sligo and later I was transferred to Limerick. Then, when [baby] was three months I was moved to Carrick-on-Shannon. So from there I had [second child] and I moved to [Silverwood]. (Mother, Nigerian, Silverwood Primary)

> My son had moved from India to Middle East where we lived for five and a half years before we came to Ireland. So we had moved him from India to Bahrain and then I had moved him from Bahrain to [first Irish] school. (Mother, Indian, Beechwood Primary)

Such disruption had implications for the emotional as well as economic resources parents could draw upon in enhancing their own and their child's positioning with the school. Four of the five lone parents interviewed, all mothers, had come from countries in Africa (Congo, Somalia and Nigeria) where it was stated that the father is traditionally positioned as the authority figure in the household. This gave rise to additional pressures for these mothers in coping with their lives in Ireland:

> In the Congo ... most of the time it's the father because he has authority ... but when it comes to authority over the children ... They have more respect to their Daddies than their Mummies. (Congolese Father, Redford College)

> We are not happy here as women, she wants to have her husband ... sometimes you bring your anger out on the children, you are stressed and you bring it out ... I have a husband back there, I have a child back there. (Mother, Nigerian, Silverwood Primary)

Prior socio-economic and ethnic status influenced present economic status through the ability to settle and work in Ireland. Some parents felt (relatively) secure in their employment status, while others were working in lower paid work, which in a time of recession, rendered their social positioning fragile and insecure:

> Maybe I have been very lucky, the kind of people that have hired me have been fantastic. They are all Irish and they are very nice to me, they are like my family. (Father, Nigerian, Beechwood Primary)

> I'm on a work permit and I want to come here as a legal person ... my company brought me from the UK ... but when I wake up every day I don't know if that job will be still there ... I am also afraid for my family. (Father, Nigerian, Silverwood Primary)

Across all interviews there was evidence of a time bind either through time spent working and/or coping with minding young children, in the absence of broader social supports. Six of the twenty-five parents said that both they and their spouse were employed and had to juggle their shifts around taking care of the children. Similarly, five respondents were lone parents. The reality of their everyday lives cut across their capacity to become actively involved in their children's school:

> Both of us are working so it's a very tight schedule for us, we don't have time. If I am off, he is working and if he is off, I am working. (Indian Mother, Maryville Primary)

> I know two ladies from Poland, they work in the hospital and they just don't have time and they have to fast run for kids after school go to home and do the dinner, and sit for a fast coffee and go back to work. (Polish Mother, Maryville Primary)

The positioning of parents with respect to their children's school and education was also influenced by cultural/ethnic/linguistic background. Most considered their native language to be an important part of their identity. Sixteen out of the twenty-five parents spoke their own ethnic language at home with their children (Arabic, Romanian, Polish, Malayan, Somali, Urdu, Albanian and French), while two parents spoke bilingually:

> It is a rule that we speak our own language and again at bed time my daughter or son wants a story we would have a turn of saying stories [in different languages] … but I haven't taught them the writing and sometimes when we go to India I get someone to teach them the writing. (Indian Mother, Beechwood Primary)

Five parents spoke English with their children; all of whom were Nigerian. Finally, two parents used to speak their home language (French and Albanian) but gradually this has been replaced by English, for which there was some regret.

Gender intersected with language use, in terms of mothers' fluency in English and capacity to engage more fully with their children's learning in school. Confidence engaging with others was clearly mediated by language, but also social class, as well as being defined as 'other' by virtue of one's cultural/ethnic background:

> The first [barrier] is the language because I am easy to talk to you right now but if I don't hear one word I am embarrassed to say 'What did you say?' and the conversation goes I talk less and less, and I think language is the biggest, and the second we are foreign. (Mother, Albania, Redford Community College)

Gender was also significant in terms of expectations and responsi-bilities that derived from cultural norms related to visibility in the public (school) and private spheres (family) and there was some evidence of ethnic insularity, especially among Arabic mothers, in Oakleaf primary school. As Crozier and Davies (2006) note, while the high levels of social capital in tight community networks such as these had 'use value' in terms of practical exchange and knowledge of school, it does not necessarily translate into exchange value in terms of access to higher status educational knowledge (such as fluency in English) that is required if their children are to do well in school.[5] As we saw, gender was also significant in terms of lone mothers in separated families caring for children on their own.

Other research has identified parent's appreciation of efforts by schools to acknowledge cultural diversity in both school and classroom practices (Archer and Francis 2007; Crozier 2001; Ran 2001). This was reflected in the views of the parents in this study and dovetailed with their concerns that the children would not entirely 'lose' their cultural heritage by living in Ireland. But there was also a sense that teachers did not fully appreciate the range of diversities that existed, nor of the homogenistic constructions they held of 'African' culture especially:

Each time he [child] said my teachers said to bring 'Nigerian' music, 'Nigerian' food – that's good. He said to me that he wants to write a report on 'African' food. Tell your teacher that I don't know 'African' food, do you mean 'Nigerian' food? ... To recognise what they feel that they still belong. I really appreciate that. (Father, Nigerian, Silverwood Primary)

This need for teachers to be sensitive to cultural traditions only emerged in narratives of parents from countries in Africa and also related to culturally embodied forms of respect and demeanour that it was felt teachers could misconstrue:

I was talking to somebody and they were telling me about children hiding their face ... If the teacher really knows[6] about the child's culture, you know that he or she is not hiding anything and it is just the culture as you show your respect by not looking in the eye. You take your eyes down and you don't look at adult's eyes ... but some teacher thinks the child is hiding something, so if people could know about different culture it would be more better. (Mother, Nigeria, Silverwood Primary)

Comments such as those above highlight structured patterns of representation and legitimation (Giddens 1984) in Irish society, not only in terms of the 'otherness' that is ascribed to those who differ from Irish norms (and how this is deeply ingrained in the body) but also in terms of differences in power and what this implies in terms of asserting the right to be recognised. Yet recognition is central to the mobilisation of both cultural and social capital. As a group these parents appreciated what schools were doing in this respect, but did not indicate schools 'should' do it. Their views were invariably expressed in terms of 'gratitude' that undoubtedly comes from their minority position in Irish society but also their recognition that accommodation to Irish norms was essential for success. It is 'Irishness' which has symbolic value. Reflecting perhaps their more 'other' than other' status in Ireland by virtue of their 'visible' (being black), as well as cultural difference, this desire to integrate was most consistently and overtly expressed by parents who had come from countries in Africa, especially Nigeria:

I have been trying to understand the society, since Ireland is the society I will be living in. I have been trying to understand how I will be able to fit in. (Mother, Nigerian, Silverwood Primary)

We have to integrate, and part of that integration and I know in Ireland here you have to be involved in your children's education ... part of it is to relate to our kid, relate to our teacher, relate to the community, you know? ... and that is a priority for me. (Father, Nigerian, Beechwood primary)

Structured patterns of belonging and identity also converge with respect to religious identities, but take on an added tension when access to schooling itself is predicated on affiliation to dominant religious norms. As detailed in Chapter 2, the structuring of primary education in Ireland around assumptions of religious homogeneity has created real difficulties for certain immigrant parents in accessing local schools, when they themselves are not Catholic. It has been compounded by the absence of co-ordinated urban planning, which gave rise to the need for crisis responses in intensive growth areas, as documented by O'Gorman and Sugrue (2007). In such a context, religious identity and affiliation becomes then not just a matter of personal belief, but a key resource (form of capital) which differentiates those 'like us' and 'not like us' in terms of their right to send their child to a local school. In our parent sample, a diversity of religious identities was evident: eight parents referred to themselves as 'Muslim'; five 'Roman Catholic'; four 'Protestant'; three 'Christian'; two 'Christian Orthodox'; one 'Hindu'; one parent was 'Protestant converting to Catholicism'.[7] The shortage of school places in certain areas, coupled with the transitory nature of immigrant experience, ensured that for parents newly arrived into a local community securing a place in a local school could be difficult. School choice then was predicated on belonging to the majority faith (Catholicism), as well as being an established member of the local community, which of course many immigrants, by their nature, are not:

> My experience started when I wanted to get the first one into school. There was this barrier there, as they said if you are not Catholic, you cannot go to a Catholic school … I am a Christian – an Anglican. So they sent me to [Silverwood Primary] … Catholic schools is basically Catholic. Some Africans feel there is no alternative there because I know some friends who go to Pentecostal churches and they don't want to go to Catholic schools. (Father, Nigerian, Silverwood Primary)

Religious identity as an aspect of 'habitus' emerged primarily in interviews as an issue of capacity to access a place for one's child in school, rather than in terms of attending a school (for example a Catholic school) that was different in its religious ethos to that of the family. Parents also differed however in terms of their strength of affiliation to belief systems and this also influenced their attitudes toward the religious ethos of the school. A number of schools were distinctively open and accommodating in their attitudes toward religious formation and this mapped well to the diversity of religious beliefs that was now reflected in the immigrant parent population.

> One of the best things in Beechwood is there is no barriers … they celebrate all type of religion. Even my daughter, if there is Christmas they celebrate, if there is Muslim's Eid they celebrate, like feasts they celebrate it, Judaism, Hindus. (Sudanese Mother, Beechwood Primary)

Beechwood primary as an 'Educate together' school stood out in this regard (see Chapter 4), but so too did Oakleaf primary, a Catholic school with a now established tradition of catering for the religious formation of Muslim children through classes in Islamic instruction during the school day. Furthermore, parenting classes on Islam were also held, which encouraged mothers to come into the school during school hours. As we saw in Chapter 4, this process of accommodation by school staff to the increasing Muslim population in the school was not without difficulties and required considerable reflection and engagement in terms of the ethos and focus of the school. However even in the Muslim community there were divergent views on how far and to what extent schools 'should' accommodate to the religious diversity that existed in the school community. Mr Ahmed, who has lived in Ireland for many years expressed an assimilationist perspective thus:

> I am supposed to be Muslim, I don't practice ... what I don't like here sometimes they come here and want to do their own way, their own culture, their own ... like, if you wanted these things, go back home and ... if you are happy with it, good. If you are not happy with it, tough. (Father, Algerian, Oakleaf Primary)

The analysis highlights the differentiated patterns of belonging, affiliation and identity that existed among the parent interviewees and the significance of class, ethnic/racial background and gender to such patterns. The next section considers the impact of school cultures, as well as parent background on levels of participation and involvement in the life of their children's schools.

Leaving the door open?
School culture and parental participation

Across all interviews parents spoke positively and with considerable appreciation about the work that was being done by teachers and principals in their children's schools. This was spoken of especially in terms of an openness and approachability, which was reflective of a welcoming and friendly atmosphere in which both parents, and their children, felt known and respected:

> The teachers as well they are all very good. They explain to you everything you need to know. Even when you quickly have a question about your child, they don't shun me off or neglect you. (Nigerian Mother, Maryville Primary)

> I am feeling that I can talk to Sir Dempsey [principal] for any issue, any single issue from the parents, from me, from the kids. I am feeling that other parents, Arab parents, most of them respect Mr Dempsey [so]. (Father, Libya, Oakleaf Primary)

Given the level of disruption to children's family lives, it is not surprising that when parents spoke about their children's adaptation to school, they often did so in terms of how happy the child was and the extent to which teachers in the school demonstrated care, love and support for their children. This was reflected in an appreciation of how the children 'felt', but also a focus on the individual needs of their child:

> Teacher is very good knows my daughters. Of course, how is she learn but *she knows what she feel.* That is good because my daughters, is very … delicate. (Mother, Polish, Oakleaf Primary)

> She [teacher] wants them to feel at home and she befriended each child and their personality. (Mother, Nigerian, Silverwood Primary)

For parents a culture of inclusion was equated with a 'family like' feeling, mirroring perhaps the sense of disconnectedness from extended family/community as a result of migration, but also the particular emphasis in primary schools on community and child centred education (Devine 2005/2003).

However notable differences were evident across schools in terms of actively working toward building relationships with immigrant parents in the school. Reflecting the very open and inclusive ethos of Beechwood Primary and Oakleaf Primary, direct invitations to parent focused activities was a key element of their community focus work and consisted of for example not only intercultural festivals (now a yearly event in each school), but weekly coffee mornings, cookery events and organised classes (in English language and computing skills), all of which were commented on positively by parents. While such practices have been identified as 'gestures' toward inclusion by Crozier and Davies (2007), what marked these schools out as different was the very evident sustained/committed efforts on the part of key school staff in these schools to reach out to immigrant parents. Seven parents out of those interviewed were involved on some level in the organisation of these events:

> Whenever there is something going on in the school and someone needs the help of the parents I also love participating. (Nigerian Mother, Beechwood Primary)

> They do also have these coffee mornings on Fridays … so we do go sometimes just to get a cup of tea and relax. (Ghanaian Mother, Oakleaf Primary)

In contrast, activities for parents in Maryville Primary tended to be funnelled through a local church (Catholic) based centre that was not far from the school (but perhaps significantly not in the school), and the only formal event interviewed parents could recall directly in the school was the school play at Christmas. Silverwood Primary had only held one formal event for parents which related to an anniversary celebration of the school (which significantly few of the new 'immigrant' parent community attended, a fact that was commented upon with some regret by the principal in Chapter 4). Redford secondary did not have a tradition of overt parental involvement (this would not be unusual for most secondary schools) but under the leadership of Ms O'Mahony was now beginning to develop a policy of actively inviting members of specific minority communities through targeted 'intercultural' weeks.

Clear patterns were evident that highlighted the link between parent inclusive school cultures and the building of a sense of community among the parent body. Where there were less formal social events for parents, there was less mixing and there appeared to be a weaker sense of community in the school boundaries. In Maryville Primary for example, all six parents interviewed had less than two friends in the school, nor did they speak of a parent 'community'. Similarly, in Redford secondary and Silverwood Primary, only three out of nine parents interviewed were involved in any form of parental school activities and only two parents had two or more friends in the school. The interview with one mother from Brazil was the first occasion she had been through the school doors. Such experiences contrasted with the responses of parents in Beechwood and Oakleaf Primary, where there was a palpable sense of connectedness both with and inside the school which again drew on this metaphor of the 'family'. The very specific emphasis on building relationships with parents in Beechwood and Oakleaf Primary (noted by teachers and principals in Chapters 4 and 5) was re-affirmed in parent comments:

> They are so receptive to all the good ideas and they just change for us. (Indian Mother, Beechwood Primary)

> The principal and the staff and the teachers and the board of management and the parent's association are doing well to be like community like one family … the image of the school is to be for everyone. (Libyan Father, Oakleaf Primary)

There is a danger that intercultural and other school events themselves become symbolic markers of the divide between 'them/minority' and 'us/ majority' in multi-ethnic schools (Levine-Rasky 2009). The clustering of immigrant parent involvement into intercultural events where there are no majority ethnic parents present, can reinforce the 'otherness' of minority ethnic groups in the broader school community. Such a pattern did not appear to be prevalent in either Oakleaf[8] or Beechwood Primary and must be accounted for by the type of ethical and purposeful leadership (Walker and Shuangye 2007) which was present in both schools. It was more apparent however in Maryville Primary (as Sr Bríd, the school principal noted 'it takes time') through activities that were based in the local (Catholic) parish centre and Redford Secondary, in the emerging 'intercultural' weeks Ms O'Mahony was working hard to develop. While this is clearly an unintended consequence of school efforts to be inclusive (and reflects the often contradictory workings of power at 'capillary level'), it highlights how *integration* and indeed inclusiveness as a dimension of school culture is not a process that is devoid of power relations. Rather it is embedded in structural patterns (of racism, belonging and 'otherness') between minority/majority ethnic groups in the broader community/society.

In this respect there was evidence in some parent interviews of their managing an unarticulated tension between their levels of visibility and invisibility in the community and indeed that of the school, mirroring findings identified elsewhere (Crozier and Davies 2006/2007; Levine Rasky 2009). We saw for example in Chapter 4, how the broader 'field' in which Silverwood Primary was located had a high proportion of immigrants from African countries, especially Nigeria, giving rise to tensions in the local community. These were mirrored in the comments of the school principal to being 'overwhelmed' by the cultural shift. There was some suggestion of white flight in the area, as well as a sense on the part of some Nigerian parents that they were not welcome:

> There is a lot of migrant people who want to integrate and want to bring out what they have and let them know and understand and contribute to the system. But the point is you have to lend them a channel ... and say look, you are welcome ... I have said it to some colleagues we need to try and integrate ourselves but when we first came the heat was so high that you feel threatened to be a part of the community. Because you don't feel like you are welcome ... so that would be why we would prefer to be in the shell and just be between your own community. (Nigerian Father, Silverwood Primary)

> I remember talking to [majority ethnic] parents on the way home ... and they were expressing [concerns about] the big increase in the number of children from other nationalities. (Ms Cameron, ESL Teacher, Silverwood Primary)

This is a key issue as it gets to the heart of the real challenges that are posed when normative assumptions around school culture (how the school sees and defines itself), power (who has it and how is it exercised) and voice are 'disrupted' by the presence of those who are 'different'. Schools as organisations are not merely positioned 'in-between' as neutral observers to what is happening in the broader community in which the school is located. Through their action/inaction, schools (especially the principal, but also teachers and reception staff) foster cultures of inclusion or exclusion that has implications for levels of engagement by different groups of parents in the school, as well the nature of engagement itself. While the involvement of parents in intercultural and indeed classroom learning activities is clearly beneficial, moving beyond practical tolerance (Blackmore 2006) of minority ethnic parents involves actively encouraging participation in key decision making bodies in the school such as the parent's association as well as the school Board of Management.

Activating parental voices through formal participation

Echoing other research in this area, both racialised and gendered patterns were evident in formal participation by immigrant parents in the study schools, with mainly mothers becoming involved (Luttrell 1997; Reay 2005/1998). Four of the five schools had no member of a minority ethnic group on their Board of Management, while the fifth school (Beechwood primary) had three parents from immigrant communities, two as elected parent representatives, and the third an appointed Treasurer (see Table 6.1).

Table 6.1   *Levels of participation and representation of immigrant parents in study schools*

School	Minority ethnic representation on school board	Minority ethnic representation on parents' association
Redford Community School	None	None elected, one/two attend meetings
Beechwood Primary	50% representation	7/10 are immigrant parents
Oakleaf Primary	None – one Nigerian vacated post due to time constraints	No elected reps, but some immigrant parents involved in association activities
Maryville Primary	None	No Parents' Association due to 'lack of interest'
Silverwood Primary	None	One Nigerian mother elected, others attend meetings

Of those interviewed, three were involved at a representative level in the school. These were an Indian mother in Beechwood Primary who was on the Board of Management; a Nigerian mother was an elected representative in the Parents Association of Silverwood primary and finally; a second Nigerian mother in Silverwood who attended Parents' Association meetings but was not a formal, elected member. Both of these schools were characterised by enrolment patterns where immigrants were considerably in the majority (77% and 84% respectively) and almost by necessity immigrant parents were required to become actively involved. Patterns of participation were underpinned by socio-economic background, with each of these three parents holding a third level qualification. Classed, as well as racialised expectations around such participation were also evident in the comments of Ms O'Sullivan, the principal of Silverwood primary when she stated:

> Most of the African parents here wouldn't have any idea how schools work, the women who come into me are those who have been educated and maybe going to university here.

These parent's participation in formal school committees derived not only from their positive dispositions to education, but also their 'know how' and 'feel' for the 'game', part of the strategic mobilisation of capitals and 'script' within which they positioned themselves (and were enabled to do by their prior access to resources) in settling and living in Ireland. Evident also in the narratives of these mothers was a sense of responsibility in being positive representatives for their own 'immigrant' community:

> I remember back in Nigeria ... I was the Vice President in the Law Student's Society. So, I felt anywhere I am, I want to work with people and to understand the society ... So I also wanted to give a little bit that ... We need to get involved to understand what the system is and not to feel left out. (Nigerian, Mother, Silverwood Primary)

> But basically every parent want to [good] future and you know survive well and all these aspects. So because it is more than 80% migrant children it is very important ... we are not making any racial discrimination or anything but that is important for the school isn't it? (Indian Mother, Beechwood Primary)

The remaining twenty-two parents who were interviewed were not formally involved in any school committee structure, citing reasons of lack of proficiency/confidence in English, as well as time demands due to work and childcare, as previously discussed. Also evident however was the experience of feeling as 'other' and the resultant reluctance of making oneself visible and 'exposed' through more overt forms of participation. Mr Dempsey in Oakleaf Primary, for example, had directly approached a number of immigrant parents to sit on the board of management but they were reluctant to do so:

> Most of the parents association is women ... The board of management takes a lot of time and for my excuse is language but ... [the principal] he encourages me ... But sometimes I am shy to speak to groups. (Father, Libyan, Oakleaf Primary)

> Most of it is that the Irish parents have time to be a part of it, and some also talk about the language barrier, you know? The language, I can't speak properly in public. Then sometimes they are a bit shy, they don't want to expose themselves, too many people will see me, so they want to be quiet (Ghanaian Mother, Oakleaf Primary)

While both of these parents were appreciative of the culture of inclusion and involvement in Oakleaf Primary, most parents interviewed were not aware that parents could be involved in the school Board, or stated they would not become involved in the board or parents' association unless they were directly approached, something which was actively undertaken in Beechwood and Oakleaf Primary. This may in part derive from a lack of expectation of such involvement due to their prior experiences of education in their country of origin (Archer and Francis 2007; Ran 2001). However their lack of knowledge or understanding about expectations for representative involvement in their children's schooling in Ireland also suggests that this was not something schools themselves were explicit about. Indeed in a number of the schools (Maryville Primary, Silverwood Primary and Redford Secondary) the decision by parents to become involved was very much interpreted as an individual one, something which parents could 'chose' or not 'chose' to do, and outside the remit/responsibility of school personnel. This is perhaps most explicitly reflected in the comment of Sr Bríd in Maryville that there is no parent association 'due to lack of interest', as well as that of Ms O'Sullivan in Silverwood Primary that 'if and when the Parent Association get organised', active formal involvement in the school may increase.

While parents in general across the sample spoke very positively about their day to day interactions with teachers, this did not translate into a feeling (except for those who were confident and self assured) that they had a 'right' to or should become more actively involved in decision making in their children's schools. As Crozier and Davies note (2007), schools may be operating on the basis of normative assumptions of what 'good' parents should do, without explicitly making clear to parents what the full range and spectrum of possibilities for involvement in the school are. This is especially important for parents, relatively new to Ireland, who do not have the benefit of access to the 'grapevine' (Ball and Vincent 1998) that Irish parents, especially those who are middle class, enjoy:

> Like, I feel bad that I should be more involved. I should come and get more involved in here. I should … It's not that I don't want to, or I don't care, no it's not that. But how would I feel, will I be able to speak? Where I come from, when I was in school, we didn't have that kind of thing. (Mother, Albanian, Redford Secondary)

> Most of the parents don't know, how the system works, how the funding works, that kind of thing. We don't know really. (Indian Mother, Maryville Primary)

This absence of cultural capital and knowing the 'rules of the game' is reinforced by the absence of social capital. Social capital in order to be effectively mobilised must be activated between different networks as well as within them (Bourdieu 1984; Crozier and Davies 2006), especially when such networks have differing symbolic status in the configuration of both classed and racialised power relations which exist in society. This is the difficulty when intercultural events become occasions for minority ethnic parents only to meet, signalling a lack of interest on the part of indigenous/majority ethnic parents to engage and 'reach out'. It indicates the importance of the school in defining what 'integration' means and whether it is to move beyond gestures of inclusion. The lack of connectedness had implications for access to key networks that had a trickle down effect in terms of support for representation on parent associations and school boards.

> My own thing is that the majority carries the vote, because the Irish people knows most of the parents, and they know who they want to pick … so I always think in my own way that the Irish won't want to vote for someone like me so you will not have the chance because of the migrants or colour or all these things … But everything they do, I am happy with it. (Nigerian Mother, Maryville Primary)

The significance of the school's role should not be discounted however and there were noted differences across the study schools in how they defined and conceptualised parental voice and participation. Beechwood Primary appeared to be most explicit in this respect and this is not surprising given the underpinning ethos in 'Educate together' schools that parents should and do have a voice in school matters. Mrs Assam indicates clearly her own growing sense of confidence and familiarity with both the school system and other members of the school community through the normative assumptions in the school that all parents should become involved.

> I am the female parent representative on the Board of Management, the mother should I say![9] Initially as the years went I got more closer to the school … I had no idea like how do you do … As you get to know people more it's more freedom to talk, like most of the teachers … then somehow I put up my hand for being the parent rep like I said there wasn't very many people showing interest and then I thought my children are there so I should be able to spare time for the benefit of the school or the education or whatever so I am ready for that. (Indian Mother, Beechwood Primary)

Mrs Assam is herself an educated woman, working as a professional in a local hospital, yet her account details her own struggle to assert herself ('somehow I put my hand up') and become involved, that was very much facilitated by the culture of inclusion and emphasis on parental voice and participation in the school. In contrast, Silverwood Primary with an equally high proportion of immigrants among the school population, conceived of participation in more 'transmission' (Dale 1996) terms. Thus the absence of minority ethnic parental representation on, for example, the parent's association or board of management was construed as an impediment to the communication streams necessary for the school to function, rather than necessarily in terms of broader concepts of inclusion, social justice and the representation of diversity in school life:

> *How successful do you think letters going home are?*
> Well, in our case they don't seem to be successful at all. ... one parent suggested that we should – which we will probably have to do now – invite them in and tell them of the rules of the school. Just orally tell them. *And that's why we need Africans in the parent's association so we can tell them and they can go and tell the other parents.* (Ms O'Sullivan, Principal, Silverwood Primary)

In Redford secondary, it was the initiatives of the language co-ordinator Ms O'Mahony, who was actively encouraging levels of parental contact with the school, unusual in the context of secondary schooling. We have seen how Oakleaf primary also actively sought to build parental involvement and relationships with the school, and was very successful in doing so with respect to intercultural activities and involvement in classroom learning activities, yet struggled to locate minority ethnic parents who would become more formally involved on school boards and committees. The situation is further complicated by the voluntary nature of participation in a context of the intensification of everyday life in modern society (Beck 2006), a challenge that exists across many schools today, regardless of their immigrant intake, but most especially in schools in marginalised communities. A number of parents interviewed in Oakleaf Primary indicated that they also needed to take responsibility for involvement once the school 'left the door' open:

> It is up to the migrant parent to be more active – they have to participate because they leave the door open, so whatever you want to do they will allow you. (Mother, Ghana, Oakleaf Primary)

'Leaving the door open' in itself suggests a more passive approach to parental involvement that does not fully capture the efforts that were being made by both staff and principal in Oakleaf Primary to encourage parental involvement and participation in the school. Nonetheless as a metaphor it captures the challenge that exists for schools in activating parental participation (or not) of minoritised groups and the seriousness with which minority ethnic representation and voice is taken by individual schools.

Concluding discussion

This chapter documented the perspectives of a small group of immigrant parents across five schools of their experiences and perceptions of the education system in Ireland and the key influence of factors related to both parental background, as well as school cultures in mediating both perceptions and practice. The analysis highlights differences across the parent interviewees in terms of the capitals they bring with them to their children's education. For some, their sense of 'place' and belonging in the field of education, obtained from their own location in the higher socio-economic groupings in their home country, ensured that they navigated the education system in Ireland with a sense of confidence and expectation that they would benefit from the investment made. While it is difficult to make generalisations across ethnic groups, such patterns were especially evident among immigrants who had come from Asia (Indian, Pakistan) as well as Africa (especially Nigeria). This is not to say that such parents did not encounter difficulties, some cultural and some structural (access by virtue of denominational status to schools in their local area, insecurity of status and employment, racism) but they demonstrated determination and savvyness in navigating the system, seeking to retain or improve their class position, either through contacts at work and in their neighbourhoods, or (mostly) directly through becoming involved and known in the school. They worked hard to ensure the preservation of their class position. This was especially acute where mothers became involved, and was strongly mediated by their own knowledge and acquisition of the English language, as well as their ability to find carers where they had young children, that freed them up to get involved in school. Such practices highlight the generative dimension of the habitus, these parents actively seeking to position themselves overtly in the field of education, aware of the benefits for their children's life chances either in Ireland or elsewhere. For others, the time-bind of work and caring for young children, especially lone parents, meant that they had little time to engage with their children's school, in spite of their recognition of its importance to their children's education. This was further embedded in anxieties around levels of 'visible' difference and normative assumptions in Ireland around 'whiteness', that ensured only the most confident 'black' parents would consider becoming publicly involved in school activities. As Modood (2004) notes, for minority ethnic groups social class is not the only indicator which determines levels of positioning and acceptance within the school community. It is also predicated on forms of social capital within ethnic communities, as well as the capacity to overcoming and resist colour based racism, influencing levels of confidence, feelings of acceptance/recognition in a context where many are trying to just survive (Crozier and Davies 2006).

Given the barriers that exist to participation that were referred to by parents, there is an onus on schools themselves to actively work toward the inclusion of minoritised groups. Schools need to reflect on who currently becomes involved, track that involvement and work actively with parents to promote and extend the involvement of those who are reluctant to do so. Similarly parent representative organisations also have a key role to play in supporting and encouraging the work of schools and in reaching out to all within the parent community who may be reluctant to become involved. Assumptions of 'tolerance' on the part of school leaders and teachers by 'leaving the door open', while well intentioned, in practice may only result in the exceptionally confident and socially skilled parents becoming involved. Practices of 'welcome' that do not include strategies for and monitoring of involvement, merely reinforces both classed and racialised patterns of participation and representation, and represents a missed opportunity for schools to engage, develop and grow in response to changes in the broader school community.

There are however real challenges for schools in doing so, and across this study, clear differences were evident in how successfully individual schools engaged with parents, and in the resultant levels of connectedness parents experienced relative to the school itself and to other parents in the school community. As we saw in Chapter 4, schools have their own 'logics of action' that derive from prior history and relationships in the local community, school demographics as well as the dispositions of teachers and the school principal. Many schools with immigrant populations are already struggling with marginalised and fractured communities, itself influenced by state policies in the economic and social arena. Even however where schools were highly proactive in 'leaving the door open', gradually drawing immigrant parents out of their 'shell', this did not necessarily result in such parents putting themselves forward for representative positions in the school. A balance needs to be struck between the generation of both social and cultural capital among such parents through facilitating connections informally both within and between parent clusters/groups (through school led initiatives), as well as formalising the representation of immigrant/minority ethnic parents through the establishment of, for example, quotas of representation on parent committees and school boards. The representation of minority ethnic groups on school boards and committees is itself part of a broader policy debate that needs to take place in terms of the role of schools in fostering a deliberative democracy (Blackmore 2006) that prioritises respect and active recognition of all members of the school community. This needs to move beyond tokenistic engagement that centres on the management of diversity in schools (often in very challenging circumstances), to an acknowledgement of the leadership role which can also be played by parents and of the fundamental link between meaningful engagement with parents (and indeed students) and the broader goals of education for and in citizenship, that should underpin the educational process.

Notes

1 Migrant parents are defined as those who have not undergone their primary or secondary education in the Republic of Ireland. Migrant children refer to their children, even if they were born in the Irish state. The project conducted with the Immigrant Council of Ireland is entitled 'Pathways to Parental Leadership' and seeks to develop a toolkit to facilitate schools in reaching out to immigrant parent communities. I am grateful to Sarah Sheridan, Fidele Mutwarasibo and Lucey Jessel of the Immigrant Council for their co-operation on the project.

2 Two parents were in the process of studying for a degree (law and MA in surveying), and two had pursued Fás or FETAC (Further Education and Training Awards Council) courses in Ireland (childcare and technical support). In order to get his existing qualifications recognised, one father took a part-time course for eight months in Dundalk IT. He is currently pursuing a Masters degree in a University during the evenings.

3 It is most likely however that those who presented for interview were those who are most positively disposed to the school and toward the experiences of living in Ireland.

4 The GAA (Gaelic Athletic Association) is an all-Ireland voluntary based organisation that provides training for children in football, hurling and camogie.

5 This is a complex issue however as within such communities there was also an emphasis on weekend schooling – giving rise to some concern expressed by Ms Macken in Oakleaf Primary at the level of pressure that was being placed on the children.

6 Lack of certainty over cultural norms was evident in teacher (Chapter 5) perspectives and connects with the need for professional development and training in this area.

7 In light of the significance of religious background to access to schooling in Ireland, further research is warranted to determine the extent to which religious identity and conversion may be used as part of the strategies of parents to improve the life-chances of their children in a denominationally structured school system. It could also derive from children's own desire to be 'the same' as their peers (see Chapter 7 and also Chapter 4).

8 A field visit during the intercultural week indicated the mixing of all communities, both indigenous and immigrant on this day and the celebration of Irish culture and traditions alongside others.

9 In order to ensure some gender balance, boards of management are required to have one mother and one father representative.

7

Migrant children's perspectives on policy and practice in schools

You can't talk about yourself or your culture, you have to hide. *It's like living another life.* (Senior Male Student, Parkway College)

This chapter focuses on the perspectives of immigrant children and youth. Much of the analysis I have conducted on children's voice in education stems from my work in the broader field of Childhood Studies and the recognition that greater attention needs to be given to the social and contextual factors which shape children's lives, as well as children's own competency and skill as social actors in society. Such a perspective is also informed by provisions in the United Nations Convention on the Rights of the Child (UNCRC 1989) which enshrines children's right to be consulted on matters which directly affect them. The 'new' focus on children and childhood has given rise to the development of a range of indicators of children's well-being (UNICEF 2007/2009), and of how this varies not only across countries (North and South) but also across different groups of children within countries. Education continually emerges as a key factor influencing children's well-being and comparative research across countries globally (e.g. PISA studies OECD: 2006) highlights substantial differences, as we saw in Chapter 3, in children's education outcomes. Migrant children emerge consistently as one group around which there is cause for concern, yet basic accounts of 'outcomes' (related to a narrow range of indicators) fail to capture the complexity of children's responses to their learning, nor to the factors and processes which give rise to different experiences of educational well-being, broadly defined. Furthermore, in spite of the increasing recognition being given to children to be involved in decisions about their lives, education systems appear slow to embrace the idea of real and meaningful engagement with children about their educational experiences. This is then another key element of their educational 'well-being' and has very explicit consequences for children, such as those from an immigrant background, who may differ from the cultural and social norms which may predominate in schools. This chapter highlights not only migrant children's perspectives but also how they actively construct and contribute to processes of integration, accommodation (and indeed assimilation) through their work in schools. In this sense children are central players in the adaptation and integration of immigrant communities into the host society. As the quote at the heading of the chapter indicates, for many it is 'like living another life', as they move between contrasting social and cultural worlds of home and school. Two central themes are developed, related to the experience of learning and how this is influenced not only by issues related to class, gender and age, but also the desire to manage their ethnic identities. This latter is developed further with respect to social and racial dynamics in schools.

Children, migration and schooling

We saw in previous chapters how schools vary in both their practice with and perceptions of immigrant students, that is shaped by the habitus of teachers and principals, as well as the culture/ethos and 'logics' of practice which govern policy in these schools. We also saw the challenges that are faced by immigrant parents in negotiating the education system on behalf of their children, not only in terms of gaining access to and enrolling them in local schools, but also in identifying the 'rules' that govern learning and assessment in the Irish education system, and how best to position their children with respect to these 'rules'. We learned of the differentiated struggles that existed among immigrant families and how the capacity to cope with life in school is strongly influenced by the family's access to social, cultural and economic capital, as well as the structured forms of support that are provided by their children's schools. Children's educational well-being is influenced by these factors, but also by how they interpret and experience what happens to them. Gaining insights into the children's own perspectives provides a very clear indicator of the impact of policy and practices in schools, as well as the skills and complex negotiations immigrant children especially must draw upon in order to cope with school.

Much of the research on immigrant and minority ethnic children focuses on how well they are doing academically in school (Archer and Francis 2007; OECD 2006), as well as their experience of racisms and how such experience is influenced by gender, ethnicity and social class (Connolly 1998; Troyna and Hatcher 1992). Previous chapters have also highlighted how school organisational cultures, leadership and teaching practices set the context for children's experiences, dovetailing with other research in this area (Archer and Francis 2005; Chan 2007; Crozier and Davies 2007). Much of this latter research predominates in the Anglo-Saxon world, in countries such as the USA, UK and Australia which have relatively long histories of immigration, although there is an emerging literature on immigration and children/young people in Europe (Crul 2007; Evergeti and Zontini 2006; Faas 2010). Consistently what emerges in such research is the absence of deep and meaningful engagement with the perspectives and values of minority ethnic children and youth, that is reflected in an a-critical approach to multi-cultural education (Banks 2009; May 2009; Modood 2007). While there is some research on minority ethnic pupils' perspectives on the curriculum and learning (e.g. Archer and Francis 2005/2007; Chan 2007), studies of first generation immigrant children's voices in relation to schooling are rare, with the exception of some research on the area of refugee children (Bash and Zezlina Phillips 2006; Pinson and Arnot 2007; Rutter 2006). More recently in Ireland Ní Laoire et al. (2009) have conducted in-depth analysis of migrant children's experiences. They confirmed the key role of schooling in the experiences of such children but also the different patterns that exist in how children adapt and work toward 'belonging' in Ireland.

Theorising migrant children's perspectives: agency, identities and belonging

For the newly arrived immigrant child, learning to adjust to the school situation, become familiar with new subjects and languages, as well as try to negotiate relations with peers provides a difficult set of challenges with which they must cope and overcome. Such challenges are coupled with those which may also prevail in the wider community as the immigrant family seeks accommodation and work, often in the context of split families and differentiated access to financial, cultural and social supports, as documented in Chapter 6. In considering how migrant children perceive and experience their education, my analysis is informed by constructs of children as competent and agentic, framing their identities in hybrid and multiple ways (Butler 1993; Evergeth and Zontini 2006), as discussed in Chapter 3. It is also informed by an assumption that learning is not simply a cognitive event – it is also a social process that is embedded in the relationships we form with one another (Vygotsky 1978). It involves a complex set of dispositions that draw not only on some predefined 'ability' or readiness to learn, but also on sensitivity to the responses we get from others – teachers, parents and peers, in relation to our learning. This is especially so with children.

The concept of social (Bourdieu 1986; Coleman 1988; Putnam 1995), as well as cultural capital (Bourdieu 1986) is important here, providing a framework in which to analyse social relations as productive/reproductive of structural patterns in the society at large and is especially pertinent in discussions about schooling and the experiences of migrant children. Traditional accounts of social capital emphasise the key role of bonding (inward looking and involves relationships of trust and reciprocity that reinforce bonds and connections within groups) and bridging (outward looking reinforcing relationships and networks of trust and reciprocity between different groups and communities) to processes of social integration (Coleman 1988; Putnam 1995), and of how tight kinship systems and social support within immigrant families has led to the positive orientation of many to school (Kao 2004; Reynolds 2006). While important in highlighting the centrality of both kinship and other social systems to processes of integration and accommodation, the approach of both Coleman and Putnam do not fully address the significance of power to both bonding and bridging processes, and how such power is mediated by structural factors related to class, ethnicity and gender (Devine 2009). This is where Bourdieu's analyses has certain strengths. We saw in Chapter 6 how access to both social and cultural capital had significant 'use value' in terms of navigating the Irish education system among immigrant parents but also how this was mediated by their own prior (and present) economic, social and cultural status. Confidence in one's own standing, knowing the value of certain networks and opportunities, and having the resources to push 'the door open' and 'come out of the shell' were hugely significant in setting the context for levels of interaction and engagement between the broader immigrant family and the local school. We have also seen how the habitus, culture, 'logics of action' (Bourdieu 1990) inside schools facilitated or detracted from such engagement. In each instance it is adults who are shaping the nature of interaction – through their action and/or inaction navigating a complex series of relationships that impact on how children think and learn.

Yet within such adult-centred perspectives, children are typically portrayed as receptors of adult capitals (Holland et al. 2007; Leonard 2005; Morrow 1999). It is adults who mobilise their social and cultural capital to promote children's learning in school. Migrant children are constructed as the carriers of their parent's hopes and expectations for achievement and success in the receiving society. Simultaneously they represent the mechanism used by the state, through the work of teachers, in assimilating into the norms of the host society. In this sense children are constructed as the targets for adult intervention, both at home and at school. An inter-generational perspective however highlights the patterns of power and control between adults and children (Devine 2003; James and James 2004) as well as the social competency of children (Brembeck et al. 2004) and of how through their participation in school children mobilise the social and cultural capital of the family, facilitating processes of economic and social development (Devine 2009; Leonard 2005; Morrow 1999). This is especially apt when applied to the experiences of migrant children, who can be perceived as important 'bridges' between the immigrant family and the host community by virtue of their work in school. This is not a simple process of however.

Migrant children 'have' to go to school and 'integrate' in a way which their migrant parents do not. Their sense of themselves and their place in school is influenced by the broader society which 'shapes' them according to certain norms. This is both the productive and reproductive aspect of schooling in terms of 'message systems' (Bernstein 1975) related for example to what it is to be 'Irish' in modern Ireland, who has a right to 'belong' and what this means in practice in terms of value, recognition and participation. By highlighting children's perspectives, we not only open our eyes to the richness and competence of children's interaction with one another, their processes of social identification, but also become sensitive to the dynamics of power and control that operate within this (Devine 2003). As active managers of their social identities, children negotiate, manage and perform their identities in a manner which is certainly mediated by their gender, class and ethnicity, but also by the specific context or locale (Goffman 1971) in which the interaction takes place (Devine 2007). Children are not cultural dupes to be moulded unquestioningly into the 'adult' (be it parent or teacher) way of doing things. For many a tension exists as they straddle diverse worlds, seeking approval and recognition from teachers and parents, while simultaneously retaining status and recognition from peers. Participation in child and youth cultures brings with it relief and autonomy from the constraints and obligations of formal schooling, but challenges vulnerabilities in relation to the assertion of 'self' 'otherness' 'belongingness' and recognition in relations with peers. In this scenario the situation for migrant children is especially challenging. .

The remainder of this chapter presents findings from research I have been involved with in a range of primary and secondary schools over the past ten years, details of which have been outlined in other publications (Devine 2009; Devine and Kelly 2006; Devine et al. 2008). All involved interviewing children and young people in groups, typically in a semi-structured format, along with field observations in classrooms and school recreational areas. It does so with respect to two main themes. The first relates to the mobilisation of capitals through children's learning while the second details children's perspectives on social and racial dynamics in schools.

Mobilising capitals through children's learning

A number of key themes consistently emerged from interviews with migrant children in relation to how they positioned themselves with respect to the learning environment in school. These related to the significance of language to the learning process, adjusting and accommodating to the curriculum in Irish schools, and the resources and support they would like in order to do well in school. Reflecting both a strategic and pragmatic approach to schooling, students consistently spoke about their desire to achieve and make the most of the opportunities to do well in school. For some this was linked to specific ambitions expressed by their parents, for others it was about having skills they could use if they returned to their 'home' countries:

> My parents want me to be a teacher ... where I grew up you wouldn't be able to do that ... you wouldn't be able to do what your parents wanted you to do. (Ali Nigerian Girl, Riverview Primary)

> *Interviewer*: Is it good for children to come to a different country?

> *Andre*: Yes. When they go back to their own country, they'll be different ... they'll be smarter. (Andrew, Lithuanian Boy, Riverview Primary)

> I won't say we have a great life, we don't. But for those who want to try ... we believe we can make more, study, have an education. (Rwandan Boy, Bellview Secondary)

The desire to do well was, in many (but not all) cases influenced by the children's own classed positioning. Martha, a Muslim girl whose Syrian parents were both professionals, displayed a strong sense of entitlement and confidence in relation to her integration into Irish society. She was ambitious to enter politics and achieve the highest political standing as a woman, keen to assert her place in Irish history!

> First I wanted to be the President but then Mr Murphy [teacher] told me that I should be the first female Taoiseach [prime minister] so I am planning to be the first female Taoiseach and then the president ... my parents are supporting me in wanting to be the President.

This sense of expectation and valuation of education consistently emerged across all interviews and while it can be attributed to high education levels among the children's parents, this was not always the case. The children's families were clearly differentiated in terms of both the social, economic and cultural resources they could draw upon, evident for example from the children's own different experiences of access to extra curricular activities and participation in cultural and social events at weekends. As Modood (2004) notes, tight kinship networks, as well as strong 'norms of enforcement' in certain immigrant groups leading to goal directed identities, have been shown to override class effects, especially with respect to some Asian minorities. It has been difficult to make generalisations about the class positioning of different immigrant groups in the study schools, given the diversity of occupations within groups themselves,[1] as well as the difference in legal status among immigrants. As Anthias (2010) notes, traditional classed, gendered and ethnic binaries do not map easily to transnational mobilities in modern global economies. Nonetheless, the very decision to migrate, as well as capacity to do so, is indicative of 'goal directed' activity that is centred on working actively toward improving familial life chances, which will in itself be reflected in positive orientations and work effort in school.

Gender dynamics were also significant to the children's positioning as learners. For boys especially a tension had to be managed between competing constructs of masculinity, compounded in working class schools (where migrant children tend to be located) where hegemonic masculinity centred more on sporting prowess than academic success prevailed. This tension is reflected in the comments of Mahmoud, below, as he struggles not to appear 'too good' contrary to the constructs of masculinity operating among his (working class indigenous Irish) friends, while simultaneously not doing 'too bad' given his parents' expectations that he do well in school. What is also of significance is how he draws on his construction as a migrant as a basis for potential teasing:

> I used to do maths really fast but now I do it sort of slow … like not the first to finish cos some children they say you are trying to show off just because you are from a different country [other children agree] just because we are trying to do our best. (Oakleaf Primary)

For girls, as we will see later, the tension of how they positioned themselves related to contrasting constructs of femininity in terms of appropriate 'rules' for dress, freedom to roam (especially after school) and contact/romance relations with boys.

With respect to language, the acquisition of fluency was something that was mentioned by students whose first language was not English especially with respect to engaging with the curriculum to a level and standard they sought. All of the children interviewed received some form of EAL [English as an additional language] support, but this seemed to be relatively ad-hoc in second level, more structured in the primary school, reiterating comments by teachers noted in Chapter 5:

> The grammar is so hard. We're always making mistakes. We do have extra English, but we don't find the TEFL teacher good. (Vietnamese Junior Girl, Parkway College)

> In Poland I did maths and physics but when I came here I had to do business studies in second year and I had to catch up with the first year. (Polish Senior Level, Spireview Girls Secondary)

For children whose mother tongue was not English, the additional work they had to do in order to achieve well in school was evident from the language or 'code' switching (Cummins 2001) they engaged in as they sought to master the material they were learning across a range of subjects. This is evident in the discussion below where Abraham, attending Oakleaf Primary, talks about 'thinking in Arabic' while learning through English:

> I work it out in my head in Arabic ... mostly in maths but sometimes in English as well ... like if there is a passage in English and you have to answer questions I translate them into Arabic in my head and then translate it back into English.

An additional challenge for students was also learning the Irish language,[2] which most seemed to talk about in a positive way, and which teachers (noted in Chapter 5) found students adapted to very quickly, surprised by their linquistic competency relative to many of their Irish peers. While Irish was perceived as an additive extra rather than core to the children's success in the Irish system, it did have cultural and symbolic value. Their proficiency in speaking and learning Irish was reflective of a willingness to adapt to the 'rules' of schooling in Ireland, as well as to take on board distinctly 'Irish' traditions:

> I think it is really good – like English is from England so Irish comes from Ireland. (Martha, Syria, Oakleaf Primary)

> I don't have to do it but it is my choice cos I like it. (Salma, Saudi Arabia, Oakleaf Primary)

For older students in second level schools, a more circumspect view was evident, that tied in with more specific constructs of their own national/ethnic identity as 'non-Irish':

> The Irish students seem to think its not fair that we don't learn Irish ... I think its fair enough because *we already have our own language 'cos we come from our own country with our own* life but I know we live in Ireland culture and we to have learn *their rules and laws.* (5th Year Kosovo, Spireview Girls Secondary)

Homework proved challenging for many students, especially where their parents were not fluent in English. In such instances, 'durable obligations' (Bourdieu 1986: 249) built through friendships with Irish peers proved invaluable sources of support.

> Anytime I get Irish homework, I go and ask my [Irish] friends so they do it with me. (Ahmadou, Congo, Seaview Primary)

In taking account of these challenges the students placed considerable priority on their relationships with their teachers, as they were perceived as the primary sources of support and information for learning, as well as important sources of support in the event of bullying or racist incidents (Devine et al. 2006, 2008). We saw in Chapter 5 how teachers generally spoke positively about immigrant students in terms of their ambitiousness and determination to do well, as well as their respect for authority. Talking with the older secondary school students, all of whom had prior experience of education in a different system, it was clear that their positive behaviour was rooted in patterns of inter-generational relations in their home country centred on respect for adult authority, most often mentioned by girls, as well as an appreciation of their opportunity to learn in Irish schools:

> I think the manners and the education is a bit different here ... they really don't respect the teachers ... they don't appreciate that they are being taught like ... they take it for granted ... too much freedom. (Malaysian Girl, 5th year Spireview)

However this could be a double edged sword, as their relative invisibility/ silence in the classroom ensured that they could feel overlooked by their teachers and less likely to get the support they needed. Our own subsequent observation of teacher practices in schools has confirmed a tendency for less engaged teaching/learning with such children in mainstream classrooms, especially where there are a higher number of immigrant students present (Devine et al. 2010b). A related issue concerned the view that migrant students felt they were not pressed upon to do better in school, a factor which could be reinforced by being placed in a lower stream in second level, the absence of provision of instruction during 'free' periods when other students were learning 'Irish' or a class below their age level in primary school:

> The teaching is like looking, they should put more improvement about the student. (Roseanne, Ghana, Ashleaf Community College)

> Sometimes you don't have something to do in Irish class. I don't know maybe reading, or we don't know much about computers, or typing. (Mark, Nigerian, Bellview Boys Secondary)

> It's not easy, we also need to be taught ... but sometimes we need more help. (Peter, Polish, Riverview Primary)

With respect to the curriculum, secondary school students critiqued the absence of a broader focus in subjects such as history and geography. Inevitably their experiences were rooted in what they had learned in their home country, but also concerns over level of preparedness for state examinations:

> Our geography teacher writes notes basically on Europe and America, Ireland and England. In history we've done Ireland, England, Europe and America. (Leaving Cert., Rwanda, Bellview Boys)

> We have dreams but its kind of hard to achieve them ... and in the leaving certificate exams ... they don't know the paper its not from an ordinary Irish

person ... that makes it hard. (Ukrainian, 5th Year Student, Spireview Girls Secondary)

Students at this level also voiced concerns about the impact of this Eurocentric focus on indigenous Irish students in terms of their awareness of cultures other than their own. Their comments link not only to the diasporic identities of many of these migrant students, but aso their positive attitudes toward globalisation and multi-cultural identities:

> *Andreus*: They [Irish students] say: where are you from? And I say 'Moldova' and they say where is that and I ask where do you think it is and they say 'Africa'! (Junior Cert. Boy, Ashleaf College)

> *Interviewer*: Is it good there are lots of people from different countries?

> *Natasha*: Yes. You get to know about other countries and other religions ... its kind of like fruits. If you only had banana, you wouldn't know what kiwis and oranges tasted like. (Iraq, Oakleaf Primary)

Who (se) normal, who (se) culture?

However there is a tension in this issue of cultural recognition that is underpinned by processes of inclusion, exclusion and belonging for these students. We see this more clearly in the following excerpt from an interview with one group of immigrant students in Spireview girls secondary school, although similar issues arose in a number of other schools. In an attempt to embrace cultural diversity, the school had initiated a 'cultural celebration' day in which all 'foreign national' students were provided with the opportunity to come up on the school stage, in front of the entire school, dressed in their national dress to talk about their culture. Reflecting the unintended consequences of the exercise of power at capillary level (Foucault 1979), the initiative highlighted the 'otherness' of many of these students, mirroring the concept of the 'tourist curriculum' approach to cultural diversity that is often employed by schools (Banks 2009; Chan 2006/2007; May 2009). While the intention behind such initiatives may be positive, they also increase the tendency of highlighting the difference and 'otherness' of minority students, especially when the majority culture is not similarly put on 'display'. The contrasting perception of these events by the majority 'we' and minority 'them' is succinctly reflected in the voices of the young people themselves below:

> *Student 1*: Well last term we had the culture day ... people from different countries would dress up in their own costume and say where they were from ... it was good.

Interviewer: Did you get up and say where you came from?

Student 1: No it wasn't us … it was the girls from the foreign countries … *there was actually loads wasn't there* [emphasis added]

Interviewer: Would you have liked to get up on the stage and talk about where you come from?

Student 2: No it was only for the cultureds … everybody knows me. (Majority Ethnic, Seniors, Spireview Girls Secondary)

Viewed from the perspective of the migrant students, this event highlighted the tension they feel between visibility and invisibility in school. While they were not overtly critical of such events, recognising the effort the school was making to be 'inclusive', queries were raised as to their effectiveness in improving cultural tolerance in the absence of direct instruction about tolerance of difference:

> They [indigenous Irish] don't really learn like … we had a mixed show and you say where you are from and I got up and I said I was from Trinidad and then I got off the stage and someone said; 'so what part of Jamaica are you from' and: 'say something funny'. (Group Interview, Spireview Girls Secondary)

In essence their perspectives query the rhetoric of inclusion, when it is not supplemented by real and meaningful engagement with the substantive exclusionary processes and practices which can permeate school life (Bryan 2010; Kitching 2010). Further, a number of students in other schools signalled that they did not want to be made exceptions of in any way and while they saw value in indigenous Irish students learning about their cultures, they wanted to be treated the same as their majority peers:

> *Interviewer:* Do you think other students should be made aware of your cultures, if the school drew attention to your culture, like some schools have a cultural day?
>
> *Student 1:* What I'd prefer that if they teach them projects on how to accept them … we just want to be treated the same.
>
> *Student 2:* The thing is the school can teach but education really comes from your own family. There should be a course for parents as well. (Vietnamese, Males, Senior Class, Parkway College)

Younger children expressed similar viewpoints, displaying a certain ambiguity around whether or not specifics of their culture and background should be highlighted in school. This may be to do with the more integrated nature of the primary curriculum and there was evidence of incorporating migrant children's experiences through for example group project work (Devine 2007/2009). It must also be noted that cultural validation and expression appeared to be a strong component in the support that was provided to these children in their activities with the language support teachers in each of the primary schools observed. Taking place away from the 'mainstream' classroom, this may have been a 'safer' place for the children to engage with their culture and background. Nonetheless, it is this very 'separation' which precludes working with difference by all children, reinforcing the notion that diversity education is about and for 'them' rather than about and for 'us'. The children's perspectives were also mediated by their ethnic background, as well as personal experiences (related to trauma and separation) and the extent to which they differed from the Irish norm. Children from Africa and Asia were most circumspect:

> *Interviewer*: Does your teacher ever ask you about your home country?

> *Alexander*: No and I wish he would ask me. I would be happy. (Grade 4 Lithuanian Boy, Riverview Primary)

> I would not like her to talk about my language and country because I have to think back every time. I don't like answering questions. (Francis, 5th Class Boy, Sierra Leone, Riverview Primary)

> I would tell them songs and the way we dance, but we dance funny dances and they might laugh at me. They might think it's something *disgusting*. (Precious, Nigerian girl, Seaview Primary)

Implicit in the children's perspectives was the 'use value' (Bourdieu 1986) of cultural recognition for all children, as part of the general process of cultural/capital accumulation in the class, rather than as an extra for celebration and display. Where the children saw authentic engagement with their cultures and identities and the teacher was clearly comfortable with it, then they also felt at ease. In one of the field trips, for example to Oakleaf primary, this was reflected when a missionary nun came to visit the school and spoke effortlessly to some of the children in Arabic:

> *Interviewer*: So what's that like when someone comes in and speaks like that? [in your own language]

> *Sarah*: Cool! [Laughs] and she is Irish! ... it makes you feel very comfortable. (Group Interview, Oakleaf Primary).

The analysis indicates how learning for the children is as much a social as a cognitive process. The children and young people interviewed consciously sought through their engagement with their learning and their relations with teachers especially, to acquire valued cultural capital in order to do well. In this sense their orientations mirrored their construction as 'productive' children by teachers, outlined in Chapter 5. This was not without its own difficulties, in terms of the work and effort many needed to engage in, learning English, as well as adjusting to a system which for older children especially was different to what they had experienced in their country of origin. Undercutting their experiences were not only dynamics related to gender and social class but also patterns of belonging and separateness that derived from their ethnic/cultural identities. This gave rise to differing attitudes toward the level of recognition that should be accorded to their own cultures/experiences in school, the latter only spoken of favourably when it had 'use value' in terms of performance in examinations or projects, or if engaged in authentically by teachers who were fully versant with aspects of the culture itself. It also played out differently with respect to recognition and cultural validation in peer relations and social dynamics both within and between different ethnic groups.

Social and racial dynamics in children's peer relations: mobilising social capital

There is considerable research which highlights the complex dynamics that underpin children and young people's relations with one another, patterns which become strongly embedded in relationships in the adolescent years (De Goede et al. 2009; Gaganakis 2006). While friendships appear to be more fluid for younger children, more intimate relationships are evident as children make the transition to secondary school, where friendships are also more ethnically and gender bound. Across my own research in primary schools, it was clear that a varied pattern existed, with a blend of core ethnic groupings in some classes (consisting for example of a pairing or threesome of one ethnic group) combined with an inter-mingling of minority/majority ethnic children in other friendship groups. Of note however were Roma children, clustered in Riverside Primary school,[3] who were consistently observed in the school yard as playing together, or standing on their own by the school wall. Further, Muslim children in Oakleaf Primary, especially a number of girls, also tended to cluster together in paired groupings.

In secondary schools, evidence of inter-ethnic friendships was more sparse, with a clearer demarcation of student friendships along ethnic lines, that was especially evident in the clustering of students during break times. For their part, a mixed response was evident among the second-level sample of students in relation to their levels of interaction and integration with Irish peers. While some spoke of having made friends in school, others identified difficulties in making 'deep friendships' with their indigenous Irish peers:

> Miss, it's like this yeah. I think, it's not that you can't make deep friends out of them, but it takes a long time for them to get used to you and it takes a long time for us to get used to them. (Tanzanian, Female, Ashleaf College)

Where some of these students mentioned their difficulty in making friends with their indigenous Irish peers, their feeling of relative isolation, especially after school was notable:

> I've been here for one year now, and I can say everybody here is having an Irish friend, but it's in the school ... we have friends here, we have friends in our class but *I wouldn't know what they think sometimes ... They don't know anything about black, anything about me,* they don't feel comfortable inviting me to their house. (Rwandan Senior Student, Bellview Boys Secondary)

There was a recognition that friendship was something which had to be worked on, that required accommodation from 'both' sides:

> The way you are friendly to them, it's the way they are going to react back to you. So we can't say they [Irish peers] are bad, because some of them are good. (Filipino boy, Ashleaf college)

The experience of racism and exclusion in peer relationships is mediated by the dynamics of difference/sameness that operate in children's social and cultural worlds (Devine et al. 2008). Normative prescriptions related to gender, social class, ethnicity, dis/ability underpin the experience of belonging and social togetherness of children/young people of all ages, creating dichotomies in how they organise themselves socially both inside and outside of school. This can be represented figuratively in terms of four dimensions or clusters of student relatedness and children can be positioned in any one of the quadrants, depending on the configurations of power and social dynamics that operate in their peer group (see Figure 7.1).

It is the perception and experience of difference/sameness which leads to stronger bonding between children of the same ethnic/migrant background, while simultaneously making it difficult to 'bridge' with students from other ethnic groups. Children of all ages spoke of the experience of 'otherness' and sense of being different which proved challenging for them:

> I felt so shy, everybody was different to me. There was a boy who was there and he was a black boy like me, but now he left and I was the only one and I felt so shy. (Ava, Nigerian girl, Riverview)

> *Student:* Some students see us as some kind of freaks or something.

> *Interviewer:* how do they show that?

> *Student:* Wink in the first place, more psychological. I can see it in their faces.
> (Mixed Interview Group, Bellview Boys Secondary)

What is important to bear in mind is that inclusion/exclusion and sameness/difference operates along a graduated continuum giving rise to some fluidity of movement between the dimensions, that signals caution in overly

Figure 7.1   *Dimensions of pupil social interaction and ethnicity in school*

Different
'Strange' culture, religion
'Foreign' language
Skin colour
'Other'

Inclusion
Having friends
Invitations to
parties/social events

Exclusion
No/few friends
Not included
in events

Same
Sedentary, catholic,
English speaking
White,
'Norm'

Note: There are other status issues (related for example to gender, age, social class and dis/ability) which cut across these dynamics.

simplistic analyses of children's friendship patterns. Children's social world is embedded in identity work, as they position and reposition themselves, drawing on discourses related to gender, sexuality, dis/ability, social class and ethnicity in their relations with one another. For example, intensive case study analysis of friendship patterns in Oakleaf Primary indicated intra-ethnic tensions between three Muslim girls and the subsequent positioning of Karina as more like her indigenous Irish peers in terms of dress, taste, and modes of self presentation (Devine and Kelly 2006). In contrast Salma positions herself more clearly with her Muslim/Arabic peers:

> I'm a Muslim but my Mum was brought up not wearing scarves and all the Muslims jeer me because I'm not like them ... Sometimes I wear scarves when I go to the Mosque. Since me and Karla use to be friends because we are both Muslims and everyone used to think we had loads of things in common. (Karina, Syria, Oakleaf Primary)

> First I didn't know where I belong ... now I only like to be friends with Arabs cos I tried to be friends with Irish but it just didn't work ... they have really different stuff they do that we don't do [especially for girls]. (Salma, Palestine, Oakleaf Primary)

For boys, affiliation to sport proved important in friendship patterns irrespective of ethnic/immigrant status, although the latter could be used as a basis for racist name calling on the sports field.

> Please people who are listening to this, pick up some sport or you get slagged. You have to be good at sport. (Marcus, Libya, Oakleaf Primary)

> Racism mainly takes place in sport ... sometimes white people are picked first or if a coloured person hacked you or side tackled you then you could give them a punch. (Tony, Majority Ethnic Boy, Oakleaf Primary)

At its extreme, exclusionary dynamics give rise to racism, which was something all of the children were keenly aware of, most especially in their out of school lives. This gave them a practical/grounded understanding of racism (both cultural and colour based) that was not so evident in the more incomplete and disconnected (Peck et al. 2008) narratives of their indigenous Irish peers. This racial tension is also evident in the narrative of this mother (from Pakistan) who spoke of having to remove her son from his previous primary school (not included in any of the schools I was involved with) because of the racial abuse he was subjected to by one child. In referring to this colour based racism, what is significant is how she links her son's feelings to 'ownership' (*they don't feel they own the place*) and feeling 'out of place' because of this difference:

> My son had a problem with a boy who always called him 'black' and stuff like that and mentally he tortured him so much. So usually he would come to me to ask me, 'am I very black?' it's very obvious that he is not from Ireland. So, they feel that they are not comfortable with their environment, and they don't feel they own the place. (Parkistani Mother)

At secondary level, aspects of youth culture (dress, going out, relative freedom – especially for girls), coupled with the high level of 'slagging'/banter that is typical of adolescent groups, especially among boys, created difficulties for some students to integrate socially. Issues of both ethnic identity as well as social class mediated these experiences. In Spireview Girls Secondary for example, 'the attitude' of Martha from Zimbabwe, was interpreted by her as a reason for racism directed against her and which she responded to in a defiant manner, that included fighting back:

> *Sonia:* I think it's not fair that they come to you and shout at you ... because if you are a nice person it doesn't matter what colour you are ... and I was passing by the lockers and Martha was walking along and a first year kicked her and I was 'what? What are you doing?'

> *Interviewer:* And why was Martha being kicked?

> *Tara:* Because she has attitude.

> *Interviewer:* Martha has attitude?

Martha: No, but when I am talking to my friends things like that I have a different attitude than when I am talking to them (Irish girls) … if they talk to me in that way I won't allow it 'cos they call me a mean nigger … and they can't just call me that for fun … I don't take it that way … and if you don't stand up to them they just see you as a fool. (Mixed African, Females, Junior Class, Spireview Girls Secondary)

Class dynamics were also at play here, Martha's 'attitude' undoubtedly linked to her own positioning in a diplomatic family background that perhaps gave her the confidence to stand up for herself when racially abused. Her experience of racism however underlies the additional 'work' that is required because she is black in order to retain her class position, especially in a context where she is attending a mixed social class school. A similar situation was identified in a primary school with respect to Ava, a Nigerian girl who also was teased because of her overt confidence and 'being good' at Irish (Devine et al. 2008). Minority ethnic, especially non-white children, are at continual risk of racial abuse and it was something that all were aware of and sensitive to. This is not to suggest it was a pervasive aspect of their lives in school, yet it was clear that racialised dynamics most especially came into play when minority children became 'more visible', unsettling existing status hierarchies in the classroom. Confident, assertive minority ethnic children were especially at risk of racial abuse because in their 'attitude' they have queried (and resisted) their minoritised positioning. In this sense they have crossed over normative boundaries to remain relatively invisible, in spite of/or because of their 'visible' difference, mirroring the comment of one of the parent interviewees in Chapter 6 of 'being in the shell'. Standing up for oneself, putting oneself 'out there' can be a threat to 'our own' and derives from insider/outsider status that is a challenge for migrant children to negotiate. This was also evident in an interview with a number of immigrant students in Bellview boys secondary, who recounted the 'slagging' one of their peers was subjected to by some Irish boys, when he had participated in a school drama.

Interviewer: Were you involved in the drama you had here?

Student 1: He played the piano

Interviewer: Was that good?

Students (in unison): Yeah

Student 1: When he was doing his act, a lot of Irish said he was crap or whatever, but he was trying. They wouldn't say that about an Irish.

Student 2: It's just the way it is … and there's no point in calling them names back. Like what he was saying about playing the piano and all that

... you will get that in most schools because *they feel like we are coming
to take over their country.* We're not, we all want to learn nicely and all
that but. (Minority Ethnic, Juniors, Bellview Boys Secondary)

Similar experiences emerged for young people from the Vietnamese
community in Parkway College, a number of whom had been born in
Ireland, or who had attended primary school in Ireland, yet still remained
'on the outside'. The disjuncture between their family and school lives is
evident in Lee's comment below:

You can't talk about yourself or your culture, you have to hide it. It's like
living another life. (Vietnamese, Senior Level, Parkway College)

Some of these students spoke of their frustration with the stereotypes they
faced in relation to being 'foreign, that ranged from 'not having a sense of
humour' to being seen to be abusers of the 'system'. This was more evident
in interviews with secondary school students, whose reaction to such stereo-
typing was often a desire to position themselves academically in school:

I want to do well in school ... get a good job and more money. We're being
slagged now but that would make us happy, proud if we did well in our
exams. (Vietnamese, Male, Senior Class, Parkway College)

One day I was sitting somewhere and the cleaner came downstairs and ...
knocked my glasses from the desk and they got broken. All she said was: 'oh
the social will replace them'. She is invariably telling me now that whatever
I am today, is the 'social' ... which is not proper, as a matter of fact. What it
does seem as a statement is what impression she has of me. (Rhwandan, Senior
Class, Bellview Boys Secondary)

Perceptions must also be understood in the context of broader community
and class dynamics that were evident in our discussion with parents in
Chapter 6 and teachers in Chapter 5. Students spoke of the tensions they
experienced, most especially in marginalised urban communities where
competition for resources is scarce and lack of trust, that is essential for
building strong social capital, is evident:

There's too many immigrants [in this area]. They [Irish] think the government
is going to feel sorry for them all [immigrants]. They are making money and
getting the jobs and all that. They'll lose out and they are afraid of immigrants
taking over. They don't look at it from both sides. (Polish Boy, Bellview Boys)

Neither should it be assumed that the experience of racism occurs only
between majority/minority ethnic groups, or indeed that 'whiteness'
conveys automatic privilege, which in relation to for example Traveller
children is clearly not the case (Devine et al. 2008). Notwithstanding these
challenges, there was also evidence of integration among migrant children
and their indigenous Irish peers and this led to forms of social capital which

enabled them to cope better with life in school. In Oakleaf primary for example, children talked not only about how their Irish friends helped them with their work in school, but also stood up for them when they were being racially abused:

> We stand up for each other. They [Irish friends] told them [racist name callers – fellow peers] to leave me alone and stop bossing me around and said to them: 'if you were that colour you wouldn't like if they were saying that to you'. (Ava, Nigerian Girl)

In secondary schools, it was opportunities often outside of the formal curriculum – participation in team sporting and social events which facilitated more authentic social engagement. In Ashleaf college for example, the work of the student council in putting together a fashion show allowed a blending of diverse traditions (a form of cultural hybridity) and a valuation of what could happen when the students themselves worked on creating hybrid forms of being and doing:

> *Student:* We have fashion shows. Not only to involve European fashion shows but we could also involve African things like ... but we can use even modern things, we can also even use entertaining things, to mix the Irish and the African styles.

> *Interviewer:* Not just to mix the traditions but also to mix the modern African and the modern Irish.

> *Pupils (all):* Yeah! Yeah! (Mixed Ethnic Group, Females, Ashleaf College)

Concluding discussion

The analysis highlights the inter-linkages between children's views and perspectives and those of their teachers and principals. This chapter has documented the issues which were to the forefront of the children's experience: the impact on their friendships, the opportunities created for wider learning (about themselves and others) as well as broader questions related to the dynamics of power and control in social interaction that was influenced by perceptions of and attitudes toward cultural and ethnic difference. The strong motivation the migrant children and youth displayed toward learning and achieving well in school can be understood in terms not only of their immigrant status, but also the influence of family social background and expectations on the part of their parents that they do well in school.[4] However in most instances, the children's struggle to integrate into their schools was their own – they did so often in the absence of parent's knowledge of the Irish school system as well as lack of fluency in English. There were many instances of the children having superior English language skills to their parents, placing them in patterns of responsibility and control that cut across typical patterns of inter-generational relations – mediating between the home and the school. Through their school activities then the children were acquiring new forms of knowledge (cultural capitals) with the intention of improving their own life-chances, as well as that of their entire family. While the ambition to do well may come from their parents, the generative aspect of habitus is reflected in the children's own labour and effort in school. A significant component of this work was the formation of positive social relationships and the building of social capital through relations with teachers and peers in school. Consistently there was evidence of positive relationships with teachers, derived from the children's positioning in ideal type terms, as productive and obedient in their approach to school. Such relations had important exchange value, providing access to valued cultural capital in the educational field. The general ambitiousness to do well was evident in their desire for continual focused instruction and correction from their teachers, as well as a willingness to learn and adapt to 'Irish' ways of doing things. The children were for the most part reluctant to be critical of their experiences of teaching and learning, appreciative of the efforts being made by schools, but also indicative perhaps of culturally embedded inter-generational patterns which foreclosed criticism of what teachers, as adults, were doing. Yet the comments of older secondary school students related to the need for focused instruction and correction mirrors our own observational data of teacher practices (Devine et al. 2010b) that suggests less engaged/challenging teaching and learning in classrooms with increasing numbers of immigrant students.

The children were also met with considerable challenges in their adjustment and accommodation to life in school. They bring to school a repertoire of cultural and educational experiences that especially for first generation migrant children, render the Irish system at once strange and challenging. More authoritarian child rearing regimes in their home countries ensures that the comparatively liberal tradition in western education contrasts sharply with many of these children's traditional experiences of school, raising questions for them as to the nature of pupil/teacher relations in the classroom. Further the western and distinctively Irish focus in most of their learning provides further challenges as they seek to marry new forms of learning with that gained in their home countries. While students spoke of the value of recognising their culture and experiences in school, nonetheless they were clear that they did not want to be treated differently to their Irish peers, nor have their difference promoted in a manner that rendered them more 'visible' and 'curious' to their fellow students. Some noted the need to educate indigenous Irish students toward greater tolerance of difference, challenging stereotypes of minority groups and making them more aware of the myriad of contexts of immigration into Ireland. Systemic difficulties identified by senior level minority ethnic students included their anxieties over examinations and the allowances that may be made for students who do not have English as their first language, as well as concerns over access routes to Higher Education. Frustration with bureaucracy was also noted by some students especially those who were seeking or had been granted legal asylum, adding to their difficulties of adjusting to a new society and education system, often in the absence of a family support structure (OOC 2010).

What is evident also is that there are as many differences between immigrant children as there are similarities, suggesting that a one size fits all approach to diversity in schools is not sufficient. Neither is 'diversity' about and for immigrant children, rather it is embedded in all children's lifeworld in school and should be taken as normative in itself. Further common experiences of dislocation and cultural discontinuities should not detract from both intra- and inter-group variability in migrant children's responses to school. A range of identity signifiers related to for example age, gender, social class, ethnicity, ability and sexuality intersect as the children position and reposition themselves in their relations with teachers, peers and parents. Recognition is key however to the children's educational well-being – in terms of visibility as persons with a voice to be heard and expressed, as well as in being validated, monitored and meaningfully supported in their efforts at work and play in school.

Notes

1 If we consider the Nigerian group for example, some worked within the IT sector, while others worked as taxi drivers, others had come through the asylum process and were still waiting for their applications to be processed.

2 Irish is compulsory in schools, but students over the age of 12 years who have not been resident in Ireland up to that point are entitled to a dispensation.

3 More indepth analysis of these patterns is provided in Devine and Kelly 2006.

4 These are interlinked in complex ways. Ability to migrate to a country in itself demonstrates social and cultural capital on the parts of parents to access knowledge in relation to the host country and find the means and resources to travel there.

8

Making a difference?
Securing the educational well-being
of migrant children

On 4 April 2010, Toyosi Shittabey, a 15-year-old boy who had been born in Nigeria but lived in Ireland for 11 years, was stabbed to death. His killing gave rise to considerable media attention and sent shockwaves through his local community as well as nationally. Media headlines, both nationally and internationally, conveyed the outrage in the Nigerian and broader community, as well as concerns over 'growing' racism, especially during a period of economic decline: 'Racism probe after teenager stabbed' (Irish Independent, 3 April); 'Sadness tinged with anger as community grieves' (Irish Times, 5 April); 'Ireland of the welcomes is a myth' (Sunday Independent, 11 April). Tyrellstown, where Toyosi Shittabey lived, is in Dublin 15. It is one of the most densely populated immigrant localities in Ireland and has been characterised by rapid urban expansion, low rental housing and a poorly developed urban and social infrastructure. What is worth noting in the community responses to Toyosi Shittabey's killing is the significant role those in his local school played (principal, teachers and fellow students) in articulating the sense of shock, hurt and anger over his death. School, along with Church and sporting organisations appeared central spaces in which Toyosi Shittabey experienced a sense of belonging in his life in Ireland. Yet other media headlines, focused on the growing prevalence of racism in schools e.g. 'TUI says 46% of teachers aware of racist school incidents in past month' (Irish Times, 5 April 2010). Dublin 15 is an area which has been intensively researched, a testing ground for how boom and post-boom Ireland has coped with social and cultural change. Crises over school enrolment and placement have given rise to the 'piloting' of a new model of governance in two primary schools in this area that may come to be employed nationally. Yet the 'bussing' of migrant children to schools prior to the opening of these new schools, coupled with the establishment of de facto immigrant schools signals broader structural issues in Irish society related to equality, segregation and racialisation that are crystallised in this geographic area.

The chapters in this book have documented patterns, trends and experiences with respect to immigration and schooling in Ireland. This chapter brings together the analyses and situates them theoretically and practically in terms of schooling and education in multi-ethnic contexts. The analysis acknowledges and indeed signals the tensions that exist between forces of transformation and preservation in societies marked by rapid change, as well as deeply embedded structures of power and inequality. At a time of profound crisis in Ireland, I emphasise the importance of leadership and a vision of education for participatory democracy – not only in newly multi-ethnic schools, but as an underpinning principle for the promotion of children's well-being in a more socially just society.

Changing context, changing schools

The level of change which has occurred in Ireland since the 1990s is perhaps unprecedented. Radical shifts have taken place economically and socially, including shifting patterns of demographic change through immigration and now more recently the return of the more 'familiar' territory of emigration. While Ireland was never a mono cultural society it is fair to say that the intensity of immigration as well as the range of ethnic diversities among immigrant groups with whom there was no prior link is new. Schools are often at the coal face of change, experiencing social shifts directly through the changing characteristics and needs of the child population. As institutions, schools are also located contradictorily between safe-guarding the past and what is 'known', as well as shaping the future. Sociologically they are caught then between processes of 'production' and 'reproduction', mediating between diverse forces, often in the context of constrained resources and contrasting local community dynamics.

Irish society has witnessed many of the universalistic hallmarks of cosmopolitanism, such as risk, global openness and cultural contradictions (Beck 2006; Inglis 2008). This change has been mapped onto a society that is characterised by its own particularistic (post-colonial) history and socio-cultural context. We saw in Chapter 2 the social, cultural and religious forces that have played out historically in the structuring and operation of the school system. The analysis highlighted the central role of schooling in shaping an 'imaginary of the nation' (Hickman 2008). Submerged in cultural politics, policies at the foundation of the state copper-fastened a more insular and segregated approach to managing diversities, with an overarching emphasis on the construction of national identity that margin-alised those who differed from the norm. This had a profound impact not only on governance structures in education, but also on the absence of educational policy with respect to diversities. Children were viewed predominantly as a homogenous group, with little or no attention given to those at the margins of society. While a level of indifference existed in the state to social policy in general (Fanning 2007) it was especially so with respect to children (Devine 2008). This had severe implications for embedding structured patterns of inequality that were both classed and gendered (OECD 1969, Breen et al. 1990). It also had considerable consequences for those who were ethnically 'different', evident in the marginalisation of Traveller children in education, as well as in the absence of policies to support the few non-Irish immigrants who entered the country through tightly controlled refugee programmes (Lentin and McVeigh 2002; McGovern 1993).

Structurally embedded patterns of inequality influenced and set the context for responses to subsequent change. In spite of the economic development and boom, levels of relative poverty in Ireland remained high, including that of children (Russell et al. 2010), with higher rates of child poverty relative to other advanced economies (UNICEF 2009). A sea-change in discourse in relation to the promotion of children's well-being is evident since the development of the National Children's Strategy in 2000, signalled in the establishment of an Office of the Minister for Children and Youth affairs (OMYCA) and the appointment of an Ombudsman for Children. Such developments are important signifiers in the recognition of the rights and well-being of children as a social group. Yet considerable challenges remain in the translation of policy into practice. A recent report on separated children living in Ireland (OOC 2010) for example, highlights the absence of rights and 'best interests of the child' focus in recent immigration legislation. Separated children are one group of immigrants especially vulnerable and at risk, while nationally, immigrants as a group have been identified as at most risk of poverty (CPA 2007), a pattern likely to consolidate in a period of economic recession. We know that immigrants are most likely to cluster in areas of low cost housing (Fahey and Fanning 2010) and thus more likely to attend DEIS schools (Smyth et al. 2009), especially in urban areas. It is no co-incidence that a majority of the schools from which research in this book is drawn were in this category. While the profile of immigrants indicates a prevalence of those who are well-educated relative to the national population (CSO 2008; OECD 2009a), other research (e.g. Poupeau et al. 2007) has highlighted how dynamics of exclusion and marginalisation become embedded in spatial exclusion, as immigrants become segregated from the mainstream through housing and in certain cases the clustering of their children in 'immigrant' schools. While not widespread in Ireland, given the dispersal of immigrants throughout the country (Byrne et al. 2010), it is evident in certain urban communities and in certain types of schools. What is noteworthy is the absence of political debate on immigration in Ireland, although this is likely to change with the economic recession. Especially absent is an open and coherent analysis of the long term implications of any ethnic and racial segregation that currently exists, into future generations.

Discourse and counter discourse

The absence of critical engagement and reflection on matters of social policy, the resistance to name racialisation in the experiences of existing cultural and ethnic minorities and the consolidation of traditional patterns of control in Irish education set the context for state responses to the rapid and intensive immigration that has occurred in recent years. What we also see evident in the formation of policy is not only the predominance of certain discourses, but the gradual proliferation of counter discourses which have set the ground work for educational change. This latter in itself reflects not only the contradictory and often unintended consequences of what Foucault (1979) terms the capillary exercise of power, but also how policy and practice in education is 'messy' and complex, underpinned by relations of power which are never fully sedimented nor open to radical change (Dale 1989; Green 1997). What is especially significant is that ethnic diversity has traditionally been defined in Ireland in terms of religious rather than cultural diversity,[1] giving rise to a [mainly] denominationally structured education system, especially in the primary sector. O'Sullivan's (2005) analysis highlights the graduated pragmatic approach to educational change in Ireland, with the move toward a more market oriented, mercantile policy in education dovetailing with a liberal model of democracy, in which the state defines itself as 'neutral' arbitrator between competing interests. Of course this raises fundamental questions in terms of equality in and through education, as it is those who already are recognised and have value within the system, who are most likely to experience respect and recognition and have their voices heard (Baker et al. 2009). With the opening up of society from the 1960s and the vocal assertion of rights among an increasingly educated and confident parent body, a greater diversity in school choice at primary level has (very) gradually taken hold, most explicitly through the expansion of the Educate Together school sector. The rapidity of demographic growth in certain urban centres as a result of immigration, along with broader cultural and social change has consolidated its growth as a sector.

Change itself however can also come from unexpected quarters. The impetus for the expansion of a greater diversity in choice of schools and especially the piloting of the new community school model at primary level reflects in many ways 'contradictory closing cases' (Gillborn 2008), that respond to a specific need while leaving the status quo relatively intact. It co-incides however with a sea change in public discourse about the role of traditional authority structures in Irish society and whether these can continue to serve the 'public good'. The Catholic Church's position has come under scrutiny, most notably arising from the publication of the Ryan Report (2009). It is not clear what the vision of the state is in relation to the governance of schools, yet it's continued positioning as neutral arbitrator places it in a somewhat contradictory role in relation to the realisation of the core vision of the recently released Intercultural Education Strategy (2010). Current negotiations with Church authorities over the 'handing over' of primary schools in certain urban areas raise important questions about who should control schools which are funded by the state.

What is of interest is how the debate is being shaped around the rights of parents to chose a school for their children, a right which is supported by the Irish constitution through the designation of parents as the primary educators of their children. While the exercise of choice has always been dependent upon the availability of schools in a local area, it is also significantly influenced by social class and religious/ethnic identities. While pluralist in intent, the demarcation of schools along religious lines can result in the segregation of children by ethnic and migrant status. This becomes especially marked during periods of intensive immigration. As we saw in Chapters 1 and 2, this can contribute to the establishment of in effect 'immigrant' schools and racialised patterns of school choice and allocation. Such patterns are currently evident only in certain areas of high urban growth. They may however become more pronounced as the newer models of school governance take hold, leading to schools which serve the needs of the (mainly white) Catholic majority and schools which cater for the needs of minorities who fall outside of the dominant religious/ethnic and cultural norms. The 'stakes' around school choice become especially prevalent in societies characterised by high educational levels, where prestige and value is added not by the right to go to school, but by *which* school one goes to. In such instances reputational criteria related not only to school performance[2] but also student characteristics such as class and ethnicity comes increasingly to the fore. As competition for ever more scarce resources arises, choices in relation to which and what type of school one sends one's child to become increasingly important, part of the classificatory systems which distinguish those in the 'know' (regarding the 'best' schools) and those who do not. While distinct class patterns in terms of school choice became even more prominent during the boom period in Ireland, racial and ethnic dynamics will come increasingly to the fore in the coming years. Of course such patterns are already firmly embedded in the school system with respect to Traveller children who, like immigrant children tend to be clustered in DEIS schools. The issue in relation to school governance then is not simply one of 'school choice' as if this was a neutral phenomenon, but also of (in) equalities via a structurally segregated school system and the clustering of contrasting social and ethnic groups in different types of schools.

Both Bryan (2009) and Kitching (2010) point to the inherent conservatism that has permeated state policy in the area of immigration and education. As outlined in Chapter 2, the broader emphasis and construction of immigrants in neo-liberal terms, as economic self actualised 'workers' (Rose 1991), dovetails with approaches in education which primarily emphasise investment in English language training, itself among the first targets to be hit in recent education cutbacks. Discourses of Irish emigrant experience are continually drawn upon in government policy documents to convey sensitivity and understanding of the 'immigrant experience' as a natural characteristic of the 'Irish', forestalling critique of Irish attitudes that could be considered in racialised terms. As Hickman (2010) notes, this places Irishness itself as inherently embracing the *inclusion of 'others'*, rather than itself being *comprised of a range of others*. Undoubtedly, the period from 2005 witnessed greater activity and co-ordination around immigration policy, including the education of migrant children, arising mainly from the establishment of the Office of the Minister for Integration. Yet contra-dictory processes were evident as the state argued for the benefits of cultural diversity, while simultaneously minimising social and cultural change through restrictive immigration policies (Haywood and Howard 2007).

The most recent publication of an Intercultural Education Strategy (DES/OMI 2010) foregrounds the importance of education to government policy and follows a period of considerable consultation and overview of best practice in the field. As such it must be considered along a trajectory of responses by the state, as it seeks to incorporate, and accommodate multiple discourses into the formulation of policy. A comprehensive agenda is proposed that highlights diversity as a normal part of Irish society and the inter-linkages between system and local level practices to outcomes (both social and academic) for migrant children in schools. The stated need to address gaps in leadership, quality in teaching and learning and communication between parents and schools are especially important, dovetailing with many of the issues of concern identified throughout this book. The emphasis on continuing professional development and whole school planning for inclusion and diversity is also important. While the priority remains on English language acquisition, placing student experience at the centre of the strategy ensures that cultural recognition through for example mother tongue learning is recommended. Racism is also recognised as an area that needs attention in schools. The strategy is important because it provides a statement of intent, backed by a clear emphasis on the evaluation and review of practice over five years. While specific targets are absent, 'expected outcomes' over the life-time of the strategy are key signifiers of priorities. In spite of the recognition of inter-linked and inter-connected influence of for example political leadership at the national level, the strategy clearly places responsibility on local schools to effect change in a context of ever tightening budgetary constraints. This is perhaps most explicitly encapsulated in the concluding section of the strategy which states: 'It is the efforts of the single school/institution which matter' (DES/OMI 2010:68).

Yet it is this very explicit focus on school practices without a *corresponding* focus on wider structural/systemic issues that gives cause for comment. The absence for example of analysis of issues related to the governance of schools in the strategy, considered beyond its remit (DES/OMI 2010: 29) is a case in point, given the significance of such governance to patterns of segregation in the school system. The influence and priorities of the OECD must also be considered, given the very direct input it has had in monitoring and reviewing policy development in this area (OECD 2009a, 2009b). The relatively consistent underperformance of immigrant groups into the second and third generations globally (OECD 2006) is framed in terms of the loss of human capital in market knowledge driven economies, as well as the threat to social cohesion and stability (necessary for economic growth) that derives from alienation and lack of 'integration'. In OECD publications, education is consistently framed in terms of its 'use value' rather than as a good in and of itself that enhances quality of life and well-being. These tensions and contradictions in the discourse about education are evident in aspects of the Intercultural Education Strategy (DES/OMI 2010). The benefits of and respect for cultural diversity in the education sector sits alongside the need to ensure there is no infringement of 'the overall good and well-being of Irish society' (ibid.: 49). Discourses, of course, are never neutral. The decision as to what is 'good' and who decides is itself embedded in dynamics of power in the wider society. As Foucault (1979) informs us, discourses are shifting 'truths'. They are played out in repeated cycles of power that evolve, as competing pressures – local, national, global – collide and merge. Identifying the discourses underpinning the formulation of educational policy are especially important because it is in education that both distributive (in terms of economic/material resources) and recognitive (cultural resources) differences often crystallise in shaping the (under) performance of many migrant children in schools. Any discussion of policy and practice in relation to immigrant experiences of education and of policies to promote children's educational well-being must be cognisant of the diverse dynamics, strategies and power plays that underplay the educational process.

Education as a field of power:
tension between transformation and preservation

Throughout my analysis I have drawn on the work of a number of key theorists to highlight the interplay of structural/societal and individual dynamics in the experience of, and practices in, education. Bourdieu's work has been especially useful because it integrates these dynamics in the concepts of field, capitals and habitus. While this has been outlined in detail in Chapter 3, it is worth reiterating the importance of considering education as a 'field' which is governed by a series of forces that influences how individuals both are positioned and position themselves in it. For Bourdieu:

> A field is a structured social space, a field of forces, a force field. It contains people who dominate and people who are dominated. Constant permanent relationships of inequality operate inside this space, which at the same time, becomes a space in which the various actors struggle for the *transformation* or *preservation* of the field. (Bourdieu 1998: 40–41)

This raises a number of questions in relation to teasing through the implications of immigration and schooling in Ireland. Not only is education a key site for immigrants, as 'actors' to enhance their life chances and opportunities in the 'host' society, it is equally a key site for the state and other stakeholders (e.g. the churches, teachers, parents) to influence and shape what those opportunities will be. Power is never absolute however nor devoid of the possibility of change (Foucault 1979). Rather than viewing education and schools as neutral spaces we need to foreground the power dynamics in education and of the constant tension that exists between 'transformation' and 'preservation' between the various actors in this *field*. This is played out nationally through policy development and resource allocation as in for example the most recent negotiations over school governance at primary level, as well as the changing resource allocation for language support to migrant children. It is also played out locally in school practices through for example levels of engagement with immigrant communities at local school level. These national and local dynamics create differences in participation, opportunity and outcome for children across a range of ethnic groupings. Systemic influences on children's learning can be considered in layers – almost like an onion that can be peeled back, with the child placed at the core. Macro policies at the level of the state and increasingly at the level of the EU and OECD set the broader context for what takes place in schools. These shape the context for migrant children's (and indeed all children's) educational well-being. This is represented below in Figure 8.1.

Figure 8.1   *Making a difference: macro- and micro-level influences on migrant children's educational well-being*

Of course immigrant communities come with different capacities to mobilise key economic, cultural, social, and emotional resources that will help/or 'hinder' them playing the 'field'. Children from immigrant communities are themselves a diverse group. We also need to focus on which children from within which communities are deemed 'at risk'. This again raises questions about power and privilege and how these intersect in terms of gender, class, ethnicity and immigrant status, creating multiple positionings among migrant children in the negotiation of their everyday lives in school. In this sense Bourdieu's concept of 'habitus' is a powerful concept that applies to children, as much as to their parents, teachers and school principals, shaping reaction and interaction in schools. This interplay between embedded patterns of power, status and privilege in society (structure) and how it is mediated through both the habitus of the person (child, parent, teacher, principal) and practices in the field of education is reflected in Figure 8.2. The model draws also on Foucault's notion that power is central to dynamics of interaction in society, but operates in a circular flow, both/and top down and bottom up. This gives rise to a complex and as we have seen 'messy' process of both transformation and preservation. I have placed 'habitus' at the centre, to indicate not only its central place in mediating both reaction and action to schooling, but also how it derives from the interaction between structure, practice, power and agency.

Figure 8.2   *Making a difference: the interrelationship between structure, agency, power and habitus in shaping school practice*

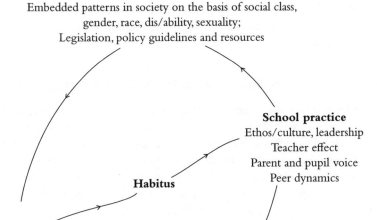

Structure
Embedded patterns in society on the basis of social class,
gender, race, dis/ability, sexuality;
Legislation, policy guidelines and resources

School practice
Ethos/culture, leadership
Teacher effect
Parent and pupil voice
Peer dynamics

Habitus

Power

Actors/agency
Identity as negotiated and fluid
Reflective

To highlight the circular and capillary nature of action and interaction in education, and actors' positioning in it, is not in any way to suggest that all actors come to the field of education with the same level of power or capacity to 'act'. Clearly they do not. It is however to highlight the interweaving of complex forces which ultimately influence both process and outcomes for migrant children. It requires a nuanced analysis of education as both a productive and reproductive space, a space that is full of potential and opportunity for empowerment and gain, as well as for the reproduction of inequalities and consolidation of social injustice. These dichotomies can operate simultaneously at systemic level, as well as at local school level. Intercultural guidelines can assert the need for respect and recognition for minorities in schools (transformation), but in the absence of investment in professional development of teachers, as well as in monitoring implementation, can lead to preservation of the status quo. Providing new school models to cater for a greater diversity of belief systems (transformation) may merely consolidate classed and racially segregated patterns (preservation) in the school system.

Two important themes emerge from the analysis presented in this book. Both are inter linked but can be divided into the significance of leadership in education and the key role of education in fostering participative democracy.

The importance of leadership in education

Leadership is at the heart of school policy and practice, shaping and guiding vision for a school which informs practice at all levels within it. The exercise of an ethical leadership that is grounded in a vision of authentic and real engagement with the community of the school is essential if real and effective learning and education in its broadest sense is to occur. The analysis of principals' experiences indicated the significance of 'habitus' to their practice, that was itself derived from their prior management experience, educational and personal histories, as well as the level and intensity of change in the school and local community which s/he served. Those who appeared most effective engaged in leaderful practices (Perumal 2009) that were rooted in a commitment to social justice and human rights, often derived from a tradition of working with and/in more marginalised communities, including with Traveller groups. They often forged a delicate balance between 'recognition' and 'risk', transformation and preservation, especially in terms of defining the school's reputation in an increasingly competitive educational marketplace. Essentialised, racialised as well as classed discourses were also evident that in themselves highlighted the embedded taken for grantedness of the dominant 'we' when met face to face with the reality of the ethnic/migrant 'other'.

Leadership in schools however is not merely the preserve of school principals. Conceived of as a distributed process, the leadership that is demonstrated by teachers both at school level in terms of contributions to whole school planning and at class level to pedagogical practice is also central to making a difference in newly multi-ethnic schools. Evident from the research is a great commitment and passion that exists among many teachers to the care and well-being of children from immigrant communities. Also evident however is the emotional challenge that is required in order to 'step' out of the usual way of doing things. As with principals, both classed and racialised constructions were also evident in teacher views. Success in working with migrant children for many teachers was defined not on their achievement *per se*, but rather their capacity to assimilate as 'normal' in the classroom, especially in terms of behaviour and respectful demeanour.

There was evidence of lower expectations and less challenging teaching in classrooms where there were larger groups of immigrant children present, as well as the tendency to cluster immigrant students in lower streams. These are practices which are of significant concern.

Pedagogy to be effective must have at its core a social justice perspective that is embedded in respect and recognition for the whole person of the child. I am reminded of a query by a student as to the relevance of social justice to teachers, when their primary concern should be pedagogy. This was a telling question that highlighted an assumption in this teacher's mind (and perhaps that of many teachers) of education as a field that is devoid of power relations, a 'neutral' space of teaching and learning. It highlights the need for professional development of teachers that is not simply about the transfer of tips and tricks for diversity and language education. What is required is a deeper appreciation of the social and cultural dimension to the development of children's learner identities and how this influences their motivation to engage with their learning in school. Pedagogical leadership requires a critical engagement with self and other, informed neither by paternalistic concern and sympathy, nor legitimation arising from the perceived productive/'added value' of the immigrant child. This has practical implications in terms of the spaces teachers create, and that are created for teachers, for reflection on their pedagogic practices. It requires consistent attention to and evaluation of progress with children of immigrant communities and a sustained sensitivity to racialised practices and patterns that can arise.

Leadership is not an end point that is fixed on any one single individual but is distributed not only within the school (through the work of teachers and principals) but also through the over-arching systems of management and control within which schools are embedded. Leadership is thus layered throughout the system and the decisions (or lack of decisions) made elsewhere influence the range of choices which both principals and teachers in schools can make.

In education, state initiatives have largely focused on the provision of English language support, as well as some (minimal) training for both language support teachers and newly appointed principals. Intercultural curriculum guidelines have been developed (NCCA 2005) and at the time of writing the 'Intercultural Education Strategy' was launched, as previously outlined. While there has been a great deal of policy making there has been much less focus on implementation, a key element of effective leadership, especially with respect to safeguarding equality and rights for minoritised groups. The focus on implementation of practice in the Intercultural Education Strategy is therefore important and timely. It needs to be counterbalanced by an equivalent focus on broader state level policies (including economic and social policies) which impact on schools' capacities to change.

Similarly Patron and school management bodies have a leadership role to play. We have seen that the role of the Churches in education is complex. Schools can be simultaneously inclusionary and exclusionary in their practices. They can legitimately prioritise the enrolment of those who are of the school's denominational status (i.e the 'same') where there is a shortage of school places locally, while embracing the wider Christian mission of welcome, care and concern for those enrolled who are 'different'. Not all Catholic schools are the same however and each implements the 'Catholic' ethos to differing degrees, depending on prior history, community context and strength of affiliation to religious orders. Challenges also arise for Protestant schools (Colton 2009), perhaps even more so, given that many are now experiencing for the first time an increase in enrolment due to the numbers of immigrants who are affiliated to the Protestant churches.

Fostering participatory democracy in newly multi-ethnic schools

Schools are not just learning spaces but important civic spaces, key locales in which diversity intersects and inter-connects depending on how the school culture is defined. Schools are also hierarchical spaces, comprised of those who are gatekeepers of knowledge, opportunity and change. Change brought about through immigration can disrupt hegemonic understandings (Youdell 2006), creating resistance and attempts to copper-fasten what is safe and known. If change is to be meaningful it needs to confront unsettling questions about power and voice. This is not an easy task and we have seen that where schools 'stepped out of the comfort zone', it was a difficult and arduous process, that was not always clear in its outcomes. Two groups have historically been positioned at the margins of decision making in Irish education: parents and children.

As with all 'parent' groups, immigrant parents are not an undifferentiated 'whole' – they come to schools with an awareness of the significance and importance of education to the life-chances of their children, but with widely different access to resources that will help them in the mobilisation of educational capital. These patterns are gendered, classed and racialised, underpinned by the struggle to adapt and accommodate self and family in the host society, alongside the psychic unease (Archer and Francis 2007) that is inevitable in settling in to somewhere new. Such patterns become especially crystallised in decisions to risk visibility in the public life of the school, through participation in classroom and school events and more fundamentally in parent associations and representation in school committees and boards. While fluency in English is a key element in facilitating such participation, it is also embedded in broader expectations and understandings about education and the role schools can play in fostering a 'deliberative democracy' (Blackmore 2006) that is centred on respect and recognition for all. The deep embeddedness of whiteness in Irish society, the tendency toward an often a–critical engagement with diversity that ultimately assumes it is about 'them' and not 'us'; the assumption that kindness and 'leaving the door open' is sufficient, requires of minoritised parents a considerable degree of confidence to extend and put themselves forward in a meaningful manner. *Laissez faire* approaches will only compound existing hierarchies as it is those with the resources to strategically mobilise opportunities who have the capacity to protect and preserve the life chances of their children. As civic spaces, schools have a significant role to play in fostering and generating cultural and social capital both within and between parent groups (both indigenous and immigrant), as well as formalising representation of minority groups on parent associations and school boards.

Children must also be viewed as key actors in schools, yet it is significant that their role in fostering community, understanding and ultimately capitals is rarely alluded to in debates and discussions around both immigrant and wider educational policy. Fundamentally democracy in education is about empowering children to realise their rights to education, as well as become aware of their rights in education. It is an important element of securing not only educational well-being, but general well-being. I have argued elsewhere of the need to consider all children as citizens and of the significant role of schooling for children's citizenship (Devine 2002, 2003). Such analyses is embedded in the concept of social citizenship and a recognition that children are not future 'becomings' but competent social beings with rights of respect and recognition for their voice and perspective.

As a signatory to the United Nations Convention on the Rights of the Child (1989), it is opportune to consider migrant children's experiences in the context of the realisation of rights to both equality and quality in their educational experiences. Issues related to access to education are important here, especially access to a school in the local community that enhances belonging and wider social integration. The importance of locality to children's everyday lives is borne out in other research (O'Connor 2009; Ní Laoire et al. 2009) and also in this book through the significance migrant children attached to locally organised activities (sports, dance etc.) that provided them with access to 'Irish' ways of being and doing. The children demonstrated savyness and determination in their efforts to integrate in schools. Caught at the intersection between often contrasting cultural scripts of home and school, they negotiated new friendships and new learning, conscious of the importance of doing so for future as well as present well-being. The children were reluctant to be critical of teachers (itself a reflection perhaps of their minority status) and were mostly grateful for the opportunities provided them in schools. Where concerns were expressed these centred on not being sufficiently challenged in their learning as well as the need to embed education for diversity into the core curriculum and assessment models used in schools. Racism was an ever-present threat that existed between minority groups as well as between minority and majority children. This led to considerable ethnic self monitoring by children, depending on the extent to which they were prepared to 'risk' visibility and the unsettling of taken for granted hierarchies and norms.

Concluding remarks

Critically reflecting on current policy and practice in schools is of crucial importance if fragmentation and segregation of ethnic 'others' is not to become consolidated as an inevitable aspect of immigrant experiences in education. Elements of good practice have been identified, as well as areas of concern. Simplistic assertions and stereotypes do no service to the complexity of schools as organisations, nor to the myriad of demands and expectations that are placed on schools to remedy the problems and challenges often created elsewhere. Structural change is more difficult to accomplish, precisely because it requires an undoing of the 'known', an interrogation of existing norms and disruption of power.

With the recent economic crisis, we are at a crossroads in terms of significant decisions being taken in the direction of our society. Education is and should be a cornerstone for change. Reform must however be embedded in key principles around the type of society we wish to create and an acknowledgement of the transformative potential within education, when adequately supported, to effect change. It is about acknowledging what is solid and good in the education system to date, but also what is in need of change. It is about harnessing both the productive and reproductive tensions in the educational field, acknowledging the central role of schooling in 'shaping the nation', explicitly stating what the guiding principles of that shaping should be. It is about recognising the fundamental role of voice, respect and recognition to the educational process. It needs to be embedded in concepts of education which place democracy (Dewey 1963), at the heart of educational practice.

Conceptually my analysis has been framed from a critical perspective, that acknowledges the inherent potential within education as social, public and civic 'good' and the accompanying responsibilities of those tasked with the project of education to realise effective change, especially among minoritised children. This is all the more pressing in light of the current economic challenges, and in light of the tendency within such contexts to marginalise 'others' further. However a critical perspective also recognises the mediating influence of power in social formation, especially in the educational sphere through the subjectivating influence of discourses, policies and practices on the motivations and identities of learners. Acknowledging the complexity of the educational field and the often competing 'logics of practice' which govern schools at the level of structures (discourse, policies, norms), as well as individual/actor response(s) should not deter those committed to education in its broadest sense from making a difference to the everyday lives of children. Securing the educational well-being of all children in multi-ethnic schools is clearly indicated in the recent Intercultural Education Strategy. Its success in five years time will be a reflection of the commitment that exists at the level of schools as well as at the level of the state in effecting meaningful change. More broadly it will reflect the priorities we place in society on securing the well-being of children generally, especially appropriate in light of the 2016 centenary celebration of the Declaration of the Republic.

Notes

1 This is reflected in the misrecognition of Traveller culture for many years.
2 This is at its most overt in the UK through the publication of school league tables, but evident also in Ireland through media driven league tables on access to third level education.

Bibliography

Adams, M. B. and Griffin, P. (ed.) (2007) *Teaching for diversity and social justice*, New York, Routledge.

Akenson, D. H. (1975) *A mirror to Kathleen's face: education in independent Ireland, 1922–1960*, London, McGill-Queen's University Press.

Alderson, P. and Morrow, V. (2004) *Ethics, social research and consulting with children and young people*, Barkingside, Barnardos.

Allen, K. (2007) 'Neo-liberalism and immigration', in Fanning, B. (ed.), *Immigration and social change in the Republic of Ireland*, Manchester, Manchester University Press: 84–99.

Allen, K. and Loyal, S. (2006) 'Rethinking immigration and the State in Ireland', in Lentin, A. and Lentin, R. (eds), *Race and State*l, Newcastle, Cambridge Scholars Press: 142–167.

Alvey, D. (1991) *Irish education: the case for secular reform*, Dublin, Church and State Books in conjunction with Athol Books.

Anthias, F. (2010) *Intersections and translocations: new paradigms for thinking about identities and inequalities*, European Conference of Educational Research, University of Helsinki.

Apple, M. W. (1979) *Ideology and the curriculum*, London, Routledge & Kegan Paul.

Apple, M. W. (1986) *Teachers and texts: a political economy of class and gender relations in education*, London, Routledge.

Apple, M. W. (2005) 'Between memory and vision: the case for faith-based schooling', *Journal of Education Policy* 20(5): 661–662.

Apple, M. W. (2006) 'How class works in education', *Educational Policy* 20(2): 455–462.

Apple, M. W. (2009) 'Is racism in education an accident?', *Educational Policy* 23(4): 651–659.

Archer, L. (2008) 'The impossibility of minority ethnic educational "success"? An examination of the discourses of teachers and pupils in British secondary schools', *European Educational Research Journal* 7(1): 89–106.

Archer, L. (2010) '"We raised it with the Head": the educational practices of minority ethnic middle class families', *British Journal of Sociology of Education* 31(4): 449–469.

Archer, L. and Francis, B (2005) '"They never go off the rails like other ethnic groups": Teacher constructions of British Chinese pupils' gender identities and approaches to learning', *British Journal of Sociology of Education* 26(1): 223–244.

Archer, L. and Francis, B. (2007) *Understanding minority ethnic achievement*, London, RoutledgeFalmer Press.

Archer, L., Francis, B. and Mau, A. (2010) 'The Culture Project: diasporic negotiations of ethnicity, identity and culture among teachers, pupils and parents in Chinese language schools', *Oxford Review of Education* 36(4): 407–426.

Baker, J., Lynch K., Cantillon, S. and Walsh, J. (2009) *Equality: from theory to action*, London, Palgrave Macmillan.

Ball, S. J. (2003) 'The teacher's soul and the terrors of performativity', *Journal of Education Policy* 18(2): 215–233.

Ball, S. J. (2009) 'Privatising education, privatising education policy, privatising educational research: network governance and the competition state, *Journal of Education Policy* 24(1): 83–99.

Ball, S. J. and Bowe, R. (1995) 'Circuits of schooling: a sociological exploration of parental choice of school in social class contexts', *Sociological Review* 43(1): 52–78.

Ball, S. J. and Vincent, C. (1998) '"I Heard It on the Grapevine": "hot" knowledge and school choice', *British Journal of Sociology of Education* 19(3): 377–400.

Banks, J. (ed.) (2009) *The Routledge international companion to multicultural education*, New York, Routledge.

Barrett, A. and Bergin, A. (2007) 'The economic contribution of immigrants in Ireland', in Fanning, B. (ed.), *Immigration and social change in the Republic of Ireland*, Manchester, Manchester University Press.

Barrett, A., Bergin, A. and Duffy, D. (2006) 'The labour market characteristics and labour market impact of immigrants in Ireland', *Economic and Social Review* 37(1): 1–26.

Bash, L. and Zezlina-Phillips, E. (2006) 'Identity, boundary and schooling: perspectives on the experiences and perceptions of refugee children', *Intercultural Education* 17(1): 113–128.

Bauman, Z. (1991) *Modernity and Ambivalence*, Cambridge, Polity Press.

Bauman, Z. (2001) *Community: seeking safety in an insecure world*, Cambridge, Polity Press.

Beck, U. (2006) *Cosmopoliton Vision*, Cambridge, Polity Press.

Beck, U. (2010) *Risk society: towards a new modernity,* London, Sage.

Bell McKenzie, K. and Scheurich, J. (2008) 'Teacher resistance to improvement of schools with diverse students', *International Journal of Leadership in Education* 11(2): 117–133.

Bernstein, B. (1975) *Class, codes and control. Vol. 3. Towards a theory of educational transmission*, London, RoutledgeKegan Paul.

Bernstein, B. (1996) *Pedagogy, symbolic control and identity: theory, research, critique*, Oxford, Rowan and Littlefield.

Birenbaum-Carmeli, D. (1999) 'Parents who get what they want: on the empowerment of the powerful', *Sociological Review* 47(1): 62–69.

Blackmore, J. (2006) 'Deconstructing diversity discourses in the field of educational management and leadership', *Educational Management Administration & Leadership* 34(2): 181–199.

Blair, M. (2002) 'Effective school leadership: the multi-ethnic context', *British Journal of Sociology of Education* 23(2): 179–191.

Bloemraad, I. (2006) *Becoming a citizen*, Berkeley, University of California Press.

Boaler, J., William, D. and Brown, M. (2000) 'Students' experiences of ability grouping: disaffection, polarisation and the construction of failure', *British Educational Research Journal* 26(5): 631–647.

Bottery, M. (2004) *The challenges of educational leadership: values in a globalised age,* London, Paul Chapman.

Bourdieu, P. (1984) *Distinction,* London, Routledge and Kegan Paul.

Bourdieu, P. (1986) 'The forms of capital' in Richardson, J. G. *Handbook of theory and research for the sociology of education*, New York, Greenwood Press: 46–58.

Bourdieu, P. (1989) 'Social space and symbolic power', *Sociological Theory* 7(1): 14–25.

Bourdieu, P. (1990) *The Logic of Practice*, Stanford, Stanford University Press.

Bourdieu, P. (1993) *The field of cultural production: essays on art and literature*, Cambridge, Polity Press.

Bourdieu, P. (1998) *On Television and Journalism,* London, Pluto Press.

Bourdieu, P. (2000) *Pascalian Meditations*, London, Polity.

Bourdieu, P. and Passeron, P. C. (1977) *Reproduction in education, society and culture*, London, Sage.

Bourdieu, P. and Wacquant., L. (1992) *An invitation to reflexive sociology*, Cambridge, Polity Press

Breen, R., Hannan, D. B., Rottman, B. and Whelan, C. T. (1990) *Understanding contemporary Ireland*, London, Macmillan Press.

Brembeck, H., Johansson, B. and Kampmann, J. (eds) (2004) *Beyond the competent child – exploring contemporary childhoods in the Nordic welfare societies*, Roskilde, Roskilde University Press.

Brown, P. and Tannock, S. (2009) 'Education, meritocracy and the global war for talent', *Journal of Education Policy* 24(4): 377–392.

Bryan, A. (2007) 'The (mis)representation of Travellers in the civic, social and political education curriculum', in Downes, P. and Gilligan, A. L. (eds), *Beyond educational disadvantage*, Dublin, IPA: 36–48.

Bryan, A. (2008) 'The co-articulation of national identity and interculturalism in the Irish curriculum: educating for democratic citizenship?', *London Review of Education* 6(1): 47–58.

Bryan, A. (2009) 'The intersectionality of nationalism and multiculturalism in the Irish curriculum: teaching against racism?, *Race, Ethnicity and Education* 12(3): 297–317.

Bryan, A. (2010) 'Corporate multiculturalism, diversity management, and positive interculturalism in Irish schools and society', *Irish Educational Studies* 29(3): 253–269.

Bush, T., Glover, D. and Sood, K. (2006) 'Black and minority ethnic leaders in England: a portrait', *School Leadership and Management* 26(3): 289–305.

Butler, J. (1990) *Gender trouble: feminism and the subversion of identity*, New York, Routledge.

Butler, J. (1993) *Bodies that matter: on the discursive limits of 'sex'*, London, Routledge.

Butler, J. (1999). 'On speech, race and melancholia: an interview with Judith Bulter', *Theory, Culture and Society* 16(2): 163–174.

Byrne, D., McGinnity, F; Smyth, E. and Darmody, M. (2010) 'Immigration and school composition in Ireland', *Irish Educational Studies* 29(3): 271–288.

Campbell-Stephens, R. (2009) 'Investing in diversity: changing the face (and the heart) of educational leadership', *School Leadership & Management* 29(3): 321–331.

Castles, S. (2009) 'World population movements, diversity and education', in Banks, J. (ed.), *The Routledge international companion to multicultural education*, New York, Routledge: 49–62.

Central Statistics Office (2008) *Census 2006 population statistics*, Dublin.

Central Statistics Office (2010) *Population and migration estimates April 2009*, Dublin.

Chan, E. (2006) 'Teacher experiences of culture in the curriculum', *Journal of Curriculum Studies* 38(2): 161–176.

Chan, E. (2007) 'Student experiences of a culturally sensitive curriculum: ethnic identity

development amid conflicting stories to live by', *Journal of Curriculum Studies* 39(2): 177–194.

Clarke, M. (2010) 'Choosing post-primary teaching as a career', in Drudy, S. (ed.), *Education in Ireland: challenge and change*, Dublin, Gill and MacMillan: 168–193.

Coleman, J. (1988) 'Social capital in the creation of human capital', *American Journal of Sociology* 94: S95–120.

Collins, R. (1979) *The credential society*, New York, Random Press.

Collin, R. and Apple, M. W. (2007) 'Schooling, literacies and biopolitics in the global age'. *Discourse: Studies in the Cultural Politics of Education* 28(4): 433–454.

Colton, P. (2009) 'Schools and the law: a patron's perspective', *Irish Educational Studies* 28(3) 253–279.

Commission on Itinerancy (1963) *Report of the Commission on Itinerancy*, Dublin, Department of Social Welfare, Official Publications.

Conaty, C. (2002) *Including all: home, school and community united in education*, Dublin, Veritas.

Connolly, P. (1998) *Racism, gender identities and young children*, London, Routledge.

Connolly, P., Kelly, B. and Smith, A. (2009) 'Ethnic habitus and young children', *European Early Childhood Educational Research Journal* 17(2): 217–232.

Coolahan, J. (1981) *Irish Education: its history and structure*, Dublin, IPA.

Coulby, J. (2008) 'Intercultural education, religion and modernity', *Intercultural Education* 19(4): 293–295.

Creemers, B. P. M. and Kyriakides, L. (2010) 'Using the dynamic model to develop an evidenced based theory driven approach to school improvement', *Irish Educational Studies* 29(1): 5–25.

Crozier, G. (2001) 'Excluded parents: the deracialisation of parental involvement', *Race, Ethnicity & Education* 4(4): 329–341.

Crozier, G. (2009) 'Race and education: policy and politics in Britain', *British Journal of Sociology of Education* 30(2): 245–250.

Crozier, G. and Davies, J. (2006) 'Family matters: a discussion of the Bangladeshi and Pakistani extended family and community in supporting the children's education', *Sociological Review* 54(4): 678–695.

Crozier, G. and Davies, J. (2007) 'Hard to reach parents or hard to reach schools? A discussion of home–school relations, with particular reference to Bangladeshi and Pakistani parents', *British Educational Research Journal* 33(3): 295–313.

Crul, M. (2007) *Pathways to success for the children of immigrants*, Institute for migration and ethnic studies, University of Amsterdam.

Crul, M. and Holdaway, J. (2009) 'Children of immigrants in schools in New York and Amsterdam: the factors shaping attainment', *Teachers College Record* 111(6): 1476–1507.

Cummins, J. (1986) 'Empowering minority students: a framework for intervention', *Harvard Educational Review* 56: 18–36.

Cummins, J. (2001) 'Empowering minority students: a framework for intervention', *Harvard Educational Review* 71(4): 656–676.

Dahhlstedt, M. (2009) 'Parental governmentality: involving "immigrant parents" in Swedish schools', *British Journal of Sociology of Education* 30(2): 193–205.

Dale, N. (1996) *Working with families of children with special educational needs: partnership and practice*, London, Routledge.

Daly, E. (2009) 'Religious freedom as a function of power relations: dubious claims on pluralism in the denominational schools debate', *Irish Educational Studies* 28(3): 235–251.

Day, C. (2005) 'Principals who sustain success: making a difference in schools in challenging circumstance', *International Journal of Leadership in Education* 8(4): 273–290.

Day, C., Elliot, B. and Kington, A. (2005) 'Reform, standards and teacher identity: challenges of sustaining commitment', *Teaching and Teacher Education* 21: 563–577.

De Goede, I., Branje, S. J. T. and Meeus, W. H. (2009) 'Developmental changes and gender differences in adolescents' perceptions of friendships', *Science Direct* 1105–1023.

Dept of Education (1947) *Rules for national schools*, Dublin, Stationery Office.

Dept of Education. (1971) *Curaculum na bunscoile*, Dublin, Stationery Office.

Dept of Education and Science (2007) *Audit of school enrolment policies*, Dublin, DES.

Dept of Education and Science (2002a) *Guidelines on Traveller education in primary schools*, Dublin, Official Publications.

Dept of Education and Science (2002b) *Guidelines on Traveller education in second-level schools,* Dublin, Official Publications.

Dept of Education and Skills (2010) *Report on the revised criteria and procedures for the establishment of new primary schools*, Dublin, DES.

Dept of Education and Skills/Office of Minister for Integration (DES/OMI). (2010) Intercultural Education Strategy 2010–2015, Dublin, DES/OMI (Dept of Education and Skills/Office of Minister for Integration.

Dept of Equality, Justice and Law Reform (2005) *Planning for diversity: the national action plan against racism 2005–2008,* Dublin.

Desforges, C. (2003) *The impact of parental involvement, parental support and family education on pupil achievement and adjustment: a literature review*, Nottingham, Department of Education and Skills.

Devine, D. (2002) 'Children's citizenship and the structuring of adult-child relations in the primary school', *Childhood* 9(3): 303–321.

Devine, D. (2003) *Children, power and schooling*, Stoke-on-Trent, Trentham Books.

Devine, D. (2005) 'Welcome to the Celtic tiger?' Teacher responses to immigration and increasing ethnic diversity in Irish schools', *International Studies in the Sociology of Education* 15(1): 49–70.

Devine, D. (2007) 'Immigration and the enlargement of children's social space in school', in Zeiher, H., Devine, D., Kjorholt, A. and Strandell, H. (eds), *Flexible childhood? Exploring children's welfare in time and space*, Odense, University Press of Southern Denmark: 143–169.

Devine, D. (2008a) 'Children at the margins? Changing constructions of childhood in contemporary Ireland', in James, A. and James, A. L. (eds), *European childhoods: cultures, politics and participation*, New York, Palgrave Press: 82–105.

Devine, D. (2008b) 'Education and Intercultural Narratives in Multicultural Classrooms', *Childhood* 15(4): 570–572.

Devine, D. (2009) 'Mobilising capitals? Migrant children's negotiation of their everyday lives in schools', *British Journal of Sociology of Education* 30(5): 521–535.

Devine, D. and Kelly, M. (2006) 'I just don't want to get picked on by anybody: dynamics of inclusion and exclusion in a newly multi-ethnic Irish primary school', *Children and Society* 20(2): 128–139.

Devine, D., Kenny, M. and MacNeela, E. (2002) *Ethnicity and schooling: a study of ethnic diversity in selected Irish primary and post-primary schools*, Dublin, Dept. of Education, University College Dublin.

Devine, D., Kenny M. and MacNeela, E. (2008) 'Naming the "other": children's construction and experience of racisms in Irish primary schools', *Race, Ethnicity & Education* 11(4): 369–385.

Devine, D. Grummell., B and Lynch, K. (2010a) 'Crafting the elastic self? Gender and identities in senior management appointments in education', *Gender Work and Organisation*, On-line early view.

Devine, D., Fahie, D., MacGillicuddy, D., MacRuairc, G. and Harford, J. (2010b) *Report on the use of ISTOF (International System for Teacher Observation and Feedback): challenges, issues and teacher effect*, Dublin, School of Education, UCD.

Dewey, J. (1963) *Experience and education*, London, Collier-Macmillan.

Drudy, S. and Lynch, K. (1993) *Schools and society in Ireland*, Dublin, Gill and MacMillan.

Drudy, S., Martin, M., Woods, M. and O'Flynn, J. (2005) *Men in the classroom: gender imbalances in teaching*. London, Routledge.

Eivers, E., Close, S., Shiel, G., Millar, D., Clerkin, A., Gilleece, L. and Kiniry, J. (2010) *The 2009 national assessments of mathematics and English reading*, Dublin, Educational Research Centre.

Elwood. J. (1998) 'The use of context in examination and assessment items: a source of inequality in assessment outcomes', *British Journal of Curriculum and Assessment* 8(3): 31–38.

Elwood, J. (2006) 'Formative assessment: possibilities, boundaries and limitations' *Assessment in Education* 13 (2): 215–232.

Evergeti, V. and E. Zontini. (2006) 'Introduction: some critical reflections on social capital, migration and transnational families', *Ethnic and Racial Studies* 29(6): 1025–1039.

Faas, D. (2008) 'From foreigner pedagogy to intercultural education: an analysis of the German responses to migration-related diversity and its impact upon schools and students', *European Educational Research Journal* 7(1): 108–123.

Faas, D. (2010) *Negotiating political identities: multi-ethnic schools and youth in Europe*, Surrey, Ashgate.

Fahey, T. and Fanning, B. (2010) 'Immigration and socio-spatial segregation in Dublin, 1996–2006', *Urban Studies* 47(8): 1625–1642.

Fahey, T., Russell, H. and Whelan, C. T. (eds) (2008) *Quality of life in Ireland: social impact of economic boom*, Frankfurt, Springer.

Fanning, B. (2002) *Racism and Social Change in the Republic of Ireland,* Manchester, Manchester University Press.

Fanning, B. (ed.) (2007) *Immigration and Social Change in the Republic of Ireland,* Manchester, Manchester University Press.

Fanning, B. (2009) *New Guests of the Nation*, Dublin, Irish Academic Press.

Farren, S. (1995) *The politics of Irish education 1920–65*, Institute of Irish Studies, Queen's University of Belfast.

Foucault, M. (1979) *Discipline and punish: the birth of the prison*, New York, Vintage Books.

Foucault, M. (1980) *Michel Foucault: power knowledge*, Hertfordshire, Harvester Wheatsheaf.

Foucault, M. (2003a). *Society must be defended: lectures at the college de france 1975–76*, London, Allen Lane.

Foucault, M. (2003b). *Abnormal: lectures at the College De France 1974–1975*, London, Verso.

Francis, B. and Archer, L. (2005) 'British Chinese pupils' and parents' constructions of the value of education, *British Educational Research Journal* 31(1): 89–107

Freire, P. (1993) *Pedagogy of the oppressed*, New York, Continuum.

Gaetane, J. M. (2008) 'Leadership for social justice: an agenda for 21st century schools', *Educational Forum* 72: 340–354.

Gaganakis, M. (2006) 'Identity construction in adolescent girls: the context dependency of racial and gendered perceptions', *Gender and Education* 18(4): 361–379.

Gaine, C. (1995) *Still no problem here*, Stoke-on-Trent, Trentham.

Garner, S. (2004) *Racism in the Irish experience*, London, Pluto Press.

Garner, S. (2007) *Whiteness: an introduction*, New York, Routledge.

Garvin, T. (2004) *Preventing the future: why was Ireland so poor for so long?* Dublin, Gill and Macmillan.

Geddes, A. (2008) *Immigration and European integration: beyond fortress Europe?*, Manchester, Manchester University Press.

Giddens, A. (1984) *The constitution of society: outline of the theory of structuration*, Berkeley, University of California Press.

Giddens, A. (1991) *Modernity and self-identity: self and society in the late modern age* Cambridge, Polity.

Gillborn, D. (2008) *Racism and education: coincidence or conspiracy?* London, Routledge.

Gillborn, D. (2010) 'Reform, racism and the centrality of whiteness: assessment, ability and the "new eugenics"'. *Irish Educational Studies* 29(3): 231–252.

Gillborn, D. and Youdell, D. (2009) Critical perspectives on race and schooling in Banks, J. (ed.), *The Routledge international companion of multicultural education*. New York, Routledge: 186–199.

Gleeson, J. and Ó Donnabháin, D. (2009) 'Strategic planning and accountability in Irish education', *Irish Educational Studies* 28(1): 27–46.

Goddard, J. T. and Hart, A. C. (2007) 'School leadership and equity: Canadian elements', *School Leadership and Management* 27(1): 7–20.

Goffman, E. (1971) *The presentation of self in everyday life*, Harmondsworth, Penguin.

Goldberg, D. T. (2002) *The racial state*, Oxford, Blackwell.

Grace, G. and O'Keefe, J. (2007) *International handbook of Catholic education*, Boston, Springer.

Green, A. (1997) *Education, globalization and the nation state*, Basingstoke, Macmillan.

Grek, S. (2009) 'Governing by numbers: the PISA "effect" in Europe', *Journal of Education Policy* 24(1): 23–37.

Griffith, A. and Smith. D. (2005) *Mothering for schooling*, New York, Routledge Falmer.

Grummell, B. Devine, D. and Lynch, K. (2009a) 'Appointing senior managers in education: homosociability, local Logics and authenticity in the Selection Process', *Educational Management Administration & Leadership* 37(3): 329–349.

Grummell, B. Devine, D. and Lynch, K. (2009b) 'The care-less manager: gender, care and new managerialism in higher education', *Gender and Education* 21(2): 191–208.

Gunter, H. and Butt, G. (2007) *Modernizing schools: people, learning and organizations*, London, Continuum.

Gunter, H. and Fitztgerald, T. (2008) 'The future of leadership research', *School Leadership and Management* 28(3): 261–279.

Hammersly, M. (1999) *Researching school experience: ethnographic studies of teaching and learning*, Buckingham, Open University Press.

Hanafin, J. and Lynch, A. (2002) 'Peripheral voices: parental involvement, social class, and educational disadvantage', *British Journal of Sociology of Education* 23(1): 35–49.

Hargreaves, A. (1994) *Changing teachers, changing times*, New York, Teacher College Press.

Hargeaves, A. (2001) 'The emotional geographies of teaching', *Teachers' College Record* 103(6): 1056–1080.

Hatcher, R. (1998) 'Class differentiation in education: rational choices?', *British Journal of Sociology of Education* 19(1): 5–24.

Haywood, K. and Howard, K. (2007) 'Cherry picking the diaspora', in Fanning, B. (ed.), *Immigration and social change in the Republic of Ireland*, Manchester, Manchester University Press: 47–63.

Heinz, M. (2008) 'The composition of applicants and entrants to teacher education programmes in Ireland: trends and patterns', *Irish Educational Studies* 27(3): 223–240.

Hickman, M. (2008) 'Immigration and monocultural (re)imaginings in Ireland and Britain', *Translocations: The Irish Migration, Race and Social Transformation Review* 2(1): 1–13.

Holdaway, J. and Crul, M. (2009) 'Cross-national comparison of provision and outcomes for the education of the Second Generation', *Teachers College Record* 111(6): 1381–1403.

Holland, J., Reynolds, T. and Weller, S. (2007) 'Transitions, networks and communities: the significance of social capital in the lives of children and young people', *Journal of Youth Studies* 10(1): 97–116.

Holm, G. and Londen, M. (2010) 'The discourse on multicultural education in Finland: education for whom', *Intercultural Education* 21(2): 107–120.

Hortz. C. and Gitz-johansen, T. (2010) 'Education of ethnic minority children in Denmark: monocultural hegemony and counter positions', *Intercultural Education* 21(2): 137–151.

Hyland, A. (1989) 'The multi-denominational experience in the national school system', *Irish Educational Studies* 13(1): 89–114.

Hyland, A. and Milne, K. (1992) *Irish educational documents. Vol. 2,* Dublin, Church of Ireland College of Education.

Inglis, T. (2008) *Global Ireland, same difference*, London, Routledge.

Irish Catholic Bishops' Conference (2008) *Vision 08: a pastoral letter from the Irish Catholic Bishops' conference*, Maynooth, Columbia Centre.

James, A. and James, A. (2004) *Constructing childhood: theory policy and social practice,* New York, Palgrave.

Kao, G. (2004) 'Social capital and its relevance to minority and immigrant populations', *Sociology of Education* 77(2): 172–175.

Kenny, M. (1997) *The routes of resistance: Travellers and second-level schooling*, Aldershot, Ashgate.

King, J. (2004) Dysconscious racism: ideology, identity and the mis-education of teachers in Ladson-Billings, G. and Gillborn, D. (eds), *The Routledge Falmer reader in multicultural education,* London, Routledge: 71–84.

Kitching, K. (2010) 'An excavation of the racialised politics of viability underpinning education policy in Ireland', *Irish Educational Studies* 29(3): 213–229.

Kloosterman, R. and de Graaf, P. M. (2010) 'Non-promotion or enrolment in a lower track? The influence of social background on choices in secondary education for three cohorts of Dutch Pupils', *Oxford Review of Education* 36(3): 363–384.

Kowalczyk, J. and Popkewitz, T. (2005) 'Muticulturalism, recognition and abjection: (re)mapping Italian identity', *Policy Futures in Education* 3(4): 423–435.

Ladson-Billings, G. and Tate, W. F. (1995) 'Toward a critical race theory of education', *Teachers College Record* 97: 47–68.

Lamaison, P. and Bourdieu, P. (1986) 'From rules to strategies: an interview with Pierre Bourdieu', *Cultural Anthropology* 1(1): 110–120.

Langlois, L. and Lapointe, C. (2007) 'Ethical leadership in Canadian school organizations', *Educational Management Administration & Leadership* 35(2): 247–260.

Lareau, A. (1989) *Home advantage*, Lewes, Falmer Press.

Lareau, A. (2003) *Unequal childhoods, class, race and family life*, Berkeley, University of California Press.

Lensmire, T. (2010) 'Ambivalent white racial idenitites: fear and an elusive innocence', *Race, Ethnicity and Education* 13(2): 159–172.

Lentin, A. and Lentin, R, (eds) (2006) *Race and state*, Newcastle, Cambridge Scholars Press.

Lentin, R. (2006) 'From racial state to racist state? Racism and immigration in twenty first century Ireland', in Lentin, A. and. Lentin, R (eds), *Race and state*, Newcastle, Cambridge Scholars Press: 187–206.

Lentin, R. and McVeigh, R. (2002) *Racism and anti-racism in Ireland*, Dublin, Beyond the Pale.

Lentin, R. and McVeigh, R. (2006) *After optimism: Ireland, racism and globalisation*, Dublin, Metro Eireann.

Leo, E. and Barton, L. (2006) 'Inclusion, diversity and leadership', *Educational Management, Administration and Leadership* 34(2): 167–180.

Leonard, M. (2005) 'Children, childhood and social capital, exploring the links', *Sociology* 39(4): 605–622.

Leonardo, Z. (2002) 'The souls of white folk: critical pedagogy, whiteness studies, and globalization discourse', *Race, Ethnicity & Education* 5(1): 29–50.

Leonardo, Z. (2009) *Race, whiteness and education*, New York, Routledge.

Levine-Rasky, C. (2009) 'Dynamics of parental involvement at a multicultural school', *British Journal of Sociology of Education* 30(3): 331–344.

Liégeois, J. P. (1994) *Roma, gypsies, Travellers*, Strasbourg, Council of Europe Press.

Lingard, B. (2007) 'Pedagogies of indifference', *International Journal of Inclusive Education* 11(3): 245–266.

Lingard, B., Hayes, D., Mills, M. and Christie, P. (2003) *Leading learning: making hope practical in schools*, Maidenhead, Open University Press.

Lodge, A. (2004) 'Denial, tolerance or recognition of difference? The experiences of minority belief parents in the denominational primary system', in Deegan, J., Devine, D. and Lodge, A. (eds), *Primary voices: equality, diversity and childhood in Irish primary schools*, Dublin, IPA: 17–37.

Lodge, A. and Lynch, K. (2004) *Diversity in Schools*, Dublin, Equality Authority.

Loyal, S. (2003) 'Welcome to the Celtic tiger: racism, immigration and the state', in Coleman, J. (ed.) *The end of Irish history? Critical reflections on the Celtic tiger*, Manchester, Manchester University Press: 48–64.

Lumby, J. (2006) 'Conceptualizing diversity and leadership', *Educational Management Administration & Leadership* 34(2): 151–165.

Luttrell, W. (1997) *School smart, mother wise*, London, Routledge.

Luttrell, W. (2003). *Pregnant bodies, fertile minds*, London, Routledge.

Luttrell, W. (ed.) (2009) *Qualitative educational research: readings in reflexive methodologies and transformative practice*, London, Routledge.

Lynch, K. and Lodge, A. (2002) *Equality and power in schools*, London, Routledge-Falmer.

Lynch, K. and Moran, M. (2006) 'Markets, schools and the convertibility of economic capital: the complex dynamics of class choice', *British Journal of Sociology of Education* 27(2): 221–235.

Lynch, K., John Baker, J. and Lyons, M. (2009) *Affective equality: love, care and injustice*, London, Palgrave Macmillan.

Lyons, Z. (2010) 'Articulating a deficit perspective: a survey of the attitudes of post-primary English language support teachers and coordinators', *Irish Educational Studies* 29(3): 289–303.

Mac Gréil, M. (1996) *Prejudice in Ireland revisited*, Maynooth, Survey and Research Unit, St Patrick's College.

MacPherson, W. (1999) *The Stephen Lawrence Inquiry*, London, Stationery Office.

MacRuairc, G. (2009) '"Dip, dip, sky blue, who's it? NOT YOU": children's experiences of standardised testing: a socio-cultural analysis', *Irish Educational Studies* 28(1): 47–66.

May, S. (2009) 'Critical multiculturalism and education', in Banks, J. (ed.), *The Routledge International Reader in Multicultural Education*, New York, Routledge: 33–49

Mayock, P., Bryan, A., Carr, N. and Kitching, K. (2009) 'Supporting LGBT lives in Ireland: a study of the mental health and well-being of lesbian, gay, bisexual and transgender people', Dublin, Public Communications Centre.

McCoy, S., Byrne, D., O'Connell, P. J., Kelly, E and Doherty, C. (2010) *Hidden disadvantage? A study on the low participation in higher education by the non-manual group*, Dublin, Higher Education Authority.

McDaid, R. (2009) *Tears, teachers, tension and transformation? Minority language children reflect on the recognition of their first languages in Irish primary schools*, Dublin, St Patrick's College of Education. Education Doctorate.

McDonagh, W. (2004) 'Travellers and education: a personal perspective', in Deegan, J. D., Devine, D. and Lodge, A. (eds), *Primary voices: equality, diversity and childhood in Irish primary schools'*, Dublin, Insititute of Public Administration: 92–109.

McGinnity, F., Nelson, J., Lunn, P. and Quinn, E. (2009) *Discrimination in Recruitment: Evidence from a field experiment*, Dublin, Equality Authority and ESRI.

McGovern, F. (1993) 'The education of a linguistic and cultural minority: Vietnamese children in Irish schools 1979–1989', *Irish Educational Studies* 12(1): 92–105.

McNay, L. (1999a) 'Subject, psyche and agency', *Theory, Culture & Society* 16(2): 175–193.

McNay, L. (1999b) 'Gender, habitus and the field', *Theory, Culture & Society* 16(1): 95–117.

Modood, T. (2004) 'Capitals, ethnic identity and educational qualifications', *Cultural Trends* 13(50): 87–105.

Modood, T. (2007) *Multiculturalism: a civic idea.* Cambridge, Polity Press.

Moller, J. (2009) 'Learning to share: a vision of leadership practice', *International Journal of Leadership in Education* 12(3): 253–267.

Morree, D., Klaassen, C. and Veugeler, W. (2008) 'Teachers' ideas about multicultural Education in a changing society: the case of the Czech Republic', European *Educational Research Journal* 7(1): 60–73.

Morrison, M., Lumby, J. and Sood, K. (2006) 'Diversity and diversity management', *Educational Management Administration & Leadership* 34(3): 277–295.

Morrow, G. (1999) 'Conceptualising social capital in relation to the well-being of children and young people: a critical review.' *Sociological Review* 4(4): 744–765.

Mortimore, P., Sammons, P., and Stoll, L. (1988) *School matters: the junior years*, London, Sage.

NESC (2006), *No. 115 Migration Policy*, Dublin, National Economic and Social Council, Dublin, National Economic and Social Development Office.

NCCA (2005) *Intercultural education in the primary school: guidelines for schools*, Dublin, National Council for Curriculum and Assessment (NCCA).

NCCRI (2008). *Building integrated neighbourhoods: towards an intercultural approach to housing policy and practice in Ireland. Part one. An overview*, Dublin, NCCRI.

Ni Laoire, C., Bushin, N., Carpena-Mendez, F. and White, A. (2009) *Tell me about yourself: migrant children's experiences of moving to and living in Ireland*, Cork, University College Cork.

Niessen, J. and Huddleston, T. (2009) *Handbook on integration for policy makers and practitioners*, Paris, European Commission: Directorate General for Justice, Freedom and Security.

Nolan, B., O'Connell, P. J. and Whelan, C.T. (2000) *Bust to boom? The Irish experience of growth and inequality*, Dublin, IPA.

O'Brien, M. (2007) 'Mothers' emotional care work in education and its moral imperative', *Gender and Education* 19(2): 159–177.

O'Connell, J. (2002) 'Travellers in Ireland: an examination of discrimination and racism', in Lentin, R. and McVeigh, R. (eds), *Racism and anti-racism in Ireland*, Dublin, Beyond the Pale: 49–63.

O'Connor, P. (2009) *Irish children and teenagers in a changing world*, Manchester, Manchester University Press.

O'Connor, S. (1986) *A troubled sky: reflections on the Irish Educational Scene*, Dublin, Educational Research Centre.

OECD (1969) *Reviews of national policies for education Ireland*, Paris, OECD.

OECD (2006) *Where immigrants succeed: a comparative review of performance and engagement in PISA 2003*. Paris, OECD.

OECD (2008a) *Migration and mobility: challenges and opportunities for EU education systems*, Paris, OECD.

OECD (2008b) *Improving school leadership. Volume 1. Policy and practice*, Paris, OECD.

OECD (2009a) *Reviews of migrant education: Ireland Country Report*, Paris, OECD.

OECD (2009b) OECD *Reviews of migrant education: closing the gap for immigrant students: policies, practice and performance*, Paris, OECD.

Office of the Minister for Integration, (2008) *Migration nation: statement on integration strategy and diversity management*, Dublin, Office of the Minister for Integration.

OOC (2010) (Office of the Ombudsman for Children) *Separated children living in Ireland*, Dublin, Office of the Ombudsman for Children.

O'Gorman, E. and Sugrue, E. (2007) *Intercultural education: primary challenges in Dublin 15*, Dublin, St Patrick's College of Education.

O'Mahony, E. (2008) *Factors determining school choice: report on a survey of the attitudes of parents of children attending Catholic primary schools in Ireland*, Dublin, Irish Catholic Bishop's Conference.

O'Sullivan, D. (2005) *Cultural politics and Irish education since the 1950s: policy paradigms and power*, Dublin, IPA.

Parker Jenkins, M. (1995) *Children of Islam: a teacher's guide to meeting the needs of muslim pupils*, Stoke-on-Trent, Trentham.

Parker Jenkins, M., Hartas, D. and Irving, B. (2005) *In good faith: schools, religion and public funding*, Aldershot, Ashgate.

Peck, C. and Donaldson, S. (2008) 'Unreached and unreasonable: curriculum standards and children's understanding of ethnic diversity in Canada', *Journal of Curriculum Inquiry* 38(1): 63–92.

Perumal, J. (2009) 'Reading and creating critically leaderful schools that make a difference: the post-apartheid South African case', *International Journal of Leadership in Education* 12(1): 35–49.

Phoenix, A. (1987) 'Theories of gender and black families', in Weiner, G. and Arnot, M. (eds), *Gender Under Scrutiny: New Inquiries in Education*, Suffolk, Hutchinson.

Phoenix, A. (2002) 'Mapping present inequalities to navigate future success: racialisation and education', *Journal of Sociology of Education* 23(3): 505–515.

Picower, B. (2009) 'The unexamined whiteness of teaching: how white teachers maintain and enact dominant racial ideologies', *Race, Ethnicity and Education* 12(2): 197–215.

Pinson, H. and Arnot, M. (2007) 'Sociology of education and the wasteland of refugee education research', *British Journal of Sociology of Education* 28(3): 399–407.

Poupeau, F., Francoise, J.C. and Couratier, E. (2007) 'Making the right move: how families are using transfers to adapt to socio-spatial differentiation of schools in the greater Paris region', *Journal of Education Policy* 22(1): 31–37.

Pullen, A. and Simpson, R. (2009) 'Managing difference in feminized work: men, otherness and social practice', *Human Relations* 62(2): 561–587.

Putnam, R. D. (1995) 'Bowling alone: America's declining social capital', *Journal of Democracy* 6(1): 65–78.

Ran, A. (2001) 'Travelling on parallel tracks: Chinese patterns and English teachers', *Educational Research* 43(3): 311–328.

Raveaud, M. (2008) 'Culture-blind? Parental discourse on religion, ethnicity and secularism in the French educational context', *European Educational Research Journal* 7(1): 74–87.

Reay, D. (1998) *Class work: mothers' involvement in their children's primary schooling.* London, University College Press.

Reay, D. (2005) 'Beyond consciousness? The psychic landscape of social class', *Sociology* 39(5): 911–928.

Reay, D., Crozier, G., James, D., Hollingworth, S., Williams, K., Jamieson., F. and Beedell, P. (2008) 'Re-invigorating democracy? White middle class identities and comprehensive schooling' *The Sociological Review* 56(2): 239–254.

Reay, D. Hollingsworth, S., Williams, K., Crozier, G., Jamieson, F., James, D. and Beedell, P. (2007) 'A darker shade of pale? Whiteness, the middle classes and multi-ethnic inner city schooling', *Sociology* 41(6): 1041–1060.

Reynolds, T. (2006) 'Caribbean families, social capital and young people's diasporic identities', *Ethnic and Racial Studies* 29(6): 1087–1103.

Rijkschroeff, R., ten Dam, G; Duyvendak, J. W., de Gruijter, M. and Pels, T.

(2005) 'Educational policies on migrants and minorities in the Netherlands: success or failure?', *Journal of Education Policy* 20(4): 417–435.

Rizvi, F. (2010) *Rethinking issues of diversity within the context of an emergent transnationalism*, Keynote address, European Conference of Educational Research. University of Helsinki.

Rizvi, F. and Lingard, B. (2006) 'Globalisation and the changing nature of the OECD's educational work', in Lauder, H., Brown,. P., Dillabough., J. A. and Halsey, A. H. (eds), *Education, Globalisation and Social Change*, Oxford, Oxford University Press: 247–261.

Rose, N. (1996) *Inventing ourselves*, Cambridge, Cambridge University Press.

Rose, N. (2001) *Governing the soul*, Cambridge, Cambridge University Press.

Russell, H., Quin, E., King, R. and McGinnity, F. (2008) *The experience of discrimination in Ireland*, Dublin, ESRI.

Russell, H., Maitre, B and Nolan, B. (2010) *Monitoring poverty levels in Ireland 2004–2007: key issues for children, working groups and older people*, Dublin, ESRI.

Rutter, J. (2006) *Refugee children in the UK*, Maidenhead, Open University Press.

Ryan, A. (1998) 'Teachers, Travellers and Education: A sociological perspective', *Irish Educational Studies* 17: 161–174.

Sammons, P., Day, C., Kington, A., Gu, Q., Stobart, G. and Smees, R. (2007) 'Exploring variations in teachers' work, lives and their effects on pupils: key findings and implications from a longitudinal mixed-method study', *British Educational Research Journal*. 33(5) 681–701.

Schnefp, S. V. (2006) 'How different are immigrants? A cross-country and cross-survey analysis of educational achievement', in Parsons, C. and Smeeding, T. (eds), *Immigration and the Transformation of Europe*, Cambridge, Cambridge University Press.

Shapira, M. (2010) *An exploration of differences in educational attainment in migrant pupils in 18 OECD countries*, European Conference of Educational Research, University of Helsinki.

Skeggs, B. (2004) 'Exchange, value and affect: Bourdieu and the self', *Sociological Review* 52(2): 75–95.

Smyth, E. (1999) *Do schools differ? Academic and personal development among pupils in the second-level sector*, Dublin, Oak Tree Press.

Smyth, E., Darmody, M., McGinnity, F. and Byrne, D. (2009) *Adapting to diversity: Irish schools and newcomer students*, Dublin, ESRI.

Spillane, J. P. and Diamond, J. B. (2007) *Distributed leadership in practice*, New York, Teachers College Press.

Stefkovich, J. and Begley, P. T. (2007) 'Ethical school leadership', *Educational Management Administration and Leadership* 35(2): 205–224.

Sugrue, C. (2005) *Passionate principalship: learning from life histories of school leaders*. London, RoutledgeFalmer.

Teddlie, C. and Reynolds, D. (2002) *International handbook of school effectiveness research*, London, Routledge.

Thomson, M. and Crul, M. (2007) 'The second generation in Europe and the United States: how is the transatlantic debate relevant for further research on the European second generation?', *Journal of Ethnic & Migration Studies* 33(7): 1025–1041.

Troyna, B. and Hatcher, R. (1992) *Racism in children's lives: a study of mainly-white primary schools*, London, Routledge.

UNICEF (2007) *Child poverty in perspective: an overview of child well-being in rich countries Report Card 7*, Vienna, Innocenti Research Centre.

UNICEF (2009) *The state of the world's children*, New York, United Nations.

Vaught, S. E. and Castagno, A. E. (2008) '"I don't think I am a racist": Critical Race Theory, teacher attitudes, and structural racism', *Race, Ethnicity & Education* 11(2): 95–113.

Vincent, C. and Ball, S. J. (2006) *Childcare, choice and class practices*, London, Routledge.

Vincent, C., Ball, S. J. and Kemp, S. (2004) 'The social geography of childcare: making up a middle-class child', *British Journal of Sociology of Education* 25(2): 229–244.

Vygotsky, L. (1978) *Mind in society, the development of higher psychological processes*, London, Harvard University Press.

Walker, A. and Dimmock, C. (2005) 'Leading the multi-ethnic school: research evidence on successful practice', *Educational Forum* 69(3): 291–304.

Walker, A. and Shuangye, C. (2007) 'Leader authenticity in intercultural school contexts', *Educational Management Administration and Leadership* 35(2): 185–204.

Walters, S. (2007) 'How do you know that he's bright but lazy? Teachers' assessments of Bangladeshi English as an additional Language pupils in two year three classrooms', *Oxford Review of Education* 33(1): 87–101.

Warikoo, N. and Carter. P. (2010) 'Cultural explanations for racial and ethnic stratification in academic achievement: a call for a new and improved theory', *Review of Educational Research* 79(1): 366–394.

West, C. and Zimmerman, D. H. (1987) 'Doing gender', *Gender and Society* 1(2): 125–151.

Wilkinson, G. and Pickett, K. (2009) *The spirit level: why more equal societies always do better*, London, Allen Lane.

Willis, P. E. (1977) *Learning to labor: how working class kids get working class jobs*, New York, Colombia University Press.

Youdell, D. (2006) 'Subjectivation and performative politics – Butler thinking Althusser and Foucault: intelligibility, agency and the raced-nationed-religioned subjects of education', *British Journal of Sociology of Education* 27(4): 511–528.

Young, M. (1971) *Knowledge and control*, London, Collier Macmillan.

Zeiher, H, Devine, D., Strandell, H. and Kjorholt, A. (2007) *Flexible childhood? Exploring children's welfare in time and space*, Odense, University Press of Southern Denmark.

Zembylas, M. (2010) 'Racialization/ethnicization of school emotional spaces: the politics of resentment', *Race, Ethnicity and Education* 13(2): 253–270.

Index